Wilbur Samuel Jackman

Nature Study for Grammar Grades

A Manual for Teachers and Pupils below the High School in the Study of Nature

Wilbur Samuel Jackman

Nature Study for Grammar Grades
A Manual for Teachers and Pupils below the High School in the Study of Nature

ISBN/EAN: 9783337779719

Printed in Europe, USA, Canada, Australia, Japan

Cover: Foto ©Thomas Meinert / pixelio.de

More available books at **www.hansebooks.com**

NATURE STUDY

FOR

GRAMMAR GRADES

A MANUAL

FOR TEACHERS AND PUPILS BELOW THE HIGH SCHOOL IN THE STUDY OF NATURE

BY

WILBUR S. JACKMAN, A.B.

DEPARTMENT OF NATURAL SCIENCE, CHICAGO NORMAL SCHOOL

To me the converging objects of the universe perpetually flow.
All are written to me, and I must get what the writing means.
WALT WHITMAN

New York

THE MACMILLAN COMPANY

LONDON: MACMILLAN & CO., Ltd.

1899

INTRODUCTION.

IN preparing this Manual, it has been the author's aim to propose, within the comprehension of grammar school pupils, a few of the problems which arise in a thoughtful study of nature, and to offer suggestions designed to lead to their solution. That pupils need some rational and definite directions in nature study, all are generally agreed. But to prepare the outlines and suggestive directions necessary, and to place these within the reach of each pupil, is more than any ordinary teacher has time to do, even granting that she is fully prepared for such work. The utter futility of depending upon oral suggestions during the class hour, when the pupils are supposed to be doing individual work, is easily apparent on a moment's reflection. With a manual of directions in hand, each pupil may become strictly responsible for a certain amount of work, either in the field or in the laboratory. This removes all occasion for that interruption in his work, which is, otherwise, due to the pupil's attempt to *think* and at the same time *hear*, what the teacher says. Under the usual plan of giving oral instructions, the teacher must necessarily wearily repeat what has once been said, or, what is worse, permit the pupils to get the directions from each other. In either case, confusion is an inevitable result.

In using the Manual, the author would suggest that the teacher assign a certain topic and then give appropriate opportunity for the pupils to study it individually, either in the field or in the laboratory, along the lines suggested in the book. After such study, the pupils will be prepared to meet in general class discussion, and the subsequent steps, drawing, painting, modeling, writing, etc., may follow in proper order. It is not to be expected, of course, that every pupil will work out every suggestion. It is unreasonable to suppose that all are equally interested in the same thing. The pupils should not feel that they are to be held, absolutely, to the points enumerated under the *Queries*, but that they are to consider them merely as *suggestions* capable of almost indefinite expansion in the direction which the pupil's interest may determine.

Teachers will find many of the monographs issued by the U. S. Department of Agriculture of great use. Acknowledgment is due to the American Book Company for the use of Table IX., from Waldo's *Meteorology*. Other acknowledgments are made in the text.

CHICAGO NORMAL SCHOOL.

I.

MUTUAL RELATIONS OF PLANTS AND INSECTS: PLANTS.

FIELD LESSON.

A. *Equipment:* Baskets and small knives.

B. *Places to be visited:* Open fields, woods, thickets and marshes. Study and collect specimens of plants, including every part — fruit, flower, leaf, stem and root. (See further directions given under Number Work.)

C. *Evidences to be considered:*

1. Galls on leaves or stems.
2. Partially eaten leaves or stems.
3. Partially eaten or stung fruit.
4. Stings of all kinds upon various parts of plants.
5. Parts of plants that have been used as nest building.
6. Parts of plants that have been used as depositories for eggs.
7. Parts of plants in any way distorted by insect depredations.

STUDY OF MATERIAL COLLECTED IN THE FIELD.

A. QUERIES:

1. *Are the plants benefitted or injured by the insect's work.*

Consider
(a) The function of the part of the plant deformed or destroyed.
(b) The stage of growth when attacked by the insect.
(c) The season of the year when the insect begins its work.
(d) The extent and character of the malformation.
(e) The time when the eggs are hatched.
(f) The habits of the larvae; food.
(g) What is the specific injury likely to be sustained by the plant?

2. *If the visits are beneficial, what are the inducements offered by the plant?*

Consider, selecting some plant for special and prolonged observation:
(a) Color.
(b) Juicy secretions.
(c) Odor.
(d) Time of visitation.
(e) Special adaptation through peculiarities of growth to the needs of insects.
(f) What is the specific end to be gained by the plant through the insect visit.

3. *If the visits are injurious, what are the defenses of the plant?*

Consider, selecting some plant for special and prolonged observation:
(a) Location, wet or dry.

(b) Juicy secretions, wax.
(c) Spines, thorns, prickles, hairs.
(d) Odor.
(e) Special provisions through growth : Shape of flower, position of pistils and stamens, etc.
(f) Sensitiveness to touch.
(g) Change in form or position of part at different times, day or night.

NUMBER WORK.

Select different kinds of plants, the oak—any species—the goldenrod, the ironweed, the willow, the maple, the poplar, the dock, the prairie dock, the burdock, the lilac, the elm, the box elder ; gather data which will furnish a basis for calculating the amount of material used by insects as food.

If a small plant is selected, consider all its leaves ; if a tree, select small branches from different parts of the tree having a total of at least 100 leaves.

QUERY : *What proportion of leaf surface of various plants is destroyed by insects ?*

1. What per cent. of the whole number of leaves has been injured by insects ?

NOTE.—This problem, and the following ones, may be given as one in percentage, ratio, fractions, or whole numbers, depending upon the age and ability of the pupils, e. g: (a) What is the *ratio* of the number injured to the whole ? (b) The number injured equals *what part* of the whole?   (c) What is the difference between the number of leaves injured and the whole number studied?   The teacher will use his judgment in adapting the proper mode of comparison to the experience of the pupil.

2. What per cent. of the leaves remains uninjured?

3. What per cent. of the leaves has been stung by insects in laying eggs?

4. What per cent. has lost the leaf form as a result of the injury?

5. What per cent. has been devoured, in part, as food?

6. Examine the part of a goldenrod stem enlarged by the sting of an insect; cut out the enlarged part and weigh it.   Weigh an equal length of the stem taken from just below or above the injury; by what per cent. has the injured part increased in weight by the sting?

7. Select leaves having typical galls; the weight of the galls equals what per cent. of the weight of the leaves?

8. What per cent. of the leaves has been used in the construction of nests or cocoons?

9. Make a list of all the plants studied; which plant has the largest per cent. of leaves attacked by insects?

10. What plant has the lowest per cent. attacked?

11. Write a list of the plants examined in the order of the amount of injuries sustained.

12. Can you see any definite effects upon

the life and character of the plants due to their relations to the insects ?

REPRESENTATIVE EXPRESSION.

1. *Drawing.*

(a) The part of the plant modified, as a whole, either natural size or enlarged to *definite scale*, if necessary to distinctness.

(b) Make drawings of various sections of modified parts to show in detailed outline the distorted structure caused by the insects' injuries. Enlarge to *definite scale* when necessary for distinctness.

2. *Painting.*

(a) Landscape ; showing the condition of life as indicated by color.

(b) Tree selected for study during the year.

(c) Leaf of tree ; irregular and typical forms. Natural size. Study causes of irregularity in form.

(d) Show any modifications in color due to insect depredations.

II.

MUTUAL RELATIONS OF PLANTS AND ANIMALS: ANIMALS.

FIELD WORK.

A. *Manual Training.*

1. Insect nets.

(a) Make light handle 3 ft. long, 1 in. diameter. A broom handle may be used.

(b) Wire hoop (No. 8 wire) 8 in. diameter; bring the ends of the wire together twisted into short handle.

(c) Bore hole in end of handle to suit wire ends and insert the latter.

(d) Make mosquito netting bag 2 ft. deep and sew to wire hoop.

2. Insect cages.

(a) Procure small wooden boxes. Soap boxes may be obtained at the grocers that will answer the purpose.

(b) Fasten an upright post 1 in. square and 2 ft. high in each corner.

(c) Fill the box nearly full of moist earth into which seeds may be sown or seedlings transplanted.

(d) Cover the whole with wire netting or mosquito bar ; collect live insects and preserve them in this cage. Larvæ may also be kept in this cage.

3. Small boxes; cigar boxes, for example, to hold the insects while in the field collecting.

4. Poison bottles; prepare as follows:

(a) Use 1 oz. morphia bottle.

(b) Half dozen pieces *cyanide potassium*, size of a hickory nut.

(c) Drop cyanide into bottle and cover with water.

(d) Sprinkle into the water plaster of paris until a dry cake forms. Dust out, wipe inside of bottle and keep tightly corked.

NOTE.—It is best and safest to have a druggist prepare this bottle; the *cyanide of potassium* is a DEADLY POISON and should not be handled by children under any circumstances. Two or three such bottles will be enough for a room of 40 pupils.

(e) To use the bottle, drop the insect within and cork tightly for a few minutes.

B. *Field Observation and Collecting.*

1. Visit open fields, woods, thickets and marshes. Make a systematic search upon each plant selected for study, as follows, securing at least one specimen from each part infested.

Take but one plant at a time and without haste, make the examination without alarming or disturbing the insects at work. Remember, great patience is required; to hurry and bustle is to see nothing. For further suggestions, see

Number Work under this subject. Record
your observations on color relations in a chart
prepared according to the form of Chart I.

Consider :

(a) The leaves.
(b) The bark.
(c) The flower.
(d) The fruit.
(e) The stem, external and internal parts.
(f) The roots.
(g) Examine old logs and other decaying
matter.
(h) Hunt for beetles and crickets under
stones and rubbish.
(i) Compare the color of the insect with
that of its surroundings. Make your
notes in chart form according to the
accompanying model.

Before disturbing the insect, consider :

(a) Is the plant herbaceous or woody?
(b) The purpose of the insect visitation.
(c) The insect—eating, spinning, laying
eggs.
(d) The relative abundance of larval and
mature forms.

CHART I. MUTUAL COLOR RELATIONS OF PLANTS AND INSECTS.

1. Name of Insect 2. Name of Plant	COLORS OF INSECT.			COLORS OF PLANTS OR SURFACE.				COLOR RELATIONS.	
	WINGS.	BODY.	TOTAL COLOR EFFECT.	LEAF.	STEM.	1. FLOW'R 2. FRUIT.	SURFACE.	HARMONY CONTRAST.	
								UNIFORM-ITY.	HARMONY CONTRAST
1. Milk-Weed Butterfly. 2. Milk-Weed.	1. Open. 2. Closed. 1. Brown. 2. Grayish	Black.	Brownish.	Green.	PaleGreen	1. Pink.		Uniform-ity.	Harmo-nious.

STUDY OF MATERIAL GATHERED IN THE FIELD.

NOTE.—Encourage individual work. Much time can be gained by devoting the recitation hours to a consideration of reports made by pupils on their personal observations. Give suggestions as they are needed.

A. *Equipment.*
1. Magnifying glass or hand lens.
2. At least two dissecting needles; thrust the eye end of a needle into cedar or pine pen holder.
3. Small, sharp-pointed pair of scissors.

B. QUERIES.

1. *How do the insects obtain their food from plants?*

Consider:
(a) The jaws; shape, size, movement.
(b) Teeth; number, peculiarities; grinding, cutting, crushing.
(c) Pin the insect to a piece of cardboard or soft pine. Open the abdomen lengthwise from upper side with the scissors. It is more satisfactory to sink the board with the insect pinned to it below the surface of water in a shallow pan.
(d) The alimentary canal; note its divisions.
(e) Condition of food in the various parts.
(f) How are the insects constructed that they may secure the nectar and other liquid parts of plants?

2. *How are insects constructed that they may deposit eggs within the plant tissues?* Pin specimen to a board as before directed and

Consider :

(a) The ovipositor ; its protecting sheath; shape, size, etc.

(b) Examine, under the magnifier, the spinning apparatus.

3. *How do insects move from place to place?*

(a) Select insects that have means of flight.
Consider :

(b) Number of wings.

(c) Arrangement of wings—separate, overlapping, interlocking, etc.

(d) Where two pairs are present the function of each pair.

(e) How the wings are moved when flying.

(f) How the wings are disposed when at rest.

(g) The contrasts in wing structure.

(h) The spread of wing compared with weight and size of body.

(i) How the character of the wings affects the mode of flying.

(j) Insect flight compared with that of birds.

4. *How are insects adapted to moving about over the plant and how do they cling to it?*

Consider:

(a) The number of legs.

(b) The position and relative size of the legs.

(c) The attachment of the legs to the body.

(d) The joints of the legs; in how many planes do the legs bend at each joint?

(e) The use of so many joints; how do other animals secure an equal range of movement with fewer joints?

(f) The foot structure; claws, pads, etc.

(g) Order of movement of legs in walking or running.

5. *What are the provisions in the structure of the insect designed as means of attack and defense?*

Consider :

(a) Color.

(b) Carapace or outside shell.

(c) Odors.

(d) Bodily secretions.

(e) Stings.

(f) Means of concealment in the plant structure.

(g) Character of insect — pugnacious or cowardly?

(h) Positions and attitudes assumed when feeding or resting.

NUMBER WORK.

QUERY: *What is the evidence that the colors of insects are significant of their relations to plants or to other animals?* (See note under problem 1 in *Number Work* under head of. *Plants.*)

A. Study the same insect and consider the locations chosen for alighting in 10 to 25 instances.

B. Study 10 to 25 insects and consider their habits while they are resting or feeding.

C. Make your notes in a chart farm, ruled as in the accompanying model.—Chart I.

NOTE.—Remember these observations require both *time* and *patience.* Without exercise of the greatest care in observation the problems following are worse than useless.

Problems.

1. What per cent. of the insects observed alighted for the purpose of feeding or rest in situations that were, through color, protective?

2. What per cent. of the entire number was made more conspicuous by their surroundings?

3. In your observations upon a single insect, what per cent. of the number of situations selected by it for feeding or rest was protective?

4. What per cent. of the insects assumed, while feeding or resting, certain positions or attitudes that were protective?

5. What per cent. of the insects observed seem to lack protective coloration?

6. What per cent. of the insects observed are, through other means, able to dispense with protective coloration?

7. What per cent. of the insects examined have some special enemy which they habitually try to avoid?

8. What per cent. of the insects observed do you know certainly to be the food of other animals?

9. Compare the ratio of wing area to bodily weight in the various forms studied.

REPRESENTATIVE EXPRESSION.

1. *Drawing.* Make all drawings to exact scale. Enlarge if necessary to show parts distinctly.

    (a) The insect as a whole, showing correct form and proportions.

    (b) Parts of the insect that have peculiar interest in form or function — foot, jaws, teeth, wings, ovipositor.

    (c) The internal parts—alimentary canal.

2. *Painting.*

    (a) The insect as seen on a plant or on the ground, as feeding or at rest.

    (b) Eggs, cocoons, larvæ, nests.

III.

METEOROLOGY.

A. MANUAL TRAINING. *Apparatus-making.*

1. *The Hygrometer.* Select two mercurial thermometers which under similar conditions read the same. Fasten these, side by side, on a small board to the bottom of which (about two and one-half inches below the bulbs) is attached a shelf sufficiently large to support a wide-mouthed two-ounce bottle. Wrap one of the bulbs with clean, thin muslin and allow a bundle of twenty-five threads to reach from the muslin envelope down to the bottom of the bottle. Fill the bottle with clean water and allow the threads to enter through a hole in the cork. The water evaporating from the muslin cools the bulb. The dryer the air at a given temperature, the greater the amount of evaporation and the more the bulb is cooled, consequently the lower the reading of the wet-bulb thermometer.

2. *Thermometer.* Must be purchased.

3. *Barometer.* Should be purchased. The tube, if great economy is necessary, may be purchased and filled carefully with mercury. This may be fastened to a yard or meter stick to show the height of the mercurial column.

4. *Raingauge.** A three-inch standard gauge may be purchased for one dollar and twenty-five cents. (Henry J. Green, manufacturer of meteorological instruments, 1191 Bedford avenue, Brooklyn, N. Y.)

The U. S. standard gauge is accurately made as follows:

(a) Cylindrical tube 20 inches long, inside diameter, 2.53 inches.

(b) Cylindrical receiver, inside diameter 8 inches, with funnel shaped bottom. The sides of the cylindrical part of (b) may be about 2 inches.

(c) The receiver (b) is fitted on the under side, or funnel end, with a sleeve or short tube which slides over the tube (a), so that all the rain falling into (b) will pass down into (a).

(d) The depth of water falling into (b) is magnified 10 times when it stands in (a). That is, 10 inches of water in (a)$=$1 inch of rainfall. Use small wire in measuring depth in (a). The instrument may be made of sheet copper by a skillful tinsmith.

B. *Observation of meteorological conditions.*

1. Select convenient hours. Let certain pupils record observations, say, at 8:30 A. M; others, at 12 to 1 P. M.; others, 3 to 4 P. M.

2. The pupils should record the conditions

---

*These, and the following directions, are adapted from Instructions to Voluntary Observers, Weather Bureau, Washington, D. C.

prevailing at time of observation when possible.

3. Certain observations, dew or frost, for example, must be recorded from memory. Record the rainfall during the previous 24 hours.

4. How to use the hygrometer: Before taking a reading, cause a brisk current of air to pass over both bulbs of the hygrometer, either by fanning or whirling. When whirled before making the readings, instruments of the most diverse patterns are strictly comparable.

TABLE I.

Directions for finding the dew point: $t=$dry thermometer, $t'=$wet thermometer.

If at a reading $t=60°$, and $t'=50°$ $t-t'=$ $10°$. Turning to Table I, follow the left-hand column dry thermometer until you come to 60°. Follow column at the top of the page (difference between dry and wet thermometer) towards the right until you come to 10°; the number in the column below this opposite °60 is 40° or the dew point for the reading.

TABLE II.—RELATIVE HUMIDITY.

In Table II is given the relative humidity corresponding to the reading of the dry and wet bulb thermometers. The relative humidity of the air at any time is the percentage of moisture contained in the air as compared with the whole amount it is capable of holding at that particular temperature. Air containing no moisture is at zero relative humidity; when saturated, the relative humidity is 100.

TABLE I.—Temperature of the dew point, in degrees Fahrenheit.

(Dry ther.)	Difference between the dry and wet thermometers ($t-t'$).											
	1°.0	2°.0	3°.0	4°.0	5°.0	6°.0	7°.0	8°.0	9°.0	10°.0	11.°0	12°.0
20	17	13	8	2	-6	-19						
21	18	14	9	4	-4	-15	-47					
22	19	15	11	6	-1	-11	-31					
23	20	16	12	7	+1	-8	-24					
24	21	18	14	9	3	-5	-18					
25	22	19	15	11	5	-2	-13	-42				
26	23	20	16	12	7	0	-9	-28				
27	24	21	18	14	9	+3	-6	-20				
28	25	22	19	15	11	5	-3	-15	-54			
29	26	24	20	17	12	7	0	-10	-32			
30	27	25	22	18	14	9	+2	-6	-22			
31	29	26	23	19	15	11	5	-3	-15			
32	30	27	24	21	17	13	7	0	-10	-33		
33	31	28	25	22	18	14	9	+3	-6	-22		
34	32	29	26	24	20	16	11	6	-2	-15		
35	32	30	28	25	22	18	13	8	+1	-9	-32	
36	34	31	29	26	23	19	15	10	4	-5	-20	
37	35	32	30	27	24	21	17	12	6	-2	-14	-52
38	36	33	31	28	26	22	19	14	9	+2	-8	-29
39	37	34	32	29	27	24	20	16	11	5	-4	-18
40	38	35	33	30	28	25	22	18	13	8	0	-12
41	39	36	34	32	29	26	23	20	15	10	+4	-6
42	40	38	35	33	30	27	24	21	18	12	7	-2
43	41	39	36	34	31	29	26	23	19	14	9	+2
44	42	40	37	35	32	30	27	24	20	16	12	6
45	43	41	39	36	33	31	28	25	22	18	13	8
46	44	42	40	37	35	32	30	27	24	20	16	11
47	45	43	41	39	36	33	31	28	25	22	18	13
48	46	44	42	40	37	35	32	29	26	23	20	15
49	47	45	43	41	38	36	33	31	28	25	21	17
50	48	46	44	42	40	37	34	32	29	26	23	19
51	49	47	45	43	41	38	36	33	31	28	24	21
52	50	48	46	44	42	40	37	34	32	29	26	23
53	51	49	47	45	43	41	38	36	33	30	28	24
54	52	50	49	46	44	42	40	37	34	32	29	26
55	53	52	50	48	46	43	41	39.	36	33	30	28
56	54	53	51	49	47	44	42	40	37	34	32	29
57	55	54	52	50	48	46	44	41	39	36	33	30

TABLE I.--Temperature of the dew point, in degrees Fahrenheit.
CONTINUED.

t (Dry ther.)	Difference between the dry and wet thermometers (t—t').											
	1°.0	2°.0	3°.0	4°.0	5°.0	6°.0	7°.0	8°.0	9°.0	10°.0	11°.0	12°.0
58	56	55	53	51	49	47	45	42	40	37	35	32
59	57	56	54	52	50	48	46	44	41	39	36	33
60	58	57	55	53	51	49	47	45	43	40	38	35
61	59	58	56	54	52	50	48	46	44	42	39	36
62	60	59	57	55	53	52	50	48	45	43	41	38
63	61	60	58	56	55	53	51	49	47	44	42	39
64	62	61	59	57	56	54	52	50	48	46	43	41
65	63	62	60	59	57	55	53	51	49	47	45	42
66	64	63	61	60	58	56	54	52	50	48	46	44
67	66	64	62	61	59	57	55	54	52	50	47	45
68	67	65	63	62	60	58	57	55	53	51	49	46
69	68	66	64	63	61	59	58	56	54	52	50	48
70	69	67	66	64	62	61	59	57	55	53	51	49
71	70	68	67	65	63	62	60	58	56	55	53	51
72	71	69	68	66	64	63	61	59	58	56	54	52
73	72	70	69	67	66	64	62	61	59	57	55	53
74	73	71	70	68	67	65	63	62	60	58	56	54
75	74	72	71	69	68	66	64	63	61	59	57	56
76	75	73	72	70	69	67	65	64	62	61	59	57
77	76	74	73	71	70	68	67	65	63	62	60	58
78	77	75	74	72	71	69	68	66	65	63	61	59
79	78	76	75	73	72	70	69	67	66	64	62	61
80	79	77	76	74	73	72	70	68	67	65	63	62
81	80	78	77	75	74	73	71	70	68	66	65	63
82	81	79	78	77	75	74	72	71	69	68	66	64
83	82	80	79	78	76	75	73	72	70	69	67	65
84	83	81	80	79	77	76	74	73	71	70	68	67
85	84	82	81	80	78	77	75	74	72	71	69	68
86	85	83	82	81	79	78	76	75	73	72	71	69
87	86	84	83	82	80	79	78	76	74	73	72	70
88	87	85	84	83	81	80	79	77	75	74	73	71
89	88	86	85	84	82	81	80	78	76	76	74	72
90	89	87	86	85	84	82	81	79	78	77	75	74
91	90	88	87	86	85	83	82	80	79	78	76	75
92	.91	89	88	87	86	84	83	82	80	79	77	76
93	92	91	89	88	87	85	84	83	81	80	78	77
94	93	92	90	89	88	86	85	84	82	81	80	78

TABLE II.

Relative humidity, per cent.

t (Dry ther.)	\multicolumn{12}{c}{Difference between the dry and wet thermometers ($t-t'$).}

t (Dry ther.)	1°.0	2°.0	3°.0	4°.0	5°.0	6°.0	7°.0	8°.0	9°.0	10°.0	11°.0	12°.0
25	87	74	62	50	38	26	14	3				
26	88	75	63	51	40	28	17	6				
27	88	76	64	53	42	30	19	9				
28	88	77	65	54	43	33	22	11	1			
29	89	77	66	56	45	35	24	14	4			
30	89	78	67	57	47	36	26	17	7			
31	89	79	68	58	48	38	29	19	10			
32	90	79	69	59	50	40	31	21	12	3		
33	90	80	70	60	51	42	33	24	15	6		
34	91	81	72	62	53	44	35	26	17	9		
35	91	82	73	65	54	45	37	28	19	12	3	
36	91	82	73	66	56	47	38	30	22	14	6	
37	91	82	74	66	57	48	40	32	24	16	8	1
38	92	83	75	67	58	50	42	34	26	18	11	3
39	92	83	75	68	59	52	44	36	28	20	13	6
40	92	84	76	68	60	53	45	38	30	22	16	8
41	92	84	76	69	61	54	46	39	32	24	18	10
42	92	84	77	69	62	55	48	40	34	27	20	13
43	92	85	77	70	63	56	49	42	35	29	22	15
44	92	85	78	70	63	57	50	43	37	30	24	17
45	92	85	78	71	64	58	51	44	38	32	25	19
46	93	85	79	72	65	58	52	46	39	33	27	21
47	93	86	79	72	66	59	53	47	40	34	28	22
48	93	86	79	73	66	60	53	48	42	36	30	24
49	93	86	80	73	67	60	54	49	43	37	31	26
50	93	87	80	74	67	61	55	50	44	38	33	27
51	93	87	81	74	68	62	56	50	45	39	34	28
52	94	87	81	75	69	63	57	51	46	40	35	30
53	94	87	81	75	69	63	58	52	47	42	36	31
54	94	88	82	76	70	64	59	53	48	43	38	32
55	94	88	82	76	70	65	59	54	49	43	39	34
56	94	88	82	77	71	65	60	55	50	44	40	35
57	94	88	83	77	71	66	61	55	50	45	40	36
58	94	89	83	78	72	67	61	56	51	46	42	37
59	94	89	83	78	72	67	62	57	52	47	43	38

TABLE II.—CONTINUED.

Relative humidity, per cent.

t (Dry ther.)	Difference between the dry and wet thermometers ($t-t'$).											
	1°.0	2°.0	3°.0	4°.0	5°.0	6°.0	7°.0	8°.0	9°.0	10°.0	11°.0	12°.0
60	94	89	84	78	73	68	63	58	53	48	44	39
61	94	89	84	78	73	68	63	·58	54	49	44	40
62	95	89	84	79	74	69	64	59	54	50	45	41
63	95	89	84	79	74	69	64	60	55	51	46	42
64	95	90	85	79	74	70	65	60	56	51	47	43
65	95	90	85	80	75	70	65	61	56	52	48	44
66	95	90	85	80	75	71	66	61	57	53	49	45
67	95	90	85	80	76	71	66	62	28	53	49	45
68	95	90	85	81	76	71	67	63	58	54	50	46
69	95	90	86	81	76	72	67	63	59	55	51	47
70	95	90	86	81	77	72	68	64	60	55	52	48
71	95	91	86	81	77	72	68	64	60	56	52	48
72	95	91	86	82	77	73	69	65	61	57	53	49
73	95	91	86	82	78	73	69	65	61	57	53	50
74	95	91	86	82	78	74	70	66	62	58	54	50
75	95	91	87	82	78	74	70	66	62	58	55	51
76	95	91	87	82	78	74	70	66	63	59	55	52
77	95	91	87	83	78	74	71	67	63	59	56	52
78	96	91	87	83	79	75	71	67	63	60	56	53
79	96	91	87	83	79	75	71	68	64	60	57	53
80	96	92	87	83	79	75	72	68	64	61	57	54
81	96	92	88	84	80	76	72	68	65	61	28	54
82	96	92	88	84	80	76	72	69	65	62	58	55
83	96	92	88	84	80	76	73	69	66	62	59	55
84	96	92	88	84	80	77	73	69	66	63	59	56
85	96	92	88	84	80	77	73	70	66	63	60	56
86	96	92	88	84	81	77	73	70	67	63	60	57
87	96	92	88	84	81	77	74	70	67	64	60	57
88	96	92	88	85	81	77	74	71	67	64	61	58
89	96	92	88	85	81	78	74	71	68	64	61	58
90	96	92	88	85	81	78	75	71	68	65	62	59
91	96	92	89	85	82	78	75	71	68	65	62	59
92	96	92	89	85	82	78	75	72	69	65	62	59
93	96	93	89	85	82	78	75	72	69	66	63	60
94	96	93	89	86	82	79	75	72	69	66	63	60

TABLE III.

Grains of water-vapor contained in a cubic foot of air.

Dew Point	0	1	2	3	4	5	6	7	8	9
−20	.219									
−10	.356	.340	.324	.309	.294	.281	.267	.254	.242	.231
− 0	.564	.540	.516	.493	.471	.450	.430	.411	.391	.374
+ 0	.554	.590	.617	.545	.574	.705	.735	.767	.801	.837
10	.873	.910	.950	.991	1.033	1.075	1.122	1.169	1.217	1.268
20	1.321	1.374	1.430	1.488	1.550	1.611	1.675	1.743	1.812	1.884
30	1.958	2.034	2.113	2.194	2.279	2.366	2.457	2.550	2.646	2.748
40	2.849	2.955	3.054	3.177	3.294	3.414	3.589	3.557	3.800	3.936
50	4.076	4.222	4.372	4.526	4.685	4.849	5.018	5.191	5.371	5.555
60	5.744	5.941	6.142	6.350	6.563	6.782	7.009	7.241	7.480	7.726
70	7.980	8.240	8.508	8.782	9.065	9.355	9.655	9.961	10.277	10.601
80	10.933	11.275	11.626	11.987	12.356	12.736	13.127	13.575	13.937	14.358
90	14.791	15.234	15.688	16.155	16.634	17.124	17.626	18.142	18.671	19.212
100	19.766	20.335	20.917	21.514	22.125	22.751				

TABLE III.—WEIGHT OF VAPOR IN THE ATMOS-

PHERE.

1. By Table I, find the dew point.

2. Find the number of grains of moisture per cubic foot of atmosphere as given opposite the dew-point temperature in Table III. Example: Dew point$=43°$; amount of vapor per cubic foot$=3.177$ grains.

Special precautions to be observed in using the hygrometer.

1. Do not take a reading immediately after wetting the bulb.

2. Continue fanning or whirling until the wet bulb reaches its *lowest* reading.

3. Record the lowest reading of wet bulb.

4. Do not allow the muslin on wet bulb to become even *partly* dry.

5. Take the temperature not less than six feet above the sod.

6. Keep the instrument sufficiently far from the body to avoid the influence of the bodily temperature.

7. Do not take the observation in direct sunshine, nor in heavy shade of wall or house.

8. When the temperature is below freezing, keep the instrument indoors. To take an observation, merely wet the bulb, without using the bottle, step outside and whirl as before.

SUGGESTION.—Each pupil should keep a systematic daily weather record in a chart form prepared on the plan of the accompanying model.*

QUERIES:

1. *What are the most important weather influences that may be directly recognized in the appearance of living things?*

Consider:

    (a) Temperature.
    (b) Wind.
    (c) Clouds and cloudiness.
    (d) Humidity.
    (e) Rainfall.

---

*See the author's *Nature Study Record*.

CHART II.—METEOROLOGICAL RECORD FOR.................. 18....

DAY	DATE	FROST OR DEW.	DIRECTION OF WIND.	CLOUDINESS; FOGS	RAINFALL	TEMPERATURE	BAROMETER	SUN RISES	SUN SETS	MOON'S PHASES	MOON RISES	MOON SETS	MORNING STAR.	EVENING STAR

Weekly Summary

(f) Fogs, frost, dew. Especially note date and effect of the first frosts in autumn.

2. *What factors enter into temperature?* (See topics under astronomy.)

Consider:

(a) The extremes of daily temperature and the daily range.
(b) The daily average temperature.
(c) The time of highest temperature.
(d) Direction, veering and force of the winds.
(e) Humidity.

3. *What phenomena of life, at present, are due chiefly to the temperature?*

Consider:

(a) Landscape coloration.
(b) Activity of animal life — sluggish or active.
(c) Effect upon modes or habits of life; note the earthworm; the frogs; the insects.

4. *What is the effect of temperature on the soil?* (See detailed suggestions under Mineralogy.)

5. *What are the chief influences of the wind?*

Consider:

(a) Its relation to temperature.
(b) Its relation to clouds: Forms; degree of cloudiness.

(c) Its relation to humidity; to dew and frost.

(d) Its relation to rainfall. Rain bearing? Dry?

6. *What are the influences of clouds?*

Consider:

  (a) The appearance of plants on cloudy days; position of leaves and flowers.

  (b) Activity of animal life; worms, butterflies and other insects; birds.

  (c) Cloud forms at different hours of the day.

7. *What are the influences of humidity?* Use hygrometer to measure the absolute humidity and to determine the dewpoint. Collect data and record it according to the form given in chart III.

Consider:

  (a) Effects in forming dew; are humid days followed by dewy nights?

  (b) Effects upon animal life—especially upon one's personal comfort.

  (c) The appearance of plants; does a humid atmosphere prevent wilting?

8. *What are the effects due to rainfall— heavy and light?* Collect data and record it according to the form given in chart IV.

Consider:

  (a) Temperature.

(b) Height of barometer.

(c) Effects upon plants; position of flowers and leaves.

(d) Effects upon animal life ; worms, insects, frogs, etc.

(e) Relation to wind ; direction, veering and velocity.

(f) Relation to clouds and cloudiness. See *Number Work*.

9. *What are the conditions for fog, dew and frost, and what are their noticeable effects upon plants ?*

Consider:

(a) Humidity.

(b) Temperature ; average, extremes.

(c) Wind and clouds.

(d) The position of leaves for the reception of dew.

Chart III.—*Atmospheric Water.*

Gather the data required for this table by means of the hygrometer. From the observations made, and by the use of *Tables*, calculate the quantity of water suspended in a given space.

DATE.	Hour.	Dry Bulb.	Wet Bulb.	Relative Humidity.	Dew Point.	Grains per Cubic Foot.	Am't over one acre 100 feet above surface.	Equivalent in rainfall.

Signed,.................

CHART IV.—*Rainfall.*

Determine the rainfall by measurement, or use the records of the Weather Bureau as reported by the daily papers. Calculate the amount of water that falls upon various areas, *e. g.*, the area covering the roots of the tree studied, an acre of grain, etc.

DATE AND TIME OF DAY.	Average T'mp'rature	Total precipitation and hours of rainfall.	Gallons on root area of a tree; state radius.	Gallons of water per square yd.	Barrels of water per acre.	Barrels of water per square mile.	Cubic feet of water per acre, per sq. mile.

Signed,..............................

STUDY OF THE UNITED STATES WEATHER MAPS.

NOTE.—In order to more clearly understand the local changes of weather, the pupils must master the interpretation of the daily record as presented in these maps. Study carefully the explanation of the symbols as given on the margin of the maps.

1. Locate the *Low Areas*, i. e., the areas of least atmospheric pressure.

2. Locate the *High Areas*, i. e., the areas of greatest atmospheric pressure.

3. What is the direction of the isobars with respect to these two areas?

4. By means of the *scale of miles* given on the margin of the map, measure the distance from both the *Low* and the *High* to the outermost isobar that curves about each. What area is included within this circle?

5. By a study of *all the arrows* within these circles determine the general direction of the wind.

6. What difference noticed, in the general drift of the arrows, between the *Low* and the *High* regions?

7. Consider the direction of the wind in the different quarters of the general whirl.

    (a) East of the *Low*, what is the direction?

    (b) Northeast of the *Low;* what is the direction?

    (c) North of the *Low;* what is the direction?

(d) Northwest of the *Low;* what is the direction ?

(e) West of the *Low;* what is the direction ?

(f) Southwest of the *Low;* what is the direction ?

(g) South of the *Low;* what is the direction ?

(h) Southeast of the *Low;* what is the direction ?

8. What movement as a whole does the storm make from day to day? Consult successive maps.

9. If the storm is moving eastward, how would the wind veer at a place that is north of the path traversed by the *Low?*

10. How would the wind veer at a place lying south of the path of the *Low* area?

11. If the storm is moving northeast or north, consider how the wind must veer on different sides of the *Low?*

12. Suppose at your place of observation, the wind is observed to be southeast (i. e., from the southeast) and that it veers to east and northeast; describe the position and path of the *Low Area.*

13. Suppose the wind is southwest and veers west and northwest; describe the position and path of the *Low Area.*

14. A storm passing northward along the Mississippi river and northeast along the Ohio river, would bring moisture to Chicago from

what direction? How would the wind veer with the passing storm?

15. Carefully note the paths of the *Low Areas* for the month; which storms bring rain and which ones are dry?

16. In which half or quarter of the storm is the rain?

17. In which quarter is the highest temperature?

18. In which quarter is the lowest temperature?

19. In which quarter are the clouds? Why?

20. Which quarter is clear? Why?

21. Can you tell in which quarter of a storm you are located? Consider:

    (a) Temperature; rising or falling?

    (b) Character of clouds; cloudiness increasing or diminishing?

    (c) Veering of the wind?

    (d) Barometer; rising or falling?

22. Compare the *High Area* with the *Low Area* as to temperature, direction of the wind, its path, cloudiness and rainfall.

23. Note the direction of the isotherms with respect to the two areas? What do the curves indicate?

24. Compare the direction of the isotherms with that of the parallels; where is the greatest divergence between the two? Look closely for the first appearance of the *frost line* in the United States.

25. Where are the condensing areas of the

TABLE IV

GENERAL RULES, PREPARED BY E. B. GARRIOTT, WEATHER BUREAU, CHICAGO.

BAROMETER. Reduced to sea level. *	WIND DIRECTION.	CHARACTER OF WEATHER INDICATED.
30.00 to 30.20 and steady.	W.	Fair, with slight changes in temperature for one or two days.
30.00 to 30.20 and rising rapidly.	W.	Fair and cooler, followed within three days by rain or snow, depending upon the season.
30.00 to 30.20 and falling slowly.	S.	Warmer, with rain or snow within two days.
30.20, or above, and falling rapidly.	E. to S.	Warmer, with rain or snow within thirty-six hours.
30.20, or above, and rising rapidly.	W. to N.	Cold and clear, quickly followed by warmer, and rain or snow.
30.20, or above, and steady.	Variable.	No immediate change.
30.00, or below, and falling slowly.	S. to N. E.	Rain or snow within twelve hours, that will continue at least a day or two.
30.00, or below, and falling rapidly.	S. to E.	Rain or snow, with high wind, followed within two days by clearing, colder.
30.00, or below, and rising.	S. to W.	Clearing and colder within twelve hours.
29.80, or below, and falling rapidly.	S. to E.	Severe storm of wind, and rain or snow within twelve hours.
29.80, or below, and falling rapidly.	E. to N.	Severe northeast gales, and heavy rain or snow. In winter, cold wave within twenty-four hours.
29.80, or below, and rising rapidly.	Going to W.	Clearing and colder within twelve hours.

Rapid changes in the barometer indicate marked and early changes in the weather.

*To reduce the barometer to sea level at the elevation of Chicago (690 feet), add to the observed reading the fraction given with the temperature at time of observation. For complete table, see *Instructions to Voluntary Observers.*

Temperature	−20o	−10o	0o	10o	20o	30o	40o	50o	60o	70o	80o	90o	100o
Fraction to be added	.754	.737	.719	.702	.686	.672	.667	.643	.629	.617	.605	.693	.581

United States as shown by the areas of rainfall?

26. Whence is the vapor derived that furnishes the rain to the United States in the interior? On the coasts?

NOTE.—By kind permission, the author gives a few general rules for predicting the weather which have been prepared by Prof. E. B. Garriott, of the Chicago Weather Bureau. The signs hold good, with slight modifications, for all regions east of the Rocky Mountains. (See page 33.)

NUMBER WORK.

NOTE.—*Use the data recorded in the charts when it is possible to do so.*

A. *Temperature.*

1. Find the average temperature for the week.

2. What is the greatest range of temperature during any day of the week?

3. What was the greatest range of temperature during the week?

4. What is the greatest range of temperature during the month?

5. What is the average temperature for the month?

6. Compare the average temperature of each week with the average for the month.

7. What was the greatest change in temperature noted after rainfall?

B. *Barometer.*

8. What is the average height of the barometer for the month?

9. What was the greatest *daily* range of the barometer during the month?

10. What was the greatest range during the month?

11. What is the average height of the barometer during the rainy days?

12. The average height during the rainy days equals what per cent. of the average height during the clear days?

C. *Rainy, cloudy and clear days.*

13. The number of rainy days is what per cent. of the entire month?

14. The number of cloudy days is what per cent. of the entire month?

15. The number of clear days is what per cent. of the entire month?

16. The number of rainy days equals what per cent. of the number of cloudy days?

17. The number of rainy days equals what per cent. of the number of clear days?

18. The number of cloudy days equals what per cent. of the number of clear days?

D. *Rainfall.*

19. What is the average daily rainfall for the month?

20. The daily average for the month is what per cent. of the average for the rainy days?

21. The average for the rainy days is what per cent. of that for the cloudy days?

22. How many gallons of rain fell during the month per square foot?

23. How many barrels of water fell during the month per acre? Per square mile?

24. How many tons of water fell per acre? Per square mile?

25. The water which fell during the month upon an acre would fill a tank 100 feet square to what depth?

26. To what depth would such a tank be filled by the water which fell during the month upon a square mile?

27. Construct tanks of other dimensions but having the same volumes.

28. Is the rainfall for the month above or below the average? How much water is in excess or lacking this month, per square foot?

E. *Frost, Dew and Fogs; Humidity.*

29. The frosty mornings are what per cent. of the entire month? The dewy mornings?

30. Using the data obtained by the hygrometer, calculate the amount of water, in barrels, over an acre within 100 feet of the surface. The amount over a square mile at same height.

31. Suppose this amount of water were to descend in rain, what depth of rainfall would it make?

32. Find the relative humidity, i. e., the percentage of saturation; how much water would there be, per cubic foot, in the atmosphere if it were saturated at this temperature?

33. How much water, at the same rate, would there be over one acre, 100 feet above the surface? A square mile?

IV.

ASTRONOMY. A STUDY OF SUNSHINE DISTRIBUTION.

MANUAL TRAINING.

A. *A Color Chart.**

1. Upon a sheet of cardboard, aboxt 14×16 inches, rule off a series of two-inch squares in such a way that each square will stand for *one* day, as in the ordinary wall calendar.

2. From a selected series of colored papers, cut a number of two-inch disks and allow each color to stand for a certain phase of weather.

3. At the close of each day (or on the following morning) paste in the proper square the colored disk which will most appropriately represent the weather.

4. The following colors (named according to the Bradley Educational Colored Papers) are suggested: (a) Clear, yellow. (b) Fair (three-tenths clear), orange yellow. (c) Cloudy, cool gray No. 1. (d) Rainy, cool gray No. 2. (d) First frosts of autumn and last frosts of

---

*For this suggestion, acknowledgment is due Miss Florence Fox, a student in Cook County Normal School. The author knows of no more graphic way of representing the meteorological conditions for a year, month by month. With Chart II it forms a valuable supplement to the landecape work. The color chart may be modified in many interesting ways.

spring, small white disks in center of the large ones. (e) Snow, white. (f) An arrow drawn across each disk will show direction of the wind. (g) At the end of the month, paste a narrow strip of paper on the card, near the margin, of proper length to show depth of rainfall.

B. *The Skiameter.*

The Skiameter.

This instrument, illustrated in the accompanying cut, has been devised as an easy means of measuring the distribution of a given beam of sunshine at any slant. This is accomplished by measuring the area of the *shadow* cast by the cross section of the stick *a*, when the latter has the same slant as the sun's rays. For this reason, the name skiameter (Greek *skia,* shadow, and *metron*, measure) is suggested. Almost any one can make the apparatus, and the mode of using it will be understood from the·following explanation :

A, beam of wood 10 units (centimeters suggested) square and about 30 cm. long; *b*, brass protractor; *c*, plumb line; *d e*, meter stick; *x*, bottom board 10 cm. wide; *y*, side board 10 cm. high; *p*, copper or tin strip for adjusting (*a*); *t*, block of wood; *o*, compass; *l*, level ; *v*, hinge.

To take an observation of sunshine distribution at noon: Place the skiameter at *noon* on *north* and *south* line on a *level* surface, *a* pointing south ; adjust *a* until shadow of edges *w* and *w'* coincide on *x* in line *f m*; beam *a* then has the same slant as the sun's rays; *f m n g* equals the area covered by a beam of sunlight having the same slant and sectional area as *a*; measure the edge *f g* by reading distance *h i* on *d e*; find degree of slant of *a* by means of the plumb line *c*.

To take an observation of sunshine distribution at any other hour, place the skiameter so that the line of shadow (*g f*) is in the plane of the corresponding side of *a* and proceed as before.

QUERIES :

1. *What is the variation in sunshine distribution at various points between the equator and the poles?*

A. *Distribution of noon sunshine at the time of the equinox.*

Collect and record data according to the form prescribed in Chart V.

Consider :

(a) The position of the sun at noon with

Chart V.—*Distribution of Sunshine.*

Measure slant with skiameter in successive weeks. Calculate area of distribution of sunshine at each angle found. Compare areas. Compare the varying intensity. Compare mean daily temperatures at time of measurements.

DATE.	Slant.	Area of Distribution.	Average Temperature.	Ratio of Areas.	Ratio of Intensities.	Ratio of Temperatures.

Signed,..

respect to an observer at the equator.

(b) The slant of the rays.

(c) The area covered by a beam of sunshine the size of (a) in the skiameter.

(d) If the observer moves 1° north, what
would be the angle of the rays with
the vertical? If he moves 10° north?
40° north? 70° north? 90° north?

(e) The relation of the slant of the rays at
noon at the equinox to the observer's
⌐ latitude.

B. *Distribution of noon sunshine before and
after the equinox.*

Consider:

(a) The sun's noon rays vertical north of
the equator; if north 10°, what
would be the slant to the observer at
that point?

(b) Under such conditions what would be
the noon slant to an observer at 40°
north latitude? 60° north latitude?

(c) The sun's noon rays vertical 10° south
of the equator; what would be the
slant to an observer on the equator?

(d) The slant to an observer 40° north
latitude? 70° north latitude?

(e) The area covered by a vertical beam of
sunshine the size of (a) in the skiameter is $10 \times 10 = 100$ square units; what
would be the areas respectively covered at the slants mentioned in (b)?
At the slants mentioned in (c)? In (d)?

C. *Distribution of sunshine at a given place at different hours of the day.*

Consider:

(a) The slant at 9 o'clock A. M.

(b) The slant at 10 o'clock A. M.; at 11 o'clock A. M.

(c) The slant at 1 o'clock P. M.; at 2, 3 and 4 P. M.

(d) The corresponding forenoon and afternoon hours.

(e) The difference in temperature at the corresponding hours.

D. *What is the variation in length of day and night?*

Consider:

(a) Variations in time of sunrise.

(b) Variation in time of sunset.

(c) Different latitudes. (The pupils should have access to the Nautical Almanac* for data under [c].)

NUMBER WORK.

QUERY: *What is the relation between the different areas representing the distribution of a given beam of sunshine in different latitudes?*

1. Find the area showing the distribution of a beam in your latitude. Use the skiameter.

2. Compare the area obtained in (1) with the corresponding area 10° south; 10° north.

3. The sunshine exactly covering, at noon, an

---

*Government Printing Office, Washington, D. C.

acre in central Illinois, will cover how much ground in southern Louisiana?

4. How much will the same sunshine cover in northern Minnesota?

5. The sunshine covering an acre at 9 o'clock A. M. will cover how much ground at 10 o'clock A. M.? At 11 o'clock A. M.? At 12 o'clock noon?

6. The sunshine covering an acre at 12 o'clock, noon, will cover how much at 1 o'clock P. M.?

7. How much will it cover at 2 P. M.?

8. How much will it cover at 3 P. M.?

9. How much will it cover at 4 P. M.?

10. How much will it cover at 5 P. M?

11. The sunshine covering an acre of ground on the first day of September, will cover how much the last day of the month?

REPRESENTATIVE EXPRESSION.

1. *Drawing.*

    (a) The sun is approximately 864,000 miles in diameter; the earth 8,000 miles; draw circles representing the circumference of each. If the diameter of the earth is represented by a line one inch long, how long a line must be used to represent the sun's diameter?

    (b) The actual distance between the sun and earth is, approximately, 96,000,-000 miles; on a proper scale how far apart should the two circles above described be placed?

(c) Draw a square two inches on a side to represent a given noon sunshine distribution at the equinox on the equator.

(d) On this scale represent the noon sunshine distribution, same date, at latitude 10°, 20°, 30°, 40°, 50°, 60°, 70°, 80°.

(e) By a rectangle two inches wide and proper length represent the sunshine distribution at the beginning of September.

(f) On this scale, represent the sunshine distribution at the end of the month.

V.

MINERALOGY. STUDY OF SOILS.

A. Mechanical Constituents.

1. *Manual Training.*

   (a) Make two sieves, say, six inches square and two inches deep; in one, use brass wire gauze one-fiftieth inch mesh and in the other use gauze having one-tenth inch mesh.

2. *Apparatus.*
   (a) Scales (Harvard Trip Balance recommended).
   (b) Bunsen burner or alcohol lamp.
   (c) Battersea dish (clay) or porcelain crucible. A small *stamped* tin cake dish will answer the purpose.
   (d) A vessel in which water may be boiled.

3. Query : *What is the proportion of coarse gravel found in the soil?*

   (a) Sift, say, 50 grams through the coarse sieve; wash, dry and weigh what remains in the sieve.

4. Query: *What is the proportion of gravelly sand in the sample of soil?*

(a) Rub through the fine sieve the part which *passed through* the coarse sieve.

(b) Wash, dry and weigh the part too coarse to pass through the fine sieve. This is the *gravelly sand.*

5. QUERY: *What is the proportion of coarse sand in the soil ?*

(a) Take a few grams of the soil that passed through the fine sieve and boil it in water to thoroughly separate the particles.

(b) Rinse water and soil out of the flask into a tall wide-mouthed jar.

(c) Set this jar in a larger one to catch the overflow and by means of a tube reaching to the bottom of the jar, pour water into it, gently agitating the sediment.

(d) When the overflow is *clear*, pour off the water, dry and weigh the remainder for the *coarse sand.*

6. QUERY: *What is the proportion of fine sand ?*

(a) Repeat the process described in (5) with the overflow, agitating the water less ; the result will be the *fine sand.*

7. QUERY: *What is the proportion of clay in the soil ?*

(a) Subtract the weight of the *coarse* and fine sand from the weight of that which passed through the fine sieve and the result will be the weight of clay.

8. QUERY: *What is the proportion of organic matter ?*

(a) Heat, until it ceases to smoke, a known weight of what passes through the fine sieve and weigh; the loss represents the weight of the organic matter.

B. TEMPERATURE OF SOILS.

1. QUERY: *What is the surface temperature of various kinds of soils?*

(a) By means of a stick slightly larger than the thermometer (chemical with scale on glass stem) make a small hole an inch deep.

(b) Insert bulb and take temperature.

2. QUERY: *What is the rate of decrease in temperature as the depth increases and at what depth is the temperature practically uniform ?*

(a) Repeat the experiment described under (1), taking the temperature at different depths.

C. MOISTURE IN THE SOIL.

1. *Manual Training.*

(a) Make a cubical box, one or two inches square; it may be made of stiff cardboard or wood.

CHART VI.—*Loss of Water from Soil.*

Fill a tin or iron pan with earth; measure the area of surface exposed and weigh the earth it contains. It should be 4 to 6 inches deep. Bury it in the ground to a level with adjacent surface. After a given time, weigh again and calculate the loss of moisture per square foot of surface; per acre; per square mile. Observe under different conditions of weather. Repeat experiment, covering soil in pan with sod, to determine effect of growing grass.

DATE.	Area measured.	Character of surface.	Weight of soil.	Hours exposed.	Relat. Humid- ity.	Winds? Cloudy? Day or night?	Temp- erature.	Loss per square foot.	Loss (bbls.) per acre; per sq. mile.	Equiva- lent in rainfall.

Signed,..............

(b) The apparatus needed will be rulers, scales and measures of volume.

2. QUERY: *The water in the soil forms what part of its weight and volume?*

(a) Measure several samples of the soil with the box described above. Select these samples from various depths.

(b) Take the weight of each sample while fresh.

(c) Thoroughly dry the samples and weigh the dry soil.

(d) Find by subtraction the weight of water lost by drying.

(e) Allowing one pound of water to the pint, find the *volume* of water lost by drying the soil.

(f) Calculate the weight and volume of water per cubic foot.

3. QUERY: *How much moisture escapes from the soil through evaporation?* (Chart VI.)

(a) Procure a box of tin or iron (wood will not do) having at least one square foot of surface and a depth of six inches.

(b) Fill it with soil and shake it so that it will have its normal compactness.

(c) Weigh the box with its contents.

(d) Sink the box in some selected spot, where the conditions may be studied, so that the surface of the soil in the box is on a level with the general surface.

(e) At the end of a given time, weigh the box and its contents and calculate the loss per square foot of surface exposed.

4. QUERY: *How much is the loss accelerated or retarded by the presence of sod?*

(a) Prepare the box as described under (3), but cover it with a layer of sod. This should be watered for a few days until growth has well begun, then proceed as before.

NUMBER WORK.

A. QUERY: *What are the proportions of coarse gravel, gravelly sand, coarse sand, fine sand, organic matter and clay in the soil?*

1. The clay is what part of the whole?

2. The fine sand is what part of the whole?

3. The organic matter is what part of the whole?

4. The gravelly sand is what part of the whole?

5. The coarse sand is what part of the whole?

6. The coarse gravel is what part of the whole?

B. QUERY: *What is the absolute quantity of water present in soil within given depths?* (See Query (2) p. 49.)

1. How much water by weight is in a depth of one foot of soil in an area of one acre?

2. How much, same depth, area one square mile?

3. Give the results found in (1) and (2) in gallons.

4. Give the results found in (3) in barrels.

5. Give the results found in (3) in cubic feet.

6. The quantity of water found in (5) would fill a tank 100 feet square to what depth?

7. Calculate the amount of water in the soil to the depth of one foot and with one square rod area; what depth of rainfall would this equal on the same area?

8. Suppose the roots of forest trees to have an average depth of six feet; how much water would be about the roots of a forest one mile square? Give the result in barrels.

9. Give the result found in (8) in cubic feet.

10. How deep would the amount of water found in (9) fill a tank 500 feet square?

C. QUERY: *What is the absolute quantity of water lost from various areas within given times under varying conditions?* (Use data recorded in Chart VI.)

1. How many gallons evaporate from one acre during the hours of daylight? (Consider different conditions; see chart.)

2. How many gallons evaporate from one square mile in daytime.

3. How many cubic feet in the quantities of water found as results in (1) and (2)?

4. How deep would the water fill a tank 200 feet square?

5. The loss from an acre in one day is equal to what depth of rainfall?

6. The loss during a night in clear weather equals what part of the loss during a clear day?*

7. The average loss during cloudy days equals what part of the loss during clear days?

8. The loss from the bare surface in the pan of soil equals what part of the loss from a sodded surface?

REPRESENTATIVE EXPRESSION. (Use data previously collected.)

1. *Drawing.*
   - (a) Draw a square 12 inches on a side and allow it to stand for the entire sample of soil measured.
   - (b) On this scale draw other squares which shall correctly represent the clay, the organic matter, the coarse sand, the fine sand, the gravelly sand and the coarse gravel.
   - (c) Draw a square 12 inches on a side to represent a cubic foot of soil.
   - (d) On the base of the square construct a rectangle which will correctly represent the water in the cubic foot of soil.
   - (e) Draw a square 12 inches on a side to represent a square foot of surface.
   - (f) Draw upon the upper side of the square, as a base, a rectangle showing the depth of water lost by evaporation in twenty-four hours.

2. *Painting.* Landscape work.

---

*In problems of this kind, the pupil must give due consideration to *all* the modifying conditions. See Chart VI.

VI.

THE DISSEMINATION OF SEEDS.

FIELD WORK.

Visit areas having different geographic features, such as, a marsh, a hillside, the banks of a stream, woodland and open fields. Collect specimens of the branches bearing seed pods. Note the relative height of the different plants. Remember that close observations are required upon the plant as a whole where it may be studied in its relations to the soil, air, water and animal life. It is perhaps needless to insist that the observations must be extended as widely as possible.

NOTE.—Nothing but *actual* and *exact* observations should be considered in answering the queries.

QUERIES :

1. *Do the seeds possess the same relative importance for all the plants observed?*

Consider :
  (a) The character of the roots.
  (b) The character of the stem.
  (c) The relative number of seeds borne by the different kinds of plants noted under (a) and (b).

2. *Do the plants, found growing in your*

vicinity, show any well defined arrangement, as to localities, implying some adaptation on their part? That is, can you find evidences of plant communities?

Consider:

    (a) The banks and margins of streams; edges of wet-weather rivulets.

    (b) The ponds and streams—floating and submerged plants.

    (c) The edges of marshes.

    (d) The marshes; the ridges; hillsides.

    (e) The roadsides.

    (f) Hedge rows and fences or other barriers, as logs and stumps.

    (g) Crevices in rocks.

    (h) Proximity to other plants—i. e., the trailers, creepers and climbers.

3. *In what respects is the location occupied by the parent plants likely to become unsuited for the same plants in succeeding years?*

Consider:

    (a) The demands of the plants upon the soil.

    (b) The plant's relations to light.

    (c) The plant's relations to its insect and other enemies.

    (d) The plant's climatic relations.

    (e) The effect, upon each other, of great numbers of germinating seeds of the same kind within a small area.

4. *Upon what means may the plants, in part or wholly, depend as aids in disseminating their seeds ?*

Consider :

(a) The wind.
(b) Streams or bodies of water.
(c) Animals.
(d) Mechanical contrivances found in structure.
(e) The configuration of the surface of the ground.
(f) Artificial means afforded by the accidents of cultivation, roadways, railways, etc.

5. *Which of these agents of distribution is likely to be the most effective ?*

Consider:

(a) Its constancy, steadiness, and range of its operation.
(b) The facility with which plants may take advantage of it.
(c) The chances of the seed's being destroyed by the agent.
(d) The chances of the seed's falling upon a spot suitable for germination.
(e) The chances of the seed's being planted.
(f) The barriers limiting the various agents.

6. *By what adaptations do plants take advantage of the wind as an agent of distribution?*

Consider:

    (a) The height of the plant, both in flowering and at seeding time.

    (b) The shape of the fruits. Shape as related to the direction and movements of the seed in falling. Note the peculiar movements. Account . for them.

    (c) The weight of the fruits.

    (d) The various appendages favoring buoyancy; look into the structure and attachments of pappus, wings and supporting membranes.

    (e) The nature of the plants bearing winged fruits—height, etc.

    (f) The nature of the plants bearing seeds with pappus or down-like appendages.

    (g) The habits of pappus-bearing seeds in damp weather and at night.

    (h) By experiment, the relative distances which the various seeds are borne under the same conditions.

    (i) Which kind of plants seems to be most abundant in your neighborhood? Make an actual count.

    (j) Which kind is most widely distributed over the earth? Consult your geography.

(k) *Suggested for observation:* Dandelion, thistle, asters, fleabane, cat-tail, thoroughwort, wild lettuce, milkweed, basswood, elm, hornbeam, maples, pines.

7. *By what adaptations do plants take advantage of the water as an agent for distributing their seeds?*

Consider:

(a) The specific gravity of the seeds, i. e., will they float?

(b) The behavior of the seeds if allowed to remain in the water; i. e., do they sink or continue to float? Or, if they sink at first, do they rise later?

(c) The contrivances for rendering the seed buoyant; do they belong to the seed itself or its appendages?

(d) The effect of rain or dew upon ripened pods—does it close or open them?

(e) The means by which seeds may be scattered in water where currents are absent.

(f) The proximity of the growing plant to the water; the incidental relation of the surface of the ground; the shape of the seed.

(g) The chances for the seed to be planted in a location suitable for its germination and the later development and growth of the plant.

(h) The principal limiting influences to this mode of distribution.

Suggestion : Test, for buoyancy [see (a) and (b)], all the seeds and fruits not showing special structures adapting them for wind distribution ; such as, all kinds of nuts ; small solid seeds ; fleshy fruits ; the water lilies and other aquatic plants. Distinguish between those seeds that have special adaptations for water dispersal and those that are accidentally disseminated by this means.

8. *What animal life is found in the vicinity of the plants being studied?*

Consider :

(a) The kinds of birds.
(b) The insects.
(c) The mammals.
(d) Other forms.

9. *Through what habits are the animals, found in this locality, related to the plants — especially to the seeds?*

Consider :

(a) Food and feeding habits ; also the coverings of hair, fur and feathers.
(b) Migration.
(c) Burrowing. Storing food.
(d) Wading.
(e) Swimming.

(f) ·Vagrant wanderings—search for food, escape from enemies.

10. *Can you find out if the edibility of fruits is directly related to seed dispersal?*

Consider the edible portions of:

(a) Nuts.
(b) Fleshy fruits—berries, apples, cherries, grapes.

Also consider:

(a) The colors of the ripe and unripe fruit.
(b) The colors of the leaves and branches while the fruit is green and also when it is ripe.
(c) The length of time that it hangs on the plant.
(d) The flavors of the unripe and the ripe fruit.
(e) The odors of the fruit, unripe and ripe.

11. *What are the chances for the seed in edible fruits to escape destruction?*

Consider:

(a) The edibility of the seed itself; its shell or rind.
(b) Its digestibility if eaten along with other parts.
(c) The teeth, gizzard, and other parts of the digestive apparatus of the animals that eat the fruits.
(d) The cud-chewing habits of certain fruit-eating animals.

(e) The chance dropping of the seeds or fruits.

(f) The storing of fruits.

12. *Do any of the inedible fruits show any adaptations to animal life that bear upon seed dispersal?*

Consider :

(a) The burs; what parts of these fruits are hooked?

(b) The various prickly appendages of fruits.

(c) The height of plants bearing prickly or bur fruits.

(d) The kinds of animals likely to infest the locality; their food.

(e) How and why the animals would likely rid themselves of such fruits, if once gathered by them.

(f) The animals infesting the locality which would in no way gather such seeds; their food.

(g) The chances of seeds being carried in the mud that may be gathered by waders and other animals.

(h) The barriers and obstacles which limit this mode of distribution.

13. *Can you find any reason for the curling, twisting, or rolling up of various seed pods that may be found?* Watch the opening of such a fruit and

Consider:

    (a) How the pod opens.

    (b) The effect of touching the ripened but unopened pod.

    (c) The effect of birds or other animals brushing against such ripened pods.

    (d) The effect of the wind.

    (e) The distance the seed is thrown.

    (f) The influences limiting this mode of distribution.

14. *How do the occupations of man favor the dispersal of plants.*

Consider:

    (a) The railways—shipment of live stock, grain and hay.

    (b) Roadways—droves of live stock, local transportation of grain and hay.

    (c) The effect of tilling the soil.

    (d) The interchange of seeds and the various grains among farmers.

    (e) The feeding of live stock on the various grains.

15. *In what seeds and fruits is man interested in autumn?   How are they preserved?   How and to what places are they shipped?*

Consider by observation :

    (a) Those gathered in your own locality. By reading and study of geography,

    (b) Those gathered in other parts of the country and the world.

(c) The wheat area.
(d) The oats area.
(e) The corn area.
(f) The rye area.
(g) The flax area.
(h) The buckwheat area.
(i) The tobacco area.
(j) The cotton area.
(k) The apple area.
(l) The grape area.
(m) The peach area.
(n) The pear area.
(o) The cranberry area.
(p) The plum area.

16. *Can you find any means employed by the plant to bury its seeds in the ground?*

Consider :

(a) The shape of the seed.
(b) Its various hairy or bristly appendages.
(c) The effects of moisture and dryness upon such appendages.

In this connection also

Consider :

(d) The means employed in sowing wheat, rye and other autumn crops.

17. *What is the relative importance in the world at large of the various plants found in your vicinity? By reference to geography and to books on distribution of life on the globe,*

Consider:

- (a) Whether their distribution is more widely east and west or north and south.
- (b) Which plants are most widely distributed?
- (c) The means by which the most widely distributed plants disperse their seeds.
- (d) The relative number of seeds produced by such plants.
- (e) The effect of mountains upon the distribution of the various plants; of seas; of rivers; of climate; of other plants; of forests.
- (f) How the plants in your locality become modified when they grow under different geographic or climatic conditions.
- (g) Vegetation as modified by removal of forests.
- (h) What plants that grow elsewhere are allied closely to those in your vicinity?

FINAL QUERY: *Which is the more favorable agent for the plant in dispersing its seeds, the one which scatters multitudes of seeds over limited areas or the one which carries a few seeds over widely extended areas?*

Consider:

- (a) The similarity of soil.
- (b) The similarity of climatic conditions.

(c) The probable ultimate effect upon the plant of having a few seeds deposited in widely different latitudes with greatly contrasted climatic divisions.

(d) The chances for variation.

(e) The chances for pollination of flowers.

(f) The chances of adverse climatic conditions.

NUMBER WORK.

The pupils should carefully collect entire specimens of various plants and find out approximately the number of seeds each produces. This may be done, either by actual count or by counting a given weight of seeds and then estimating the entire number from the weight of all the seeds found on the plant.

Select a square yard or square meter of surface where the plants occupy the ground entirely and count the number per square unit (yard or meter).

In Kerner's Natural History of Plants the following data are given:

An average hedge mustard plant (*Sisymbrium sophia*) yields 730,000 seeds.

Fleabane (*Erigeron canadense*) yields 120,000 seeds.

Shepherd's Purse (*Capsella bursa-pastoris*) yields 64,000 seeds.

Plantain (*Plantago major*) yields 14,000 seeds.

Henbane (*Hyoscyamus niger*) yields 10,000 seeds.

QUERY: *At what rate would the various plants increase if all the seeds that are produced were to ripen and grow?*

1. Supposing all the seeds produced by the henbane to ripen and grow, and allowing 40 plants to the square yard, at this rate of production how long would it take the plant to cover the State of Illinois?

2. How long would it take it to cover the United States?

3. How long would it take the plant to cover the land surface of the earth?

4. Find a small community of shepherd's purse and count or estimate the number per square yard; supposing all the seeds to ripen and grow, how long would it take it to occupy the land area of the earth?

5. Find a well-grown Spanish needle and make similar calculations.

6. In the same way make calculations for the burdock.

7. In the same way make calculations for the amarantus or pig-weed.

8. If opportunity offers, gather the acorns from a single oak and make similar calculations.

9. In the same way, estimate the rate of increase of a hawthorn.

10. Estimate the rate of increase of an apple tree.

QUERY: *What is the relative importance of the various means of dispersal to the plants you have studied?*

11. How many of the plants studied depend

mainly upon the wind as a means of dispersal of their seeds?

12. How many different kinds may *incidentally* use the wind, water and animals in scattering their seeds?

13. How many different kinds have you found that have no obvious means for dispersing their seeds?

14. The number of inedible fruits equals what part of the number of those that are edible?

15. The number of fruits that are adapted for clinging to the coverings of animals is what part of the number edible for the same animals?

16. The number of fruits that may be eaten by birds equals what part of the whole number studied?

17. The number of fruits that are not buoyant in water is equal to what part of the number of those that float?

18. The number of fruits that float in the air equals what part of the number of those that have no adaptation for this means of dispersal?

19. What part of the whole number of fruits studied would be able to take some advantage of certain conditions of surface in becoming dispersed?

20. What part of the whole number studied have some mechanical adaptation discharging them from the pods?

QUERY: *What are the counter influences at work which prevent the rapid spread of plants supposed in problems 1 to 10? To what extent are these influences effective?*

21. Catch a number of thistle and dandelion downs and note the presence or absence of the seeds; what part of the number so caught still carries the seeds? Try the experiment with other floaters.

22. What part has lost the seeds?

23. Gather at random several hundred acorns; what part of the number examined has been destroyed by worms, i. e., the larvæ of insects?

24. What per cent. of the plants whose fruits are provided with hooks and prickles grow in places not infested with animals adapted to carrying them in their coverings?

25. If you have the opportunity of observing a tree having winged fruit under proper conditions, measure the radius of the circle around the tree outside of which you find no fruit on the ground.

MANUAL TRAINING.

Gather specimens of the seeds studied and sew them, or branches bearing the seeds, to stiff card-board. In this way mount a series of two dozen or more, each, of the various winged fruits; keep a sharp lookout for variations in form and size of wings. Interpret these variations from the standpoint of the plant, i. e., are they favorable or unfavorable? Try the sailing power of the various odd forms.   Is the seed in the odd form fully matured ?

REPRESENTATIVE EXPRESSION.

1. *Drawing.*
   (a) Show the *structures* by which the various kinds of seeds adapt themselves to the different agents of distribution.
   (b) Show in a series the various odd forms that have been found.

2. *Painting.*
   (a) The various colored fruits showing the color relation of the ripened fruits to the surrounding foliage or branches.
   (b) Nuts, showing their color relation to the ground or the grass and leaves upon which they lie.
   (c) The landscape, showing the withdrawal of color with the approach of winter.

3. *Modeling.*
   (a) Show, in clay, the various forms assumed by fleshy fruits and nuts.

4. *Writing.* Gather up in one paper a summary of observations and express yourself as to the probable meaning of the various odd appendages to seeds.

VII.

THE FORMS OF TREE-TOPS: RELATION TO GROWTH.

FIELD WORK.

QUERIES:

1. *What causes operate to determine the various forms found in different tree-tops?* Select, if possible, for study trees standing in isolation, i. e., apart from other trees, and

Consider:

    (a) The relation, in length, of the transverse to the vertical diameter.

    (b) The point on the vertical diameter where it is crossed by the transverse.

    (c) The various shapes as related to the relative length of the diameters, and to the point of intersection; whether it is at the middle of the vertical or above or below it.

    (d) The effect upon the shape if the point of intersection of the diameters is very near the bottom or very close to the top.

2. *What habits of growth determine the relations of the different diameters of tree-tops?*

Consider:

(a) The growth from terminal buds; the shape where the growth is chiefly terminal.

(b) The growth from lateral buds; the shape where the growth is chiefly lateral.

(c) The relation of the terminal to the lateral growth in the various forms of tops.

(d) The angle which the branches make with the main stem or plant axis.

(e) The flexibility of the branches.

3. *What conditions operate to cause a variation in the length of the twigs in any year's growth? Is this variation constant for different seasons?*

Consider:

(a) Light; is there any part of the tree-top that does not receive sunshine during the day while the twigs are growing?

(b) Adjacent trees or other objects.

(c) Influences affecting spread of roots.

(d) Prevailing wind.

(e) Try to recall the conditions which prevailed during the growing season. If necessary consult the summaries furnished by the Weather Bureau.

CHART VII.—*Growth of Twigs.**

NAME OF TREE. SHAPE OF THE TOP.	TERMINAL GROWTHS.			LATERAL GROWTHS.			
	Present Year.	Preceding Year.	2d Preceding Year.	3d Preceding Year.	Present Year.	Preceding Year.	2d Preceding Year.	3d Preceding Year.

*The side of the tree measured may be indicated by the appropriate letters, E. W. N. S.

NUMBER WORK.

QUERIES:

1. *How much have the branches of different kinds of trees grown in length during the past year?*

(a) Select 25 twigs, at least, from each side of the tree and measure from the tip back to the ring in the bark which marks the position of the terminal bud when the year's growth began. Also measure the growths of the two or three preceding years. Make a carefully tabulated list of results. (See Chart VII.)

(b) Measure in the same way the lateral twigs, i. e., twigs from lateral buds.

(c) Measure twigs, both lateral and terminal, that have grown inside the general circumference of the tree; i. e., near the trunk or body.

(d) Measure in a similar manner twigs near the top of the tree, if possible.

(e) Measure on the ground on different sides the distance from the trunk to the point vertically under the tip of the longest branches.

(f) What figure is formed by connecting these points with a regular curving line? Note the relations of the diameters of this figure.

QUERY: *What are the exact relations of the terminal to the lateral growth in the various forms?*

1. Find the average length of the terminal and lateral twigs on different sides of various trees and record the results in a form like *Chart VII.*

2. The average length of the lateral twigs in the orbicular-formed tree-top, equals what part of the average length of the terminal twigs?

3. Find the same relation in the cone-shaped top; in the oval top.

4. What is the ratio between the average length of twigs on the north side of the tree to the average length on the south side; in the same way compare the twigs on all sides of the tree. (Use data from *Chart VII.*)

5. Measure the angle formed by the twigs with the trunk; is there uniformity?

6. What is the ratio of the growth this year to the growth last year?

7. What is the ratio of the depth of rainfall during the growing months this year to the depth last year for the same months?

REPRESENTATIVE EXPRESSION.

1. *Drawing.*

    (a) Show in outline the shapes of the tops of different kinds of trees.

    (b) Show by a drawing of a branch the relation of the lateral to the terminal growth ; make a series taken from different trees.

2. *Painting.*
    (a) Make a careful sketch of a landscape showing the condition of life as indicated by color. Compare closely with the appearance in September.

VIII.

AUTUMNAL CHANGES: CONSTITUENTS OF PLANTS.

QUERIES:

1. *What becomes of the material in the leaves after they fall from the tree ?*

Consider :

(a) Their condition when they fall.

(b) The influences operating upon them after they fall.

(c) Their chances of being preserved as fossils.

(d) Their chances of being removed.

2. *By what means may the materials in the leaf be revealed so that they may be studied ?*

Consider :

(a) The disadvantages in observing the leaves as they undergo the usual processes of decay as they lie on the ground.

(b) The natural means that may be employed to hasten the separation of the elements : heat; soaking in water.

(c) The means of collecting and measuring the elements or simple compounds as they become disengaged from the leaves.

EXPERIMENTS.

Equipment. Scales for weighing; a *stamped* shallow tin pan or cup, to be used as a crucible; alcohol lamp or bunsen burner; a retort stand or other support for pan over the flame.

A.

1. Weigh about 25 grams of *completely dry* autumn leaves. Count the leaves, also. Different pupils may select leaves from different kinds of trees and plants. It will be interesting to take the leaves of some aquatic plants, also.

2. Place the dried leaves, crumbled as finely as possible, in the tin pan; cover with a lid and heat *slowly* at a *low temperature* until the mass is thoroughly blackened. During this heating process the temperature must be so low that little or no *smoke* will pass off and no ash must be formed.

3. Weigh the blackened mass and note the amount lost by heating.

4. After weighing, heat again strongly without the lid, until nothing but grayish white ash remains.

5. Weigh the ash and note the loss due to second heating.

6. Make accurately from cardboard a cubical box 1 inch square; with this, *measure* the ash.

B.

1. Place the ash on filter paper folded funnel shape; support this and pour distilled water through it, catching the *filtrate* in a glass or porcelain vessel; or better, stir the ash up well in a tumbler of water and then pour the mixture into the filter.

QUERY: *Has any of the ash dissolved?*

Consider:

(a) Color of filtrate; i. e., the liquid passing through the filter.

(b) Its odor.

(c) Its taste. (This test in laboratory work must be employed with the greatest caution; never where there is the slightest probability of danger.)

(d) The effect upon litmus paper—red and blue. (Red turning blue indicates a substance termed an alkali. Blue turning red indicates an acid.)

(e) Dip the end of a glass rod, that has been cleaned by holding it for a moment in the flame, into the liquid and then hold it in the bluish bunsen flame. Look sharply for the flame tinge.

(f) The litmus test indicates the *nature* of the substance dissolved—an alkali —and the flame test indicates a *particular* one—potassium.

(g) What remains (the *residue*) after carefully evaporating the filtrate.

C.

QUERY: *How much material was dissolved?*

(a) Dry the residue left undissolved upon the filter paper.

(b) Without removing from the paper, weigh—balancing the filter by a similar paper. Note loss of weight.

D.

QUERY: *Does any easily soluble matter remain on the filter?*

(a) Again pour through the ash on the filter dilute hydrochloric acid. (HCl.) Note any action as the acid comes in contact with the ash.

(b) Dry and weigh the residue, i. e., what remains on the filter, and note if there is loss in weight.

(c) Evaporate the filtrate to dryness and note the residue.

(d) If the amount found in (c) is great enough for you to weigh, can you account for any apparent discrepancy when the weight is compared with what was shown to be lost in (b)?

(e) After drying the residue obtained in (c) expose it to the action of the atmosphere for a short time and note the result. Can you detect the odor of a familiar substance?

QUERIES:

1. *How many different kinds of substances do the foregoing experiments reveal in the leaves?*
2. *What will likely be the fate of these substances as they become separated through the slower processes outdoors?*

Consider:
   (a) The nature of the materials separated in invisible form.
   (b) The nature of the materials dissolved in the water. What would become of them when in the earth?
   (c) The nature of the material dissolved by the acid.
   (d) The probable fate of the apparently insoluble substances.

3. *Can you picture in your mind the redistribution of all these materials when they are separated from each other? What becomes of the ash? What will determine its distribution?*
4. *Can you picture their chances for being built up into leaves another year?*
5. *In the course of the various changes traced, does it appear likely that any of the materials are actually lost or totally destroyed?*

E.

As a supplementary experiment, a small bunch of leaves may be placed in a Florence flask and partly covered with water. By means of glass and rubber tubing this flask may be connected with an inverted jar, according the common method employed for collecting gases over water. (See any chemistry.) As decay or disintegration of the leaves goes on, gas will pass off into the receptacle prepared to receive it. The flame test may be applied to this.

QUERY: *What are the materials (and how much of each) built by the plant into the fleshy fruits?*

Consider as examples:

(a) Apple, pear, quince, peach, grapes, squash, cranberries, melons.
(b) Also, the materials built into other parts of the plant as, potato, turnip, cabbage stalk, beet, carrot, parsnip.
(c) Different specimens may be assigned to different pupils.

EXPERIMENTS.

A.

MANUAL TRAINING. To make a drying tray that will serve the entire school proceed as follows: From $\frac{1}{4}$-inch pine make a rectangular frame $16 \times 10\frac{3}{4}$ in., outside measurement, and

2 inches deep. Divide this lengthwise with 5, and crosswise with 8 partitions. This divides the tray into 54 spaces, each 1½ inches square and 2 inches deep. Tack fine wire gauze (mosquito netting will serve) over one side of the tray for a bottom; make a light frame of the same dimensions as the tray and cover it with the netting for a lid.

Assign each pupil a space in the tray. The fruit may be kept in this until dry without danger of loss.

B.

1. Weigh about 5 or 10 grams of fresh fruit and dry it without scorching. (It may be convenient for the teacher or some pupil to put the fruit tray in the oven of a kitchen stove over night.)

CAUTION.—Dried fruit is usually hygroscopic; that is, it readily absorbs moisture from the atmosphere. The pupil will see the necessity of promptness in weighing.

2. After drying, weigh again and note the change. How much ? *What does the change mean?*

3. With the dried fruit, proceed to repeat the experiments given previously in the study of leaves and obtain the amount of charcoal or carbon, ash and organic matter.

SUGGESTION: Tabulate all the results obtained according to the form given in Chart VIII.

CHART VIII.—*Plant Constituents.*

NAME. Leaves or Fruit.	No. of Leaves.	Weight of Fresh.	Weight of Water.	Weight of Dry Solid.	Weight of Ash.	Weight of Charcoal.	Weight of Organic Matter.

REPRESENTATIVE EXPRESSION.

1. *Drawing.*

   (a) Draw a square, 10 centimeters on a side, and allow it to represent the amount of material in fresh leaves or fruit.

   (b) On one side as a base, draw an inner square that will correctly represent the proportion of *ash.*

   (c) In the same way, represent by an inner square the proportion of *water.*

   (d) Represent in the same way the proportion of *organic matter.*

   (e) Represent in a similar manner the proportion of *dry solid.*

   (f) Represent, also, the proportion of *carbon or charcoal.*

   (g) Represent the above proportions by straight lines.

2. *Painting:* The various proportions may be more clearly shown by coloring the different figures drawn under (1).

3. *Modeling.*

   (a) Take a given weight of clay, 2 lbs. will suffice, and divide it into parts which will correctly represent, by weight, the proportions of *water, dry solid, ash* and *organic matter* found in different leaves and fruits.

   (b) Mold from the clay a series of cubes

which will correctly represent the relative volume of the different plant constituents.

NUMBER WORK.

QUERY: *How much of each substance found in the fruits and leaves is actually built up by the plant in one season?* Use the data tabulated in Chart VIII.

1. Gather a definite part, say one-fourth, of the leaves that have fallen from a tree; dry and weigh and compute the weight of leaves for the entire tree.

2. How many pounds of ash do they contain?

3. How much potash do they contain?

4. How much insoluble matter in the leaves?

5. How much matter that may be dissolved by dilute acid?

6. How many pounds of organic matter? What becomes of this as the leaves decay?

7. How much charcoal in these leaves?

8. The ash equals what part of the dry weight of the leaves?

9. The organic matter equals what part of the dry weight of the leaves?

10. The charcoal equals what part of the weight of the leaves?

11. How many trees, such as you have studied, could stand, without crowding, upon an acre? How many could stand, at the same rate, upon a square mile?

12. Compute the amount of each substance, found in the leaves, that such forests would build into their leaves.

QUERY: *How much of each substance, found by experiment in the fruits, is built up by the plant in one season?*

1. Calculate and actually measure into some vessel the amount of water in a bushel of apples.

2. An apple tree may yield five barrels of apples; how much ash would they contain? How many pounds of organic matter? Of dry solid?

3. How much water in a bushel of grapes? Actually measure it into a vessel.

4. How much ash in a bushel of grapes?

5. The water in a bushel of grapes equals what part of the whole weight?

6. The ash in a bushel of grapes equals what part of the whole weight? Lift these two weights—one in each hand.

7. How much water in a bushel of pears? How much dry solid? How much ash? Lift these weights.

8. The water in apples equals what part of the weight of the water in the same weight of pears?

9. Compare the amount of water in grapes with the amount in apples and pears.

10. Compare the quantities of dry solid, ash

and organic matter found in the various fruits studied.

11. Compare the amounts of these substances as found in potatoes, turnips, beets and other vegetables.

12. Suggestion. As the quantity of each substance in the common units of measurements, as the peck, gallon, bushel, etc., is found, the pupil should have their relations impressed by actually handling the weights. The picture should be further developed and enlarged by computing the amount produced in an average crop. (See the tables given in any good geography for crop statistics.)

IX.

METEOROLOGY FOR OCTOBER.

QUERIES:

1. *What portions of the United States show most clearly the approach of winter?* (Use Weather Bureau Maps.)

Consider:

(a) The southern limit of the freezing point; trace a line connecting the most southerly points where 32° Fah. was noted.

(b) The agricultural crops that grow within this area.

(c) The fruits that grow within the same area.

(d) Trace in the same way the snow line for the month.

(e) The region where the isotherms depart farthest from the parallels of latitude. What does this mean?

(f) The isotherms that cross the greatest number of parallels. What does this mean?

(g) The general position of the isotherms as compared with corresponding dates of September?

(h) The changes brought about in the landscape in various parts of the country during the past month.

2. *What influences have worked the changes in the local landscape?*

Consider:

(a) The extremes of temperature; the range.
(b) The average temperature; the frost dates.
(c) The prevailing wind.
(d) The sunshine, cloudiness, rainfall, average relative humidity.

NUMBER WORK.

QUERY: *How have the meteorological influences changed during the month?*

1. The number of clear days equals what part of the month? Compare with September.

2. The number of cloudy days equal what part of the month? Compare with September.

3. The number of partly cloudy days equals what part of the month? Compare with September.

4. The number of rainy days equals what part of the month? Compare with September.

5. What was the amount of water per square yard that fell in October? Compare with September.

6. What was the amount of water per square

yard on the average for the rainy days? Compare with September.

7. What was the amount of water per square yard on the average for the cloudy days? Compare with September.

8. Which averages the more water, and how much per square yard, a rainy day in September or one in October?

9. Which month averages the more water per cloudy day to the square yard, and how much, September or October?

10. Compare the average barometer for September with the average for October.

11. Compare the greatest range in temperature in September with the greatest range in October.

12. During 24 hours, Sept. 29th and 30th, a rainstorm covered an area in the north central part of the United States about 450 miles long and 400 miles broad; based upon the reports from 21 cities within this area, the average depth of rainfall was found to be 1.83 inches. Compute the amount of water that fell, per acre, per square mile, and upon the whole region, in barrels, tons and cubic feet. How long a lake one-half a mile deep and two miles wide would the whole amount of water fill?

REPRESENTATIVE EXPRESSION.

1. *Drawing.*

(a) Draw a circle 6 inches in diameter;

represent upon this by sectors the relative amount of clear, cloudy and rainy weather. This may be made more striking by pasting on sectors of colored paper.

(b) Upon a similar circle, represent the number of days when there was frost.

(c) By two lines represent the depth of rainfall for September and October.

2. *Painting.* A landscape sketch showing characteristic coloring this month.

X.

ASTRONOMY FOR OCTOBER.

QUERY : *How has the distribution of sunshine changed during this month ?*

1. Use the *Skiameter*. (See page 38.)

2. Compare the area covered by a given beam of sunshine at noon with the area covered by the same beam one month ago. Compare the heat effects on the two dates.

3. Compare the noon slant of sunshine on Oct. 23d with the slant on Sept. 23d.

NOTE.—The difference in slant will show in degrees how far south on the meridian the sun has apparently moved during the month. This *added to the latitude* of any place north of the equator will give the slant of the noon sunshine at that place.

4. Find the relative intensity of a given beam of sunshine at different points on the isotherm that departs most widely from the parallels on a given date.

5. The sunshine that covered one acre a month ago covers how much surface now ?

6. The sunshine on this date that covers one acre at New Orleans covers how much at Chicago; at Boston; at London; at St. Petersburg?

7. Compare the area covered one month ago by a given beam of sunshine at 9 o'clock with

the area covered now at 9 o'clock by the same beam.

QUERY: *How much has the day changed in length during the month?* (Consult the almanac for time of the rising and the setting of the sun.)

Consider:

    (a) The change in the morning; in the evening.

    (b) The relative length of night and day.

    (c) The variation in the rate of change in length of day and night.

REPRESENTATIVE EXPRESSION.

1 *Drawing.*

    (a) Draw a series of rectangles which will show the variation in the area covered by a given beam of sunshine on the equator and on every 10th degree northward.

    (b) Draw two lines which will show the relative length of day and night.

2. *Painting.*

    (a) Paint a characteristic landscape for this date.

    (b) Paint characteristic clouds and sunsets.

XI.

MECHANICS. HEAT AS WORK POWER OR ENERGY.

SPECIAL OBSERVATIONS.

Visit an engine that is actually in operation and very carefully study how it does the work required.

QUERIES:

1. *How is the engine connected with the machinery that it is required to run?*

Consider:

    (a) Belts. Pulleys.
    (b) Shafts.
    (c) The piston. The cross-head. The fly-wheel.
    (d) The crank; note how the back-and-forth motion of the piston is changed into circular motion.

2. *By what arrangement of parts does the steam move the piston back and forth?*

Consider:

    (a) The steam pipe.
    (b) The exhaust or escape pipe.

NOTE.—The steam chest and the cylinder should

be pointed out to the pupils and the inner working parts should be explained and illustrated by models, diagrams or pictures.

  (c) The outer mechanism which moves the sliding valve.
  (d) The governor.

3. *By what means is the steam supplied to the cylinder?*

Consider:

  (a) The throttle valve.
  (b) The course of the steam pipe to the boilers.
  (c) The means employed to prevent loss of heat from the steam while it is in the pipe.

4. *How is the boiler supplied with water?*

Consider:

  (a) The pump.
  (b) The injector, if one is used.
  (c) The water gauge.
  (d) The steam cocks.

5. *How is the pressure of steam in the boiler determined and regulated?*

Consider:

  (a) The steam gauge; its use?
  (b) The safety-valve; its use?
  (c) The pressure at which the steam blows off.

6. *How is the heat applied to the boiler?*

Consider:

(a) The fire-box.
(b) The flues in the boiler; their use?
(c) The ash-box.
(d) The grate-bars.
(e) How the ashes are gotten out of the fire-box.

7. *Under what conditions does the fire burn best?*

Consider:

(a) The various doors opening into the furnace.
(b) The grate-bars.
(c) Where are the openings kept clear when strong heat is required?
(d) The location of the apertures kept open when it is desired to cool the furnace down.

8. *What is the evidence that air passes into the furnace?*

Consider:

(a) The movements of a piece of paper held before the openings when a strong heat is required.
(b) The same before the openings when the fires are cooling off.

9. *What seems to be the course of the draught when the fire is hottest?*

10. *What seems to be the course of the draught when the furnace is being cooled off?*

11. *What similarity and what points of difference do you find in the construction of other things in which fuel is burned?*

Consider :

(a) The cook-stove.
(b) Open fire place with or without a grate.
(c) A candle.
(d) A lamp with a chimney.

12. *In each case what seems to be the purpose of the various openings? What uses for grate bars?*

Consider the following experiments :

(a) Light a short candle and lower it to the bottom of a fruit jar.
(b) In a similar manner lower the candle into a lamp chimney or globe.
(c) Wrap a cloth about the base of a lamp burner in such a manner as to close all the holes; try again and close *nearly all the holes;* again, closing but few of the holes.

13. *From the foregoing observations and experiments what things seem to be required that we may have a fire?*

14. *Under what* CONDITIONS *will the fire begin to burn? Why will it not start when a*

current of air blows against a wood pile or a coal pile?

Consider what takes place when a piece of wood or coal lies on *top* of a stove as the latter becomes gradually heated.

NOTE.—The point at which it begins to burn is called its kindling temperature.

15. *Does the kindling temperature vary in different substances?*

EXPERIMENT:

(a) Place a small piece of wood, a small piece each of cannel, bituminous and anthracite coal, a piece of cotton cloth and a match upon a piece of tin or thin sheet iron (a thin shovel will serve the purpose) and heat over a bunsen burner or over live coals.

(b) Note the order in which they begin to burn.

(c) Why is the end of a match covered with the phosphorus mixture. By what means is it ordinarily raised to its kindling temperature?

16. *In the burning of the coal and wood in the furnace what substances are produced?*

Consider:

(a) The contents of the ash-box.
(b) The soot lining the flues and chimney.
(c) The smoke; what is smoke?

Experiments :

(d) Light a splinter and lower it into a fruit jar. When it is extinguished, pour into the jar half a pint of clear lime water and shake. Note the changed appearance.

(e) Pour a like amount of lime water into a jar of air and shake; compare with the result found in (d).

(f) Through a tube blow the breath into a little clear lime water; compare the result with (e) and (d).

17. *What is the proof that the gaseous or air-like substance which is in the jar after burning the splinter is not quite like pure air?*

NOTE.—The lime water used as directed furnishes a simple test for a gas called *carbon dioxide.*

EXPERIMENTS. *Apparatus:*

(a) Large sized test tube fitted with perforated rubber cork.

(b) Glass tube, one-eighth inch bore, six inches long, bent at a right angle; insert this through the cork. Also rubber tube same size one foot or more in length.

(c) One ounce each of chlorate of potash and manganese dioxide.

(d) Half fill the test tube with equal parts of the potash and manganese; and, with the cork fitted, heat the mixture over a lamp.

(e) Collect the gas formed over water. (See any chemistry.) This gas is called oxygen.

(f) When the jar is full of the gas repeat the tests described under (16-d).

(g) Also, lower a candle into a jar of the fresh gas; try a small piece of coal that has been kindled.

(h) Tie small splinter to a fine iron wire and after lighting the former lower it into the jar.

(i) After each experiment, test for *carbon dioxide* in the jar. Does the result obtained in (h) show the same?

18. *In what way does oxygen behave like common air?*

19: *In what way does it behave differently?*

20. *What would be the probable effect if a strong current of oxygen, instead of air, were forced up through the coals on the grate bars in the furnace?*

21. *What is the proof that the oxygen undergoes some change in the jar when the splinter burns?*

22. *What proof that the air is changed in the jar by the burning splinter?*

23. *What likely takes place when the draught of air passes up through the coals in the furnace?*

24. *What is the real purpose in bringing*

about these changes of air and fuel in the furnace ?

Consider:

(a) The work done by the engine.

25. *Among the several things produced by the changes in the air and fuel in the furnace, what is really used? What things are not used?* Review the preceding queries.

26. *Is all the heat derived by the changes in the air and the fuel in the furnace used ?*

Consider :

(a) The temperature of the air in front of the furnace.
(b) The temperature in the ash-box.
(c) The temperature on all sides of the boiler.
(d) The temperature of the smoke-stack.
(e) The temperature at the upper end of the chimney of the escaping gas and smoke.
(f) The heat that passes into the water in the boiler.

27. *What must the heat do before the water is changed into steam ?*

EXPERIMENT:

Apparatus needed : Chemical thermometer, registering at least 212°; small vessel holding a quart; bunsen burner or some other source of heat.

(a) Half fill the vessel with water.

(b) Take the temperature and heat gradually.

(c) Note the point on the thermometer where the mercury ceases to rise? What is this fixed temperature?

28. *Until this fixed temperature was reached what was the heat doing which passed into the water?*

Consider:

(a) The gradually rising temperature.

(b) The escaping steam.

29. *What is the heat doing that passes into the boiler from the furnace after the boiling point is reached?*

NOTE.—Consult the steam gauge. The working parts of this instrument should be explained by means of drawings or a model. The fact that it registers something different from that shown by the thermometer should be made clear.

Consider:

(a) How the pressure is transmitted from the boiler along the steam pipe.

(b) How the steam is admitted alternately on the opposite sides of the piston head; its movements.

30. *The changes going on in the fuel and air in the furnace, bring about what results in the boiler and through the engine?*

Consider :
(a) What the thermometer indicates.
(b) What the steam gauge tells.
(c) What is told by the moving machinery connected with the engine.

Consider, also, the loss of heat,
(a) About the steam pipe and cylinder.
(b) The loss in the steam that escapes from the cylinder. If possible, take its temperature with a thermometer.

31. *Do the various fuels used have the same relative value in the production of power ?*

EXPERIMENTS: *apparatus:* Stamped tin cup; (See page 45) scales; bunsen burner, and support for pan.

(a) Weigh out equal quantities of *dry* wood, cannel, bituminous and anthracite coal.
(b) Powder the coal finely and heat each in the pan over the flames until nothbut a grayish ash is left.
(c) Compare the weight of the ash with the original weight of the coal and wood.
(d) What has become of the part or parts found in the coal and wood not found in the ash ?

NOTE.—The pupil will reflect that the workpower which is directed by the engine finds its starting point in the changes which take place in the air and fuel in the furnace; that one of the results of these changes is *heat*; that only such part of the heat thus formed *which passes into the water in the boiler* is useful, and only so much of this as may be retained within; that much of this escapes before the steam reaches the piston head, and finally, that after the steam has done its work against the piston head it is still very hot when it escapes into the air. Very much of the heat, therefore, which actually arises by the changes of the coal and air in the furnace is lost; that is, it does not show itself as work power.

It is said that the very best engines yet made cannot utilize more than 15 parts out of every hundred, or 15% of the actual work power there is in coal.

The National Electric Light Association recently tested 80 modern electric light and power plants and found that, on an average, 97.4% *of the actual power in the coal was wasted.* The electric current obtained in these plants, thus represents but 2.6% of the actual power value of coal.

(For an interesting article on this point, see Harper's Monthly, December, 1896—*Electricity direct from coal.*)

NUMBER WORK.

QUERIES. 1. *What is the value, in pounds, of the steam as indicated by the steam gauge?* (The steam.gauge indicates pressure per square inch).

1. Find the dimensions of the boiler and calculate the area of its surface; according to the steam-gauge, what is the total pressure upon its inner surface?

2. Find the area of the piston-head; accord-

ing to the steam-gauge, how many pounds of pressure are exerted against its surface ?.

3. Find out, by inquiry, how much coal, per day, is required to run the engine studied, and calculate the cost of the fuel for one year.

4. If the engine can utilize but 15% of the power value of the coal, (see note above) how many dollars per day are paid out for heat that is not used as power? How many dollars per year?

5. If an engine were to drive the dynamo in an electric plant, how many dollars would represent the waste in producing the electric current?

6. How much coal would be needed to run the engine studied, if all the power value in the fuel could be obtained and used as work power ?

7. How much coal would be needed to generate the electric current, that is possible with this engine, if the whole power value of the coal could be utilized ?

8. What is the difference between the weight of the bituminous coal and the weight of its ash? The latter is what per cent. of the former?

9. What is the difference between the weight of anthracite coal and the weight of its ash? The ash is what per cent. of the coal?

10. What is the difference between the weight of cannel coal and the weight of its ash? The ash is what per cent. of the coal ?

11. What is the difference between the

weight of the dry wood and the weight of its ash? The ash is what per cent. of the wood?

12. How much ash, per ton, in each of the above kinds of fuel?

13. How much ash is formed, per day, in the furnace studied in these lessons?

14. In the process of burning, what becomes of that part of the coal not left behind in the ash? How much of the fuel thus escapes, per ton, in each kind above mentioned?

15. Judging from the quantity of ash, which is the cheapest kind of fuel? Which the most expensive? (The market price of each must be taken into account).

REPRESENTATIVE EXPRESSION.

1. *Drawing.*

(a) Make drawings of the furnace and boiler, showing by arrows the draught when a hot fire is required. Show in the same way the course of the draught when the furnace is cooling off.

(b) Make a drawing of the engine, showing its connection with the boiler, how the steam is applied and how it escapes.

(c) Draw a square 2 inches on a side and let this represent the total power value of coal; within this figure draw a square or rectangle which will in proper ratio represent the actual amount utilized in the best engines.

(d) By similar figures, represent the proportion of the power value of coal in the electric current.

(e) Draw a figure 2 inches square and let it represent a ton of fuel; upon this figure, by squares, represent the proportion of ash in each kind mentioned above.

(f) Draw a figure 2 inches square, and let it stand for the cost of a ton of bituminous coal; upon one side of this as a base, represent by rectangles the proportionate values of the other kinds of coal and of wood.

2. *Modeling.* Instead of drawing the rectangles mentioned above in (c), (d), (e), and (f), cubes representing the proper proportions may be modeled in clay.

XII.

HEAT.—A STUDY OF VENTILATION.

Observations. The pupils should make a careful note of the various means employed in heating and ventilating rooms, public buildings, street-cars and railroad coaches. The size of the rooms, and the size and location of the openings for the ingress and egress of air should also be observed. The pupils should also observe whether the means employed are sufficient to furnish a constant and adequate supply of fresh air to those who occupy the rooms.

QUERIES:

1. *In what ways do we become aware of the presence of impure air ?*

Consider:

(a) The odors; note the evidences which may be detected upon entering the room from outdoors.

(b) The effects upon the feelings; dullness, depression, headache, sickness.

(c) What it means to remain long enough in a room with impure air to become *accustomed* to it.

(d) What it means to live habitually in rooms, work-rooms, for example, until one becomes *accustomed* to the bad air.

NOTE.—The pupils may refer to *Chapter XI, Query 16,* (*f*) for an experiment showing the presence of carbon dioxide (CO_2) in expired air. If necessary, repeat the experiment here.

"Air which has been breathed till it contains more than .2 per cent of CO_2 is injurious, not so much on account of the CO_2 present, but on account of the poisonous nature of the organic matter which is given off by the lungs." (Physiology for Beginners: Foster and Shore.)

2. *What evidence is there of CO_2 in the school-room?*

EXPERIMENT: Collect a bottle full of air in various parts of the room: near the floor, near the door, near the ceiling, near the openings which admit and discharge the air. In order to do this, first fill the bottle with water; take it to that part of the room from which it is desired to obtain the air and empty the water out. The bottle, of course, at once fills with the air to be tested. Add a gill of lime water and allow the bottle to stand in the place for fifteen minutes. In the same way, test the air outdoors.

Consider:

    (a) The turbidity of the lime water in the various places tested.

    (b) The regions in the room which seem freest from CO_2.

Note.—Exact measurements have shown that ordinary atmospheric air when breathed in contains in 100 parts, by *volume*, Nitrogen, - - 79.0
Oxygen, - 20.9
Carbonic acid gas, .04
Water vapor, a variable amount.

When expired from the lungs 100 parts, by volume, of air contain, Nitrogen, - 79.0
Oxygen, · 16.0
Carbonic acid gas, 4.0
Water vapor, to saturation.

3. *How much air is required for each respiration?*

EXPERIMENTS:

A. Procure a large bottle holding at least 2 quarts. Find its exact capacity in cubic inches by measuring the amount of water it will hold. (231 cubic inches = 1 gallon). Fill with water and invert in a basin of water as for the collection of gases. By means of a bent glass tube, one arm of which reaches well up into the bottle, let the pupils exhale naturally into the bottle. Mark with a small paster the height at which the water stands after being partially displaced by the breath, and calculate the volume of air in the bottle. This may be done by measuring the water left in the bottle and subtracting the result from its total volume.

B. Invert the same bottle filled with air in the pan of water. Using the bent tube, the arm inside being long enough to reach up nearly the length of the bottle, allow the pupil to inhale naturally, withdrawing the air from the bottle. By measuring the amount of water that rises in the bottle, determine the quantity of air inhaled.

NOTE.—Repeat these experiments until the pupils can get a fair idea of the average amount of air required by each person in a respiration. By the same means, let the pupils exhale and inhale as deeply as possible. Note the difference between the amount of air used in quiet breathing and that used when the breathing is forced. The air passing in and out in quiet breathing is called *tidal* air; that in addition, taken by a *forced* inspiration, is called *complemental* air; that in addition to the tidal air which may be forcibly expired is called *supplemental* air. The pupils should determine the volume of each.

4. *What means are employed to produce a rapid and certain change of air in the rooms you have observed?*

Consider :
  (a) Whether there is a forced draft.
  (b) The location and size of the openings used in heating and ventilation.
  (c) The direction the pure air must take after entering the room to reach the places of exit.

5. *In what way may the means employed in heating a room be made to assist in its ventilation?*

Consider:
  (a) By means of light pieces of paper or

cotton the direction of air currents about the stove or register.

(b) Follow these currents as far as possible throughout the room.

(c) Whence the supply of air that approaches the stove or registers.

EXPERIMENT: Lower a large-sized lamp chimney over a short piece of a candle, allowing its edges to rest upon small supports, thus preventing the rim from standing upon the table. By means of smoking paper, determine the currents of air about the chimney.

NUMBER WORK.

QUERIES: A. *What is the quantity of pure air needed by those who occupy the room ?*

1. Calculate the volume of air in the room in cubic feet.

2. Count the number of your usual respirations per minute; how many respirations per hour?

3. Using the data gathered from the experiments (*see Query 3*), calculate the quantity of air breathed by each person in one minute.

4. How much air, at the same rate, is consumed in breathing in one minute by *all* the occupants of the room?

5. How long will it take the occupants to use a quantity of air equal to the entire volume contained in the room?

6. How many times should the air in the room be changed in an hour?

7. How many times should it be changed during the school hours of one day?

8. By reference to the data given in the note under *Query 2*, it will be found that the CO_2 equals 4 per cent. of the volume of air expired; according to your measurements, how many cubic inches would this be?

9. If the air is rendered injurious when .2 per cent. CO_2 is present, how many cubic inches of air do you render impure by each respiration?

10. How many cubic feet do you render impure per hour?

11. How many cubic feet are rendered impure per hour by *all* those in the room?

B. *Will the means employed provide a sufficient quantity of pure air to those who occupy the room?*

12. Measure the area of the openings provided for the admission of pure air; what is the total area?

13. Imagine a column of air entering the room, the end of which has the same area as the opening for the admission; at what rate will it have to flow, in order to change the air of the entire room in one hour?

14. At what rate will the column have to enter the room in order to change the air as often as necessary to keep up a fresh supply? (See problem 6 above.)

15. What is the ratio of the quantity of tidal

air to that of the complemental or supplemental air ?

1. *Drawing.*

(a) Draw a 10-inch square and allow it to stand for the complemental air; upon this draw another square which will show the relative amount of the tidal air.

(b) Draw a square 10×10 inches which may represent 100 parts of ordinary air; draw upon this a series of rectangles which will represent the relative amounts of nitrogen, oxygen and carbon dioxide.

(c) Represent by figures similar to those in (b) the relative amounts of the different parts *after* the air has been breathed.

(d) Upon a figure 10×10 inches, represent by a similar figure the quantity of CO_2 which will unfit it for breathing. (*See Query 1, note.*)

(e) Represent the air breathed out in one respiration by a ¼-inch square; represent by a similar figure the relative amount of air that is rendered by it unfit for breathing.

2. *Modeling.* Instead of the figures suggested under drawing, cubes may be modeled from clay which will show the same proportions; or they may be cut from cardboard.

XIII.

HEAT: A STUDY OF ILLUMINATION.

Visit, if possible, the gas-works that furnish the supply of gas for the town. The pupils should be shown the retorts where the coal is heated; the means employed for purifying the gas and method of storing in the gasometer from which it is distributed to consumers.

EXPERIMENTS:

A. Fill a clay pipe three-quarters full of powdered soft coal and seal the top with plaster of paris. The coal should be weighed before being sealed up. Place the pipe in the flame of a bunsen burner or alcohol lamp. By means of rubber and glass tubing connect the pipe-stem with a mason jar or bottle prepared in the usual way for collecting gases over water.

When the gas ceases to form, disconnect the tubing and remove the flame.

QUERY: 1. *What is driven off by heating the coal?*

Consider:

    (a) The volume of gas obtained, by marking on the bottle with a small paster the space filled with gas. Measure as directed in the preceding lesson.

NOTE.—Bend a piece of glass tubing into U shape. One arm should be long enough to reach up into the inverted jar or bottle nearly to the top of the space occupied by the gas. The end of the other arm should be drawn out to a small point. Instead of thus tipping the glass tube it may be extended by means of a rubber tube in the end of which there may be placed an ordinary lava gas tip. With one arm of the bent tube inserted in the inverted jar, push the jar down slowly into the pan of water and note

(b) Any odor that may appear at the end of the tube.
(c) Whether it will burn.
(d) Its resemblance to other flames.

2. *What remains in the pipe after heating the coal?*

After opening the pipe, consider:
(a) The color and texture of the residue; it is called coke.
(b) Its weight; compare with its fresh weight.
(c) The odor and character of any substances that may collect in the pipe-stem or bowl.

B. Fill the pipe with a given weight of dry oak wood cut into very small pieces. Seal and follow the directions given under (A).

Consider:
(a) The amount, by volume, of the gas formed.
(b) The nature of the gas formed.

(c) The contents left in the pipe ; compare with the weight before heating.

3. *Why are the coal and wood not consumed when thus heated in the closed pipe as they are in a stove or furnace?*

Consider :

(a) The various openings in the stove and furnace; their purpose.
(b) The opening in the clay pipe; its purpose.

NOTE.—The separation of the coal into its elements by strongly heating it, as in the clay pipe, is called *destructive distillation.* The burning of the coal in the furnace is called *combustion;* what seems to be the essential difference between the two processes ?

C. Procure a tallow candle having a large wick. Light it and make a careful study of the flame. After it is well started,

Consider :

(a) The shape assumed by the top of the shaft of tallow.
(b) The melted tallow.
(c) The unscorched portion of the wick.
(d) The shape of the flame.
(e) The extreme *outer surface* of the flame; hold a white sheet of paper behind the flame to observe this.
(f) The inner dark part.
(g) The yellowish luminous part.

4. *Where is the hottest part of the flame?*

Lower a white sheet of paper down steadily upon the flame and quickly remove.

Consider:

(a) The area scorched most.

(b) That scorched least.

Thrust a splinter or burnt match through the flame and remove.

Consider:

(a) The scorched portions.

D. Draw one end of a piece of small glass tubing to a tapering point; thrust the other end into the dark center of the flame.

5. *Can anything by this means be drawn from the center of the flame?*

Consider:

(a) The odor at the upper end of the tube.

(b) Whether it will ignite.

(c) Is anything found that is recognizable?

(d) The result by holding the end of the tube in other parts of the flame.

(e) What seems to be in the central part of the flame?

(f) Is the wick being consumed?

(g) Why you have to occasionally snuff a candle.

E. Lower a piece of fine wire gauze down over the candle flame. Hold the gauze steadily in place until it becomes hot. Watch any changes that may occur above the gauze.

6. *What is it that passes up through the gauze?*

Consider :

   (a) ˙The odor.

   (b) Whether it will ignite from a lighted match.

   (c) When there is a flame *above* the gauze, move the latter so that the flame will be under a new place.

   (d) Why the flame disappears. (Refer to what was said in XI, 14. Note about the kindling temperature.)

F. Roll the wire gauze once around a lead pencil and lower the tube thus formed over the candle flame.

Consider :

   (a) Why the flame is diminished or finally extinguished.

NOTE.—Read the history of Sir Humphrey Davy's safety lamp.

7. *To what form is the tallow in the candle really reduced before it is burned?*

8. *What is being done in the central part of the flame?*

9. *Why is the hottest part of the flame on the outside?*

10. *What is the use of the wick in the candle? Why is it not reduced to ash?*

11. *Why will tallow not burn well without the wick?*

G. Lower a dry splinter, a burnt match is suitable, over the top of the chimney of a lighted lamp. Observe very closely the way it ignites.

Consider:

(a) The place where the blaze first forms.
(b) What this indicates.

NOTE.—Use the suggestions given for the study of a candle in a study of an oil lamp.

12. *How is part of the flame rendered luminous?*

H. Lower a cool piece of glass or porcelain flatwise into the flame.

Consider:

(a) The part of the flame that deposits the carbon.
(b) What is necessary in order to collect carbon from this part of the flame.
(c) The effect of lowering the wire gauze tube over the flame upon the amount of light given. Refer to (F) above.
(d) The luminous part of the gas flame.

13. *What becomes of the carbon in the luminous part when the flame is left undisturbed?*

Consider:

(a) The smoke.
(b) What takes place in the thin blue outer part of the flame.

14 *In what respects are all the flames studied alike in formation ?*

Consider:

(a) The nature of the substance from which the inflammable part is derived in each case.

(b) The changes which the substances undergo.

(c) The kindling temperature.

(d) The results as shown by the lime water test. [Refer to XI, 16, experiments (d); (e) and (f).]

NOTE.—Read in any chemistry what is said upon the subjects of *combustion, carbon, oxygen and carbon dioxide.*

NUMBER WORK.

1. From the results obtained with the coal in the clay pipe, calculate the amount of gas, that, at the same rate, could be made from a ton of coal.

2. At the gas-works they can make about 10,000 cubic feet of gas from a ton of soft coal. Find out from your gas meter how much gas is consumed in one month and calculate the amount of coal needed to make it.

3. Compare the price paid for the gas with the market value of the coal; the cost of the coal is what per cent. of the cost of the gas?

4. What becomes of the difference between the cost of the coal and the cost of the gas ? Consider:

· (a) The cost of manufacture.

(b) The cost of transmitting.

(c) The interest on the money invested in the gas plant and pipes.

NOTE.—The *gas* is not the only thing of value obtained by the gas companies from the coal; read an account of gas manufacture in any chemistry for a description of other substances known as by-products.

5. An ordinary gas tip burning five cubic feet of gas per hour will vitiate with .2 per cent. of CO_2 5,000 cubic feet of air in one hour; count your gas burners at home and by calculation find out to how many people they are the equivalent in this respect.

6. Count the gas burners in some church or public building and compute the number of cubic feet of air per hour that they will render unfit for breathing.

7. Find out what it costs to pay the gas bill for your city or town for one month. This represents the consumption of how much coal in its manufacture?

8. The gas bill, in (7), is the interest on what sum of money?

9. The cost of the coal is the interest upon what sum?

10. One cubic foot of coal is equal to about 70 lbs.; how much gas could be produced from an acre of coal, if the coal vein is nine feet thick and the rate of production is the same as that given in problem (2)?

11. At the current price what would the gas be worth?

12. Find out how many cubic feet of gas are consumed in your home in one year; how long would that produced from an acre of coal supply your home?

13. Find the gas bill of your city or town for one year; how much coal, in acres, is needed in its production.

NOTE.—This must not be considered as the actual amount of coal consumed, as much of the gas used is water gas which is mingled with that obtained from coal.

REPRESENTATIVE EXPRESSION.

1. *Drawing.*

(a) Represent the volume of a ton of coal by a ¼-inch square. Represent by another square, or rectangle, the volume of the gas it will produce. (One ton of coal, broken, is equal to about 40 cubic feet. See problem (2) Number Work.)

(b) Represent the essential part of the apparatus used in the manufacture of gas.

2. *Painting.*

(a) Represent carefully in color the different parts of the luminous flame in the candle, gas, lamp, and burning splinter.

XIV.

AUTUMN AND WINTER HABITS OF ANIMALS AND PLANTS.

QUERIES:

1. *In what ways does the gradual lowering of the temperature affect animals?*

Consider:

(a) The food supply; its certainty and uncertainty.

(b) The necessity for bodily protection—nests, burrows, shelter and coverings.

(c) The chief conditions which give rise to migration.

(d) The chief conditions which give rise to hibernation.

(e) The chief conditions which enable certain animals to remain active in their usual haunts during the winter season.

(f) The provision made for the following season by the animals that are killed by the winter.

2. *How do the animals that belong to the various classes mentioned above differ from each other?*

Consider:

(a) Kinds of food needed.

(b) Powers of locomotion.

(c) Adaptation of coverings to the changing season.

(d) Ability to take advantage of surrounding conditions favoring protection, such as, mud, water, rock-ledges and hollow trees.

(e) The condition of an animal when in a state of hibernation; his food; breathing; circulation; covering.

(f) The changes in the food supply of the animal that remains active during the winter.

(g) The care bestowed upon eggs and larvæ that must be preserved during the winter.

3. *How does the changing season affect plant life?*

Consider:

(a) The reduction in the area and amount of the living parts—the leaves, the fruits.

(b) The hardening of the bark over the new and soft growths.

(c) The minute living portion in the buds.

(d) The protection of the living parts: the bark, the bud scales, the seed coverings.

4. *Which class of animals mentioned under (1) do plants most resemble in their winter habits?*

Consider :
- (a) The food supply.
- (b) Means of obtaining it.
- (c) The need of food.
- (d) Locomotion.
- (e) Possibilities of protection.
- (f) The preparation for the following season.

REPRESENTATIVE EXPRESSION.

1. *Drawing.*
   - (a) Make a drawing showing the arrangement and structure of buds.
   - (b) Make a drawing showing cocoons on the branches and elsewhere.

2. *Painting.*
   - (a) A landscape showing the effects of the winter season upon the colors of living things.
   - (b) A careful painting of dissected buds and twigs showing the position of the living or green parts.

XV.

METEOROLOGY.

QUERIES :

1. *In what parts of the United States is the winter the most severe?* (Use the Weather Bureau maps.)

Consider :

(a) The general course of the isotherms; compare with October and September.

(b) The most southerly places through which the isotherm of 32° passed during the month. Compare this with the same isotherm for October and September.

(c) The most southerly limit of the zero isotherm.

(d) Through what places does the isotherm pass this month which passed through Chicago in September, marking its lowest temperature for the month?

(e) Compare the most southerly position of the isotherm 50° Fah. in November with its corresponding place in September and October.

2. *In what parts of the United States has the rainfall been heaviest?*

Consider :

(a) The area east of the Mississippi and south of the Ohio.

(b) The area east of the Mississippi and north of the Ohio.

(c) The States which border on the Gulf of Mexico.

(d) The States bordering on the Atlantic ocean.

(e) The States west of the Mississippi and east of the mountains.

(f) The great Basin States.

(g) The Pacific slope.

(h) The area east of the Mississippi and west of the Allegheny mountains.

(i) The area east of the Allegheny mountains.

(j) The number and direction of the Low Areas which crossed these areas during the month.

3. *What is the chief occupation of the people this month in each of the above mentioned areas? Compare city and country.*

Consider:

(a) How the occupations have changed since September.

(b) What preparations are being made for the next year?

NUMBER WORK.

QUERIES:

A. *What have been the temperature conditions this month.*

1. What is the average temperature for the month?

2. What was the highest temperature? The lowest?

3. What was the greatest range of temperature during the month?

4. What is the difference between the average temperature for November and that for October? That for September?

5. Which of the three months had the greatest range of temperature? Which the least range?

6. In which month is a great range of temperature likely to do the most damage?

B. *The Barometric Record.*

7. What is the average reading for the month?

8. What is the greatest range during the month?

9. What is the difference between the average reading for November and that for September? October?

C. *Rainfall and moisture conditions.*

10. What is the number of cloudy days during the month? The number of clear days?

11. The number of cloudy days equals what

part of the month ? The number of clear days equals what part?

12. The number of rainy days equals what part of the month ?

13. The number of rainy days equals what part of the cloudy days?

14. What is the total rainfall for the month ?

15. What is the average rainfall for each rainy day during the month?

16. What is the average rainfall for each cloudy and rainy day ?

17. What is the average rainfall for each day during the month?

18. Find out from the weather maps for the month the total amount of rainfall given for the stations of the Weather Bureau within each of the areas mentioned under A (2), above.

19. What is the average amount for each station ?

20. Calculate how much water fell upon each area included by these Weather Bureau stations.

21. Compare the average rainfall in (a) with the average in (b).

22. Compare the average rainfall in (c) with that in (d).

23. Compare the average rainfall on the Pacific slope with that on the Atlantic slope.

24. Compare the rainfall on the opposite sides of the Allegheny mountains.

25. Compare the rainfall between the Rocky

mountains and the Mississippi river, with that in the area lying east of the river.

D. *The Autumn months compared.*

26. What was the average temperature for the autumn months?

27. What was the greatest range of temperature during autumn?

28. Can you find places on the globe with an *annual* temperature about equal to that of our autumn?

29. What is the average barometer reading for autumn?

30. What was the greatest range in reading?

31. How many cloudy days in autumn?

32. At the same rate, what would be the number for a year?

33. How many clear days in autumn? Compute, at the same rate, the number for a year.

34. What is the total number of rainy days in autumn?

35. At the same rate, what would be the number in a year?

36. The rainy days in autumn equal what part of the cloudy days?

37. What was the rainfall during autumn? Compute, at the same rate, what it would be for a year.

38. What was the average rainfall per cloudy day?

39. What was the average rainfall per rainy day?

40. In which month did the cloudy days average the greatest rainfall?

41. In which month did the rainy days average the greatest rainfall?

42. In which month did the cloudy days give the most rainy days?

NOTE.—The pupils should carefully consider the relation of the barometric reading to the cloudiness and rainfall.

43. What per cent. of the precipitation during the autumn was in the form of snow?

REPRESENTATIVE EXPRESSION.

1. *Drawing.*

   (a) Upon a circle six inches in diameter represent by sectors of colored paper the relative number of clear, cloudy and rainy days during November.

   (b) Represent upon a similar circle the relative number of clear, cloudy and rainy days during autumn.

   (c) Represent by lines the depth of rainfall for each autumn month; by a line the total rainfall.

   (d) Draw a six-inch square to represent the amount of clear weather during autumn; draw another similar figure which will represent the relative amount of cloudy weather; draw a third similar figure which will represent the relative amount of rainy weather.

(e) Draw a set of similar figures which will represent the same facts for each autumn month.

2. *Painting.*

(a) Paint the landscape.
(b) Paint cloud colors and sunsets.

XVI.

ASTRONOMY.

QUERIES:

1. *How has the sun changed its position, relatively, since last month?* (*Use the skiameter.*)

Consider:

    (a) The noon slant—the angle.
    (b) The area covered by the given beam of sunshine.

2. *How has the day and night varied in length?*

Consider:

    (a) The variation in the morning.
    (b) The variation in the evening.

(c) The total variation during the month.

3. *How has the sun changed its position on the horizon at the times of rising and setting?*

NOTE—By laying the skiameter down upon one side with the bottom board on a north and south line, the beam (a) (See page 38) may be directed towards the point where the sun rises or sets. When placed upright again the plumb line will give the angle between the east or west point or the horizon and that at which the sun rises and sets.

NUMBER WORK.

1. The area now covered by a beam of sunshine covered how much in October at a corresponding date?

2. How much did the beam cover in September on the corresponding date?

3. The sunshine which was distributed over one acre in September covers how much ground now?

4. The sunshine which now falls upon an acre at New Orleans covers how much ground at Chicago? At Winnipeg? At St. Petersburg?

5. The intensity of the sunshine now at Chicago is equal to what part of its intensity at New Orleans?

6. The intensity of sunshine at St. Petersburg now equals what part of the intensity at Chicago? At New Orleans? At the equator?

7. The intensity of the sunshine at this date equals what part of the intensity on corresponding dates in September? In October?

8. The day's length is what part of the length on the same date in September? In October?

9. How much has the day's length changed during autumn?

10. During which month was there the most variation? How much?

11. During which month did the sun's slant change most? How much?

12. During which month has the length of day changed least? How much?

13. During which month has the sun's slant changed least? How much?

REPRESENTATIVE EXPRESSION.

1 *Drawing.*

(a) Draw the arc of a circle with six-inch radius; upon this represent the slant of the noon sun, about Nov. 25th, at New Orleans, Chicago, Winnipeg, and St. Petersburg.

(b) Draw a series of rectangles which will represent the area covered at this date by a given beam of noon sunshine at New Orleans, Chicago, Winnipeg and St. Petersburg.

(c) Draw a circle with three-inch radius; upon this represent the relative length of day and night.

(d) Draw another circle of same size to represent the horizon; upon this represent the north, south, east and west points and also the point where the sun rises and sets on this date. (About Nov. 25.)

2. *Painting.*

(a) The landscape showing different effects produced by various kinds of clouds.

(b) Sunsets.

XVII.

HEAT: CONDUCTION AND RADIATION.

OBSERVATION. Recall the various means that were employed to prevent the loss of heat from the steam in connection with the study of the steam engine. Also, the various places about the fire-box, boiler, pipes and engine that were warmed by the escaping heat. See *Queries* on pp. 94 (c) and 100 (26). Review some of the problems, beginning on page 104, which show the value of the heat that escapes without doing any work through the engine.

QUERIES :

1. *By what means is the heat received by the boiler, and how does it escape, unused, from the boiler and pipes?*

Consider :

    (a) The contact of the fire with one side of the boiler.

    (b) The contact of the water with the interior of the boiler.

NOTE.—The iron of the boiler is said to *absorb* the heat from the furnace; the sides of the boiler in giving the heat off are said to *radiate* it; the iron, in permitting the heat to pass through it, is said to *conduct* it.

2. *Are all substances alike in their absorbing, radiating and conducting powers?*

Consider :

(a) The various substances, iron, copper, tin, stone, glass, brass, etc., which are used in contact with heat. Note board walks, nail heads in boards, stone pavements, grass plots, bare ground.

(b) In which of these, absorption is important.

(c) In which radiation is important.

(d) In which conduction is important.

(e) The *finish* of the surfaces in the instances noted in (b), (c) and (d), whether rough or polished.

(f) The *color* of the surfaces in the foregoing instances.

(g) Whether uniform conditions prevail where the one or the other end—absorption, conduction or radiation—is sought.

3. *What is the relative radiation from vessels made of different materials.*

EXPERIMENTS:

A. *Equipment.* Vessels holding about 1 pint that are made of different materials, such as glass, tin, iron, copper, brass, aluminum, stone or earthenware. A chemical thermometer. Heat a kettle of water to about 175° and fill each vessel two-thirds full and cover with several thicknesses of paper. After a minute, take the temperature of the water in each vessel. Several of these vessels for this and the next experiment can be cheaply made by any tinsmith. The vessels will be useful for many purposes.

Consider:

 (a) The amount of radiating surface of each vessel.

 (b) Whether amount of surface will affect the result; the character of the surface—smooth or rough.

 (c) The quantity of water in each vessel; will this affect the result?

 (d) Why the vessels are securely covered.

 (e) Why the temperature is not taken *immediately* after pouring the water into them.

 (f) The effect of varying thickness in the vessels.

 (g) At intervals of three to five minutes, take the temperature of the water in each.

 (h) By what process, the water becomes cooler.

 (i) Which vessel seems to retain the heat best.

 (j) Which one seems to radiate it most rapidly.

4. *Does the character of the surface—smooth or rough—affect radiation?*

B. Select two each of several different kinds of vessels holding one to two pints—one having a *rough* and the other a *polished* surface. Fill with hot water, cover and test with a thermometer as before.

Consider:

(a) The rate at which the temperature falls in the vessels made of the same material but with different surface finish.

(b) The rate at which the temperature falls in *all* the vessels with polished surface.

(c) The rate at which the temperature falls in *all* the vessels having rough surface.

5. *How may the surfaces be prepared so as to reduce the amount of radiation?*

Consider:

(a) The coverings used on the steampipes.

(b) The means of protecting the surface of locomotive boilers against radiation.

(c) The wrapping that is sometimes used about the hot-air pipes of furnaces.

EXPERIMENT: *Equipment.* Several tin or copper cups. A strip each of muslin, flannel and asbestos. Thermometer. Wrap the cups with a *single layer*, one with muslin, another with flannel, and another with asbestos; if possible, have a fourth cup with its surface unprotected. Fill the cups two-thirds full of hot water and cover with several thicknesses of paper. Take the temperature of each at intervals of five minutes and note any differences in the rate of cooling. The jackets of the cups should fit closely and smoothly. They may be held in place by wrapping with a string.

6. *Which mode of protecting the surface seems best in preventing radiation?* (See Number Work.)

Consider:
  (a) Rate of fall of temperature.
  (b) The relative expense of the different materials.
  (c) The durability of the materials.
  (d) The ease of application.

7. *How do different substances vary in conducting power?* (See Number Work.)

Examine the various materials used in the manufacture of stoves and furnaces. Notice where wood is used.

EXPERIMENT: *Equipment.* A vessel holding about 1 quart. A square of cardboard considerably larger than the top of the vessel. Rods —heavy wire—of copper, iron and brass; of glass; a slate pencil. These rods should be 8 or 10 inches long. Make holes in the cardboard lid which will allow the passage of the rods but will hold them firmly. The holes should be scattered as much as possible within the area equal to the top of the vessel. Fill the vessel nearly to the top with hot water and cover it with the cardboard lid, allowing the rods to project well towards the bottom. Lightly coat the upper ends of the rod with cocoa butter, or paraffin, or lard.

Consider :

(a) Why the lid should be considerably larger than the top of vessel.

(b) Why the rods should be well distributed in the lid.

(c) Why the rods should fit tightly in the holes.

(d) Why very hot water is to be preferred to placing the ends of the rods in a flame.

(e) Why the coating on the rods melts.

(f) What the different distance, along which the melting occurs, indicates.

(g) Which of the materials in the rods is suitable for vessels in which it is desirable to retain heat—boilers, for example.

NOTE—The vessel may be placed over a flame and the water thus be kept hot until each rod has melted the coating to its limit.

(h) Whether the *rate* of melting or the *distance* along which melting takes place indicates the best *conductor*.

8. *Why do the various materials in a room of uniform temperature give us different sensations as to heat ?*

Place the hand upon the woodwork, polished and unpolished; upon iron, marble, glass, paper, cloth—cotton and woolen, stoneware, etc.

Consider:

    (a) The varying degrees of coldness.

    (b) The conductivity of each substance.

    (c) Why a good conductor, as to heat, should give us a different sensation from a poor conductor.

9. *How is it possible to heat a house by means of hot water carried to all its rooms from a boiler located in the basement?*

OBSERVATION: Study some building thus heated and notice the arrangement of the pipes and their connection with the radiators and boiler.

If possible, notice the connection of the kitchen range with the boiler. The construction of the "water back" in the stove.

EXPERIMENT: *Equipment.* Test tube or glass beaker. Alcohol or bunsen flame. Thermometer.

A. Fill the test tube or beaker two-thirds full and heat gradually over the flame. Drop some fine particles of chalk or fine dust into the water and study the movements.

Consider:

    (a) The direction and rapidity of the motion of the particles.

    (b) The meaning of the movements.

   (c) The relation of the movements to the point where the heat is applied.

   (d) Using the thermometer, the temperature at various depths.

B. Fit a wide mouth 2-oz. ointment bottle with cork having two holes. Insert two glass tubes 5 or 6 inches long, allowing one to project into the bottle an inch farther than the other. Fill with clear, cold water and insert stopper with the tubes. Fill a beaker with colored water and arrange so that it may be heated. With the fingers over the ends of the two tubes, invert the bottle and immerse the ends of the tubes in the colored water. Suspend the bottle in this position and apply heat to the vessel.

Consider:

   (a) The movement of the colored water in the tubes.

   (b) How water by being heated may be carried to all parts of a building.

NOTE.—Water that is thus heated through the interchange of its parts by means of currents is said to be heated by convection.

C. Using a test tube of water, cautiously apply the heat to the upper end of the tube, one-half inch below the surface of the water. As before, use the thermometer to determine the temperature at different depths. The result will be more striking if a piece of ice is sunk to the bottom of the tube and held there by a small pebble or any sufficient weight.

Consider:

(a) Movements by currents.

(b) The variation of temperature at different depths.

(c) How the process of heating differs from that by convection.

(d) The likeness to the experiment with the rods. (See Query 7.)

(e) Whether the water in lakes and ponds is heated by convection or conduction.

(f) What differences might be expected if the reverse were true.

XVIII.

HEAT. TEMPERATURE.

QUERIES:

1. *What does the thermometer tell us about heat?*

EXPERIMENT: *Equipment.* Two polished vessels holding about one pint each. The thin polished lemonade shakers are probably the most easily available and the best. Obtain at hardware store. Thermometer. Snow or ice. Hot water.

Heat some water to the boiling point and pour into one of the vessels about four hundred grams and into the other twice the quantity.

Take the temperature of each. Stir into each vessel 20 grams of dry ice in small pieces, or dry snow. When melted, take the temperature of each. Add snow or ice until no more will melt in either vessel; note the lowest temperature reached. Then weigh the water in each vessel.

Consider:

(a) What is indicated concerning heat by the falling temperature as the snow or ice is added.

(b) Why the temperature was different

after *equal* quantities of snow or ice had been added.

(c) Why it took more snow to lower the temperature a given number of degrees, in the large vessel than it did in the small one.

(d) The number of *degrees* lost by each vessel of water.

(e) The *amount of heat* lost by each vessel of water.

(f) The relation of *temperature* to *heat*.

(g) What there is to show for the loss of heat in the water.

2. *Are our senses a safe guide in determining the temperature?*

OBSERVATION : Note your sensations of heat and cold on entering or leaving a room.

Consider:

(a) Whether a room which *feels* warm upon entering it is actually warm enough to be safe.

(b) How a basement room or cellar *feels* on a warm summer day.

(c) How the same feels on a cold winter day, if it is enclosed.

EXPERIMENT. Using the vessels before described, fill each partially with water. In one let the water be about 130°; in another, ice water; in the third about 65°. Hold one hand in the hot and the other in the cold for a few moments; then, remove both to the third vessel with water of medium temperature.

Consider:

    (a) The reason for the opposite sensations given by the two hands.

    (b) Which hand tells the truth.

    (c) The real value of the thermometer.

3. *Does the application of heat always result in a rise of temperature?*

OBSERVATION : Make a careful study of melting snow and ice. Find a snow bank that is melting or a pond in which the ice is melting.

Consider :

    (a) Why the melting takes place.

    (b) The temperature as given by a thermometer which is held in the water issuing from the snow bank or in the pond of ice water.

    (c) The temperature of the air around the snow and ice.

    (d) Is the snow bank or ice receiving heat? How much?

EXPERIMENTS: A. *Equipment.* Two of the tin or copper vessels used in the preceding experiments. A pan about two inches in depth and large enough in area to allow the two vessels to stand within it. Thermometer. Scales.

Fill one vessel about two-thirds full of water which has been cooled with ice down to about 32° Fah. Place in the second vessel an *equal weight* of ice cracked into small pieces. Set the two vessels in the pan and pour around them ice water to a depth of 1½ inches. Set the pan over one or more lamps or gas flames, taking care that the flame does not strike the pan immediately *beneath* either vessel. Use only moderate heat. Take the temperature accurately of the contents of the three vessels just before applying the heat. Keep the water in the pan stirred gently.

Consider:

(a) The temperature in each of the two vessels at short intervals of two or three minutes.

(b) Why the water in the pan should be stirred.

(c) The quantity of heat which enters each of the two vessels.

(d) What the thermometer shows of the heat in each vessel.

(e) What there is in the vessel containing ice to show for the heat which it receives.

(f) When the ice is melted, how much heat, judged by the other vessel, has been used.

(g) How the temperature of the two vessels corresponds after the ice is melted; continue to take the temperature of each at brief intervals until it ceases to rise in the vessel, which in the beginning contained the water.

NOTE.—Using a thin test-tube, find the melting

point of other substances, such as, butter, lard, tallow, etc. Place a small quantity in the tube and place this in a vessel of water, as before, warming the latter gradually. Take the temperature the moment it is seen to slide loosely within the glass.

NOTE.—The quantity of heat required to raise the temperature of a given amount of water one degree is called a *heat unit*. Thus the quantity required to raise the temperature of a pound of ice water 1° is called a *pound degree*. That required to raise the temperature of a gram or of a kilogram of ice water 1° is called the *gram degree* and the *kilogram degree* respectively. The heat required to raise the temperature of a *cubic foot* of ice water is called the *foot degree*. Above 40° Fah. a slightly increasing amount of heat is required to raise the temperature of a given quantity 1°. A heat unit is called a *calorie*.

B. When the temperature ceases to rise in the vessel which contained the water, remove it from the pan and place directly over the flame. Continue to take the temperature at short intervals until it becomes stationary.

Consider :
(a) The number of degrees above the melting point.
(b) Whether heat is still passing into the vessel of water.
(c) What there is to show for the heat received. (See Number Work.)

4. *Do different bodies of equal weight having the same temperature necessarily have the same amount of heat ?*

EXPERIMENTS: *Equipment.* The tin or copper vessels used in previous experiments. About 100 grams (3 or 4 ounces) of each of the following: Alcohol, glycerine, copper strip, lead strip, and, if possible, one of brass. Thermometer. Alcohol lamp or bunsen burner.

A. Pour into one of the vessels 200 grams of water at about 32°. Take its temperature accurately. Heat the same quantity of water in the other vessel to about 150°. Mix the water in the two vessels and take the temperature when it becomes stationary.

Consider:
- (a) How much the temperature of the cold water rose.
- (b) How much the temperature of the warm water fell.
- (c) What the relative change in each means.

B. Again prepare a vessel with ice water. Cautiously heat the *same weight* of alcohol to about 150°. Mingle the contents of the two two vessels as before and take the temperature.

Consider:
- (a) The rise in temperature of the water.
- (b) The fall in temperature of the alcohol.
- (c) How the difference in result may be explained.

C. In the same way try the glycerine and water.

D. Roll the lead strip into a loose coil; place

it in one of the vessels with enough water to cover it and boil. Prepare the other vessel, as before, with ice water equal in weight to the lead. Take its temperature. By means of a string or pointed pliers quickly transfer the lead coil to the cold water.

Consider:

(a) The temperature of the lead while in the boiling water.

(b) Allowances that should be made for changes during the transfer.

(c) The temperature of the lead and water after the former is transferred to the latter.

(d) The rise in the temperature of the water.

(e) The fall in the temperature of the lead.

(f) The quantity of heat given up by the lead compared with the quantity given up by the same weight of water. (See Experiment A.) In the same way experiment with the copper, brass and other substances.

(g) How allowance should be made for the containing vessels in the preceding experiments. For example, when the lead was transferred to the cold water, whether the heat given off was used in raising the temperature of the *water* only.

(h) How such allowance would affect the accuracy of the results.

NOTE.—The heat which passed into the vessel of melting snow or ice without raising its temperature is said to become *latent;* the same is true of the heat used in changing the water into steam when the boiling point has been reached. Is the *latent heat* lost?

The amount of heat required to raise the temperature of a *body* one degree is called its *thermal* or *heat* capacity. The *thermal* or *heat* capacity of a substance compared with that of the same weight of water is its *specific heat.*

NOTE.—Procure from a blacksmith shop a small piece of an iron bar, weighing about half a pound; heat until red hot and then drop it into four or five times its weight of water having a temperature of about 40°. Stir with a rod and take the temperature when it becomes steady. Iron, when heated bright red, has a temperature of about 1,600°. Consider how much heat the iron loses when it is placed in the water. (See Number Work.)

XIX.

HEAT. A STUDY OF ENERGY.

QUERIES:

1. *What changes, besides variations in temperature, take place in bodies upon the application or withdrawal of heat?*

OBSERVATIONS : Examine structures made of iron or other metals which are subject to·temperature variations; such as telegraph wires and railroad rails. If there is opportunity, visit a boiler shop, or any manufactory where iron rivets are employed, as, in boilers or iron bridges.

Consider :

   (a) Whether any allowances are made for variations in size or form that depend upon fluctuations in temperature.

   (b) Why the rivets in bridges and boilers are not put in place while cold.

EXPERIMENT. Provide rods of heavy wire, a foot or more in length, of iron, copper and brass. Provide two supports of such distance apart as to support the rods at the ends. Place one end of the rod against a firm back; a notch may be cut into the support to receive the end of the rod. Stick a darning or a knitting needle into the other support *tightly against the free end of the rod.* Apply heat, by means of the flame, along the middle portion of the rod. A small paper or brass protractor may be placed behind the needle, by which the amount of movement may be measured and the relative amount of lengthening in the different rods may be determined.

Consider:

    (a) The effect of applying heat to the middle of the rod.

    (b) The effect of applying it to its entire length.

    (c) What the movement of the end of the needle means.

    (d) Of the various rods tried, which moves the needle most.

2. *Does the application of heat affect the volume of liquids?*

EXPERIMENTS: *Equipment.* Florence flask, or stout bottle, with mouth large enough to receive a rubber cork with *two* holes through it. The weight of the empty bottle, the tubing, the cork and the thermometer must be determined. Chemical thermometer. Glass tubing—a piece 12 inches or more in length. Scales for weighing.

A. Fill the bottle or flask with boiling hot water and allow it to cool down to about 40°; keep it filled to the top. Insert the tubing and the thermometer through the holes in the cork —allowing the latter to reach down to the center of the flask. By bending the tube at its upper end at a right angle, the overflow may be caught and measured or weighed. By carefully gauging the amount of water in the flask, it may be made to rise, when the cork and thermometer are pressed in, so as to fill the tube. The latter should not project below the lower surface of the cork. When thus arranged weigh and calculate the weight of water. After taking final note of the temperature immerse the flask in a vessel of hot water. Arrange a cup to catch any overflow. If desired, the flask may be *suspended* in the vessel and the latter placed over the flame.

Consider :

(a) The movement of the water in the tube the instant the flask is immersed.

(b) What occurs as the water in the flask becomes heated.

(c) The amount of the water in the overflow. In what ways this may be determined. It will be approximately correct to consider that 1 gram of water equals 1 cubic centimeter.

(d) The number of c. c. in the flask and tube before heating.

(e) The number after heating; watch the thermometer and make note at the same time of the overflow. For this purpose a small graduate with fractions of a gram marked will be useful.

(f) When the temperature of the water in the flask has risen to the height desired, determine how much altogether has escaped.

(g) The number of degrees of heat through which the water in the flask rose.

(h) The following conditions and precautions: the use of *boiling* water in filling the flask; why the tube should not project below the lower surface of the cork; why, before heating, the water should be pressed up to *fill* the tube; why the height of water in the tube should be noted the instant the flask is immersed; what allowance should be made for the flask.

(i) The total increase in the volume of the water. (See Number Work.)

B. Prepare the flask or bottle of water exactly as before. When cooled down to about 40°, arrange the tube and thermometer in the cork and press the latter down as in A. Set the flask in a vessel and fill the space between the two with finely cracked ice or snow and salt. Closely watch the thermometer and catch the overflow if there be any. After considerable ice has formed within the flask, take it from the vessel of salt and ice, remove the cork and pour out the water not yet frozen, allowing the ice to remain.

Consider:

(a) What changes must be taking place in the water judging from the movements of the water in the tube.

(b) Whether a given volume of water is greater or less than the volume of ice which it may form.

(c) How you may determine, by proper care in measurement in the above experiment, what volume of ice is formed from a cubic centimeter of water.

(d) Why ice forms on *top* of a lake or pond, not at the bottom.

(e) Why ice floats.

(f) What would take place in lakes and streams if ice were less in volume than the water from which it was frozen.

(g) What would occur in nature if water continued to *contract* down to the freezing point.

(h) How the currents are produced in the experiment illustrating convection.

3. `*How much does air expand for every degree of heat that is applied?*`

EXPERIMENT: *Equipment.* Florence flask or bottle as in the preceding experiment; rubber cork with one hole; glass tubing two or three inches long; thermometer; vessel to hold hot water.

By weighing, as before, determine the capacity of the flask, allowing for the space occupied by the cork. Pour into the vessel provided for hot water enough water having a temperature of about 140° to admit of the immersion of the flask to the level of the mouth. Take the temperature of the air inside the flask; when it becomes steady, before taking the flask from the water, press the cork in tightly and insert the tube in it. Place the finger tightly over the end of the tube and, removing the flask from the hot water, invert it and dip the end of the tube into a vessel of water having the temperature of the air in the room.

Consider:

- (a) Why the water rushes up into the flask.
- (b) Why the water does not completely fill the flask.
- (c) The temperature of the air inside the flask when the water ceases to rise.
- (d) The fall of temperature after removing the flask from the water.
- (e) What is shown by the volume of water that has passed into the flask.
- (f) Under what conditions did the air, now in the flask above the water, fill the whole flask.
- (g) Through what number of degrees the temperature fell while the water was passing into the flask.

(h) The following precaution: the flask is kept completely immersed in the hot water until the finger tightly closes the end of the tube; the cork tight fitting. When removing the tube from the water after it has ceased to flow in, should the water in the tube be allowed to enter the flask? How the expansion of the flask will affect the experiment.

(i) How much the air in the flask expanded per degree of heat. (See number work).

NOTE.—The pupil should exercise his ingenuity in devising other experiments of a similar character which show how much the air is expanded by heat. The results to be obtained by these crude experiments are but somewhat wide approximations, but they will assist in giving some notion of what is accomplished by heat.

XX.

THE SOURCES OF HEAT.

OBSERVATIONS: Make a careful study of the means employed in producing heat in the various places where it is used. Also, note under what conditions it is sometimes incidentally produced.

Consider:

(a) The mode of obtaining heat in the furnace; in the grate; with the candle; with the lamp; in the electric light.

(b) How the above modes differ from each other; how they are alike. Are they essentially similar or dissimilar?

(c) How sparks are formed by horses' hoofs striking stones. (By percussion.)

(d) The striking of two stones together; what is the spark?

(e) The sparks which are produced by the car brake. (By friction.)

(f) How percussion differs from friction.

(g) The sun as a source of heat.

(h) What phenomena on the earth can be directly traced to *heat* derived from the sun.

Note.—For an interesting description of the source, maintenance and intensity of solar heat, refer to Young's *Lessons in Astronomy.*

Queries :

1. *How is the heat of the animal body produced and maintained?*

Consider :

- (a) What conditions were necessary in order to produce heat in the furnace.
- (b) What things were produced as a result of the burning of the fuel in the furnace. (See page 97, *Queries* 16 and 17.)
- (c) What the expired air contained as shown by the lime water test.
- (d) How the expired air differed from the air before it was taken into the lungs. (See page 109, note.)
- (e) What relation there may be of food to fuel.
- (f) The real use, probably, made of the air taken into the lungs.

2. *In what way does clothing aid in maintaining the heat of the body?*

Consider :

- (a) The facts noted in the study of *radiation.*
- (b) The facts noted in the study of *conduction.*

(c) Does color play any part; summer and winter colors in clothing.

(d) The nature of the materials in summer and in winter clothing.

(e) Why there is a difference in the *feel* of a blanket and a sheet.

(f) Why wet clothing feels cold, and why it is dangerous to wear it.

(g) Why flannel underwear is recommended for summer.

3. *Does the temperature of the body vary?*

Use, if possible, a physician's thermometer and

Consider:

(a) The temperature obtained by placing the thermometer under the tongue. Note the rate of the pulse and heart beat.

(b) The effect of 10 minutes' vigorous exercise upon the temperature, the pulse and heart beat.

(c) Why the feeling of warmth is increased by the exercise.

(d) What is indicated by the changed pulse and heart beat

(e) What is indicated by a lowered or elevated temperature in disease.

(f) Why physicians regard the thermometer as a most important instrument in determining whether disease is present.

NUMBER WORK.

QUERIES:

A. *What is the relative value of asbestos and woolen and cotton coverings in preventing radiation?*

1. The fall of temperature in a given time in water in an unprotected vessel bears what ratio to the fall in the water in a similar vessel protected by asbestos?

2. In the same way compare the asbestos covered vessels with those covered with other substances.

B. *What is the relative conducting power of metals?*

3. Taking the distance along which the paraffin melted on the copper wire as 1, compare the conducting power of each of the other rods with it, as indicated by the melted paraffin.

4. Exact experiments show that if the conductivity of silver be placed at 100, that of copper is 77.6; of brass, 33; of zinc, 19.9; of tin, 14.9; of iron, 11.9; of lead, 8.5; compare your results obtained by experiment with these figures; account for any differences that may occur.

C. *What is the amount of heat required in melting a given weight of ice?*

5. The amount of heat required to melt a pound of ice would raise how much water from 32° to the boiling point?

6. Ten pounds of water at 212° would require how much ice to cool it down to 100°?

7. If 2 pounds of ice were placed in 4 pounds of water having a temperature of 160°, what would be the temperature when it was melted?

NOTE.—Devise a way for determining how you may allow for loss of heat by radiation. Exact experiment shows that the quantity of heat required to melt 1 pound of ice is sufficient to raise the temperature of the same weight of water about 142°. Review the experiments performed by yourelf and account for any difference in results.

8. The quantity of heat required to raise 10 pounds of water from 32° to 212° would heat what weight of iron bright red hot? See note under D on specific heat of iron.

NOTE.—Accurate experiment shows that copper expands .00001866 of its length for every degree of heat applied; iron, .0000122, and brass .00001875.

9. How much expansion would there be in a ten-mile copper telephone wire in a range of 60° temperature?   .

10. How much would there be in the same length of iron wire?

11. What space should be left between 30-ft. railroad rails, to allow for a range of 80° of temperature?

D. *To what extent do air and water increase in volume when heat is applied?*

12. Referring to the experiment performed,

find out what part of its volume water expanded for every degree of heat applied.

NOTE.—Accurate experiment shows that, above about 40°, Fah., water expands about $\frac{1}{4000}$ of its volume per degree, Fah. Compare with the results obtained in your experiments and account for the difference.

13. Determine from your experiment the difference in weight between a cubic centimeter of ice and the same volume of water.

14. In melting a cubic foot of ice, how much water could be obtained?

NOTE.—Accurate experiment shows that air expands $\frac{1}{481}$ of its volume for every degree of heat, Fah. Compare this with the result of your own experiment and account for the difference.

15. When the temperature of the school room rises from 40° to 70°, how much air is forced out?

REPRESENTATIVE EXPRESSION.

1. *Drawing.*

(a) Draw a 10-inch square to represent a given quantity of ice; upon this figure construct another which will correctly represent the amount of water in the ice when melted.

(b) Draw a 10-inch square to represent a given quantity of water at 40°; upon this construct another figure which will correctly show the volume of the

water after the temperature has been
raised 100°.

(c) Draw a 10-inch square to represent a
given quantity of air, at 32°; upon
this, construct a figure that will correctly represent the volume of air
when heated to 70°

XXI.

METEOROLOGY FOR DECEMBER.

QUERY: *What are the prevailing conditions this month and how are living things affected by them?*

Consider:

- (a) The average temperature.
- (b) The range in temperature; the highest; the lowest.
- (c) The precipitation—rainfall and snow —in inches. (10 in. of snow=1 in. rainfall.
- (d) The relative amount of clear and cloudy weather.
- (e) The number of rainy days.
- (f) The depth to which the ground is frozen.
- (g) Whether the buds and roots of plants freeze.
- (h) Whether the cocoons on the trees are frozen.
- (i) Whether seeds in the soil, acorns, etc., are frozen.
- (j) The isotherm marking the lowest temperature on the U. S. Weather Maps this month.
- (k) The position this month of the lowest isotherm which passed through Chi-

cago in November; in October; in September.

(l) The southerly limits of the 32° isotherm this month ; of the zero isotherm.

(m) The area of the country continuously below freezing temperature this month. Below zero temperature.

NUMBER WORK.

QUERY : *To what extent do the conditions which prevail this month differ from those in preceeding months?*

1. What is the difference between the average temperature this month and the average for the autumn months? Compare with September, October and November.

2. The greatest range of temperature for this month, bears what ratio to the greatest range of temperature in September? October? November ? To the greatest range in autumn ?

3. What is the average precipitation in December for each rainy day? For each cloudy day? The daily average for the month ?

4. Compare the averages obtained in (3) with similar averages obtained for each of the autumn months.

5. At the December rate what would be the number of cloudy days for the year? The number of rainy days ? The annual rainfall?

6. What is the average height of the barometer for the month? Compare with the record for each autumn month.

7. What is the greatest barometric range during the month? Compare with each of the autumn months.

8. What part of the entire country fell below 32° during the month? Compare this area with the area that fell below freezing in November.

9. What extent of area in the United States was continuously below freezing in December? Compare with November.

10. What was the area in the United States that was continuously below zero in December? Compare with November.

REPRESENTATIVE EXPRESSION.

1. *Drawing.*
   - (a) Draw a 10-inch square to represent the quantity of water per square foot which fell in December; upon this construct similar figures which will represent the quantity per square foot which fell in each autumn month.
   - (b) Draw lines which will correctly represent the relative amount of rainfall for each of the months studied.
   - (c) Draw lines which will correctly represent the relative number of rainy days in each month studied. Represent in the same way the relative number of cloudy days. The relative number of clear days.

2. *Painting.*
   - (a) Paint a characteristic December land-

scape. Compare carefully with September colors.

XXII.

ASTRONOMY FOR DECEMBER.

QUERY: *What is the heat and light value of sunshine received during December ?*

Make use of the skiameter, and

Consider :

(a) The area covered by a given beam of noon sunshine.

(b) The slant of the beam at the solstice.

(c) The heat and light value compared with that on corresponding dates of previous months.

(d) The relative value of the noon sunshine on the parallels 0°, 20°, 40°, 60°, 80° north latitude.

(e) The causes which modify the direct value of the sunshine at three different places.

NUMBER WORK.

1. Compare the area covered by a given beam at the solstice with that covered by the same beam on corresponding dates in the previous months studied.

2. What is the ratio of the area covered by.

a given beam at your place of observation at the solstice to the area covered by the same beam at St. Petersburg? at London? at Chicago? at New Orleans? Mexico? Quito?

3. Find the area covered by a given beam of noon sunshine at different points on the most southerly zero isotherm for the month; the most southerly 32° isotherm for the month.

4. The quantity of noon sunshine which covered a 10-acre wheatfield on September 23d, north latitude 45°, now covers how much ground?

5. Compare the heat and light intensity of noon sunshine at the various places mentioned in (2) for each of the months studied.

6. By how many minutes has the day been shortened since the equinox?

7. How many minutes have been lost in the morning? In the evening?

8. What is the ratio of the loss in the morning to that in the evening?

9. The day's length at the solstice is equal to what part of its length at the equinox?

10. Find the number of minutes lost by the day in the morning each month since the equinox. In the evening. (Use the almanac, if necessary.)

11. Compare the amount lost by the day each month with the total loss since the equinox.

REPRESENTATIVE EXPRESSION.

1. *Drawing.*

    (a) Draw a rectangle which will represent the area covered by a given beam of noon sunshine at the solstice in your latitude ; on the same scale draw rectangles which will show the distribution of the same beam at Quito, Mexico, New Orleans, Chicago, Winipeg, St. Petersburg.

2. *Painting.*

    (a) A winter landscape showing characteristic sky colors.

XXIII.

HEAT AND ENERGY IN THE ANIMAL BODY.

THE COMPOSITION OF FOODS.

OBSERVATIONS: Make a careful written list of all the various articles that you have used for food. Visit the stores and markets.

QUERIES:

1. *In what proportion do the three kingdoms —animal, vegetable and mineral—furnish our foods?*

Make a list of the foods that belong strictly to each and

Consider:

- (a) If either class is independent of the other two.
- (b) If either is derived from one or both of the others.
- (c) Which furnishes the largest, and which the smallest list of articles of diet.
- (d) How the list in each varies with the season—winter and summer; determine this by actual count.

2. *What proportion of the list of articles*

named is composed of actually essential foods?

Consider:

(a) Those you find on the table every day or nearly so—the necessaries.

(b) Those which appear at irregular intervals—the luxuries.

(c) Those which seldom appear, not being regarded as regular articles of diet.

(d) How the proportions of these vary with the season.

(e) The proportion of animal and vegetable food in each class.

3. *What are some of the most important elements and substances of which our foods are composed?*

Consider:

(a) The number and kinds in which you can prove that there is water.

(b) The proportion of water in the different kinds tested. (See Number Work.)

Experiments:

A. *Test for Starch. Equipment.* Common starch that may be bought at any grocery. An ounce of tincture of iodine.

Stir a small pinch of starch up in half a glass of water; when well mixed add iodine, drop by drop, until, by stirring, a violet color appears. This is a test for starch.

By this means, test various kinds of foodstuffs with a view to finding if they contain starch. For example, scrape a teaspoonful of raw potato and stir it up in a glass of water; as before, add iodine and draw conclusions respecting the test. Try in a similar manner bread, oatmeal, and any other articles that may suggest themselves to you.

NOTE.—The starchy foods are called *carbohydrates; sugar*, also, belongs to this class of foods.

B. *Tests for Albumen. Equipment.* A test tube or glass beaker, lamp or bunsen burner, and an egg.

Remove the white of the egg and shake it up in about a pint of water until dissolved. Strain this through filter paper or a fine cloth.

Fill the test tube half full and gradually heat it over the flame. When warmed up to a certain point (take the temperature with a thermometer) note the change in the appearance of the liquid. The white cloudiness produced in the liquid by heat is due to the coagulation or hardening of the white of egg which is nearly pure *albumen*.

Clean the test tube and partially fill with fresh egg liquid again; add to it a little hydrochloric acid and note the result. This is another test that may be made for albumen. Repeat the preparation and add a little alcohol.

Procure an ounce of lean beef and cleanse it of blood. Mince it up in a glass of clear water and strain or filter. Test this filtered liquid for albumen. Apply the test for albumen to other articles of food that have been similarly prepared.

C. *Tests for Fats and Oils.* Using a test tube, warm gradually over a flame, without burning, a small bit of meat; try to mingle what is melted out of the meat with water. When allowed to stand undisturbed, note what collects on top.

Repeat the experiment with the kernels of various kinds of nuts.

D. Refer to Chap. VIII, pp. 75–81, for directions, and determine *the dry solid matter, the water, the carbon, the ash* and *the organic matter* in various articles of food.

Milk is so important as an article of diet that there should be a somewhat careful study of its constituents. Procure a test tube six or eight inches long. On the outside paste a narrow strip of paper ruled in centimeters and millimeters. This scale should be long enough to extend the entire length of the tube, 0 being at the top.

QUERIES:

1. *What per cent. of good milk is cream?*

EXPERIMENTS:

A. Fill the tube up to the zero point with milk known to be fresh and pure. Note the color carefully and set it aside in a cool, clean place for about ten or twelve hours. Keep free from dust. At the end of this period,

Consider:

(a) The color in various parts of the tube.
(b) The depth of the layer of cream on the top.
(c) The per cent. of cream.
(d) Carefully, the nature and amount of sediment in the bottom.

NOTE.—It has been found by experiments, which would be out of place here, that the fat does not *all* rise to the top as *cream.*

(e) What is derived from the cream or fat in milk. Read about the process of butter making. Compare the prices of milk and butter.

B. With fresh samples of milk, apply the tests for albumen. The albuminous substance in milk is called *casein.* This is the part of the milk from which cheese is made. Read about cheese making. Compare the prices of cheese and milk.

2. Does milk contain any solid matter?

C. Weigh about 20 grams of milk. Put this into a shallow dish whose weight is known and dry by means of a water bath. Use, for the latter, a tin cup with a hole punched in its side near the top to permit the steam to escape. Place the vessel of milk on top of the cup, which should be partially filled with water and kept to the boiling point. Stir the milk occasionally with a glass rod to break the film that forms. Thoroughly dry the residue and determine its weight. Calculate the amount per gallon.

3. *Does milk contain any ash or mineral matter?*

D. Place the dry residue in a small porcelain evaporating dish, the weight of which is known. Place over a moderate flame and, at as low a temperature as possible, reduce to ash. If not too small in amount determine its weight.

4. *By what means may pure milk be recognized?*

E. Place a sample of fresh milk, known to be pure, in a perfectly clean test tube.

Consider, very carefully:

(a) The color, especially at the edges as seen against the glass. The general color effect should be white, very slightly yellowish.
(b) The effect as held between the eye and the light. Opaque, translucent near edges.
(c) How a drop will cling to the end of a clean, bright knitting needle.
(d) Whether sediment as black specks may be seen scattered through it.

NOTE.—The per cent. of cream (see above, experiment A) is also a test of value and purity. Ordinary milk will produce about 10%. That from a Jersey cow will reach 30% or 40%.

5. *How do impurities or adulterations show themselves in milk?*

F. Add to a test tube sample, known to be pure, a very little water—a few drops at a time. Note the change that appears in the general color, especially around the edges. Try a drop on the end of a knitting needle and compare with the appearance noted above [4 (c)]. Test various samples of milk obtained from different sources. If sediment of any kind is found at the bottom of the sample after it has stood undisturbed for some time, the milk should be regarded with great suspicion. Test the sediment to discover what it is. It may be chalk or soda.

6. *Does milk readily absorb impurities from its surroundings?*

G. Procure a sample of pure, fresh milk and carefully

Consider:

(a) Its odor.
(b) Its odor, after it has been shut up in a closet with some strongly odorous substance—an onion, a bit of musk, or a little tobacco smoke, for example.

NOTE.—By means of litmus paper, red and blue, it may be readily shown whether the sample is acid, alkaline, or neutral.   Fresh milk is generally about neutral.

E. *Tests to show the character of water used for drinking and in cooking.*

Procure about a quart of water that it is desired to examine.   It should be taken under average conditions and kept in a clean glass-stoppered bottle.

Consider:

    (a) Transparency.

    (b) Color: fill a long test tube and allowing it to rest upon a sheet of white paper, look down through it.

    (c) Set it away in a warm place for a few hours, tightly stoppered; then remove the stopper and note the *odor*.

    (d) The sediment; after the sample has been allowed to stand undisturbed for several hours, perhaps days, note the change, if any, in transparency, and also if solid matter has gone to the bottom of the bottle.

QUERIES:

1. *How much sediment or silt is found in hydrant water?*

EXPERIMENT: Wash perfectly clean a Chamberlain-Pasteur filter.   (In almost every town where "city water" is used, there will be some pupils who have these in use at home.)   Allow the filter to operate for a given time, say 12 hours. Remove the tube and carefully wash off the fine silt that adheres to it into a small beaker or evaporating dish. Evaporate this to dryness and weigh. Determine by a careful measurement or estimate the bulk of silt obtained.

Consider :

(a) The amount of water that passed through the filter while the deposit was being made.

(b) The amount of silt per gallon; per barrel. The amount drunk by one person per day.

(c) The appearance of the silt (before and after drying) under a magnifying glass or microscope.

(d) Put a small quantity of silt on a piece of glass and wash it with a few drops of distilled water. Examine for quartz or other crystalline fragments.

(e) Under the microscope, before drying the silt, note any greenish bodies, indicating vegetable organisms.

(f) Note the presence or absence of animal life as shown by movement.

(g) Place a small quantity of dry silt upon a glass slip; add a small drop of dilute hydrochloric acid. Note very closely any effervescence or other indications of solution.

NOTE.—Effervescence denotes the presence of small quantities of lime stone.

2. *Is the water used for drinking purposes hard or soft?* Dissolve a small piece of soap in a bottle of hot water and label it *Soap Solution.*

Collect samples of water from various places, including some clean rainwater; to a test tube half full of the sample add a small quantity of soap solution and

Consider:

(a) The ease with which suds are formed.

NOTE.—Water which forms suds with soap is said to be *soft;* when the mixture curdles the water is *hard.*

(b) Shake up in rainwater some finely powdered gypsum. Filter, and test the filtrate, (that which passes through the filter) with the soap solution.

(c) Repeat the experiment, using, instead of gypsum, finely powdered limestone.

(d) The effect of boiling upon the hardness of the water (samples b and c).

(e) The source of the various samples of hard and soft water; the kind of rock with which it has been in contact.

NOTE.—A test for salt which may be present in quantities too small to be detected by taste may be made with a solution of nitrate of silver. This may be purchased for a few cents at the druggists. It may be obtained also sufficiently pure thus: dissolve a tencent piece in nitric acid; evaporate to dryness and redissolve the residue in an ounce of distilled water. Bottle and keep in a dark place. A drop of this solution will give a white cloud to a tumbler of water in which there is dissolved but a few grains of salt.

3. *How much water is needed for drinking purposes per day?* Each pupil should note the amount he uses each day for several days and take the average. Measure an ordinary tumbler and estimate the quantity.

The adult man at moderately hard work needs about 4.5 lbs. or pints. (See Table V for the water contained in various foods.)

XXIV.

HEAT AND ENERGY IN THE ANIMAL BODY—(*Continued*).

THE KINDS AND QUANTITY OF FOOD NECESSARY[*]

QUERIES:

1. *What are the uses of food in the human body ?*

Consider :

(a) The physical work performed.
(b) The mental labor performed.
(c) The maintenance of the weight of the adult body.
(d) The increase of weight in the adult body.
(e) The increase of weight and size of the growing body.
(f) The heat produced in the animal body.
(g) What occurs if the food supply falls off.

NOTE.—The chief nutritive substance found in the albuminous foods examined in the previous chapter is called *protein*. Its chemical elements are C, H, O and N. The *carbohydrates* are made up of C, H and O.

*The material in this chapter has been mostly adapted from *Foods: Nutritive Value and Cost*. By W. O. Atwater, Ph. D., Wesleyan University. Published as Farmer's Bulletin No. 23, by the authority of the Secretary of Agriculture. Professor Atwater's pamphlet and charts should be in the hands of every teacher.

The *fats* of C, H and O, but have relatively less oxygen than the carbohydrates. The ash is the mineral matter which enters into bone and in small quantities into the other tissues.

TABLE V.—*Composition of Food Materials.*

FOOD MATERIALS (As Purchased.)	Refuse, (bones, skin, shell, etc.) Per cent.	EDIBLE PORTION.						Fuel value of 1 lb. Calories
		Water, per cent	NUTRIENTS.					
			Total, per cent	Protein, per ct	Fat, per cent	Carbohydrates	Mineral	
Beef, shoulder	12 6	66 8	31 6	17 0	13 7	. .	0 9	895
Beef, rib	21 0	38 2	40 8	12 2	27 9	. .	0 7	1406
Beef, sirloin	19 6	48 3	32 2	15 0	16 4	. .	0 8	970
Beef, round	7 8	60 9	31 3	18 0	12 3	. .	1 0	855
Beef, rump, corned	5 0	70 8	24 2	16 7	5 1	. .	2 4	625
Veal, shoulder	17 9	56 7	25 4	16 6	7 9	. .	0 9	640
Mutton, shoulder	16 3	49	34 7	15 1	18 8	. .	0 8	1075
Mutton, leg	18 1	50 6	31 3	15 0	16 6	. .	0 7	935
Pork, shoulder, fresh	14 6	43	42 4	13 6	28	. .	0 8	1436
Pork, ham, salted, smoked	11 4	36 8	61 8	14 8	34 6	. .	2 4	1735
Chicken	38 2	44 6	17 2	16 1	1 2	. .	0 9	330
Turkey	32 4	44 7	22 9	16 1	5 9	. .	0 9	550
Eggs, in shell	13 7	63 1	23 2	12 1	10 2	. .	0 9	655
Pork sausage	....	41 6	68 8	13 3	42 8	. .	2 2	2066
Mackerel, whole	44 8	40 4	15	10 0	4 3	. .	0 7	365
Salmon, whole	35 3	40 6	24 1	14 3	8 8	. .	1 0	635
Cod, salt	42 1	40 6	17 6	16 0	0 4	. .	1 2	315
Lobsters	62 1	31	6 9	6 5	0 7	0 1	0 6	135
Oysters	82 3	15 4	2 3	1 1	0 2	0 6	0 4	40
EDIBLE PORTION.								
Milk	. .	87	13	3 6	4 0	4 7	0 7	3.25
Butter	. .	10 6	69	1 0	85 0	0 5	3 0	3606
Cheese, cream	. .	30 2	69 8	28 3	35 5	1 8	4 2	2070
White bread, (wheat)	. .	32 3	67 7	8 8	1 7	66 3	0 9	1280
Graham flour, (wheat)	. .	13 1	86 9	11 7	1 7	71 7	1 8	1625
Oat meal	. .	7 6	92 4	15 1	7 1	68 2	2 0	1860
Corn meal	. .	15	85	9 2	3 8	70 6	1 4	1646
Rice	. .	12 4	87 8	7 4	0 4	79 4	0 4	1630
Green Peas	. .	78 1	21 9	4 4	0 6	16 0	0 9	405
Beans	. .	12 6	87 4	23 1	2 0	59 2	3 1	1616
Potatoes	. .	78 9	21 1	2 1	0 1	17 9	1 1	375
Sweet potatoes	. .	71 1	28 9	1 5	0 4	26 0	1 0	630
Turnips	. .	89 4	10 6	1 2	0 2	8 2	1 0	185
Onions	. .	87 6	12 4	1 4	0 3	10 1	0 6	225
Green corn	. .	81 3	18 7	2 8	1 1	13 2	0 6	346
Tomatoes	. .	96	4 0	0 8	0 4	2 5	0 3	80
Cabbage	. .	91 9	8 1	2 1	0 3	6 5	1 1	165
Apples	. .	83 2	16 8	0 2	0 4	15 9	0 3	315
Sugar, granulated	. .	2 0	98	. .	. .	97 8	0 2	1820
Molasses	. .	24 6	76 4	. .	. .	73 1	2 3	1360
Flour	. .	12 6	87 6	11 0	1 1	74 9	0 5	1645

Professor Atwater says that the daily diet of a man engaged at moderate muscular labor should consist of food which will yield 0.28 lbs. *protein* and 3500 *calories.* (See page 149 note.)

The items in *Table V* are selected from tables given by Professor Atwater.

NOTE.—Using the foregoing table, the pupils should construct bills of fare, introducing the necessary variety of articles to make the meals suitable and appetizing. Experiment has shown that a working man excretes about 9.5 oz. (272 grams) of carbon and 0.7 oz. (20 grams) of nitrogen per day. The food must evidently supply this waste. As stated by Professor Atwater the required food is found in .28 lbs. of protein plus a sufficient quantity of other kinds to make up 3500 calories. A sample bill of fare for one day for one person, which agrees substantially with these requirements, is given.

BILL OF FARE (APPROXIMATE) FOR ONE PERSON FOR ONE DAY.

I. Breakfast.

Two eggs, 3.6 ounces or 92.96 grams at 24c. per dozen.

Oatmeal, ⅛ lb. or 57.2 grams at 8c. per pound.

Milk, ¾ lb. or 343.2 grams, at 3c. per pint.

Bread, ¼ lb. or 114.4 grams, at 6c per pound.

Butter, ½ ounce or 14.3 grams, at 32c. per pound.

Sugar, ¼ ounce or 14.3 grams, at 4c per pound.

One orange, ¼ lb. or 114.4 grams, at 2c.

Water, 7 ounces or 200.2 grams.

II. Luncheon.

Milk, 1 lb. or 457.6 grams, at 3c. per pint.

Bread, ½ lb. or 228.8 grams, at 6c. per pound.

Rice, 1 ounce or 28.6 grams, at 8c. per pound.
Butter, $\frac{1}{2}$ ounce or 14.3 grams, at 32c. per pound.
Sugar, $\frac{1}{2}$ ounce or 14.3 grams, at 4c. per pound.
Grapes, $\frac{1}{4}$ lb. or 114.4 grams, at 4c. per pound.
Water, 7 ounces or 200.2 grams.

III. Dinner.

Fat Ox, $\frac{1}{4}$ lb. or 114.4 grams, at 16c. per pound.
Bread, $\frac{1}{4}$ lb. or 114.4 grams, at 6c. per pound.
Beans, $\frac{1}{4}$ lb. or 114.4 grams, at 4c. per pound.
Potatoes, $\frac{1}{4}$ lb. or 114.4 grams, at 2c. per pound.
Milk, $\frac{1}{2}$ lb. or 228.8 grams, at 3c. per pint.
Butter, $\frac{1}{2}$ ounce or 14.4 grams at 32c per pound.
One apple, $\frac{1}{4}$ lb. or 114.4 grams at 2c.
Water 7 ounces or 200.2 grams.

2. *Can a bill of fare be constructed which will furnish the required amount of nutritive material, without the use of meat?*

Consider :

(a) The quantity of protein needed.
(b) The calories of heat needed.

3. *Can a bill of fare be constructed from a meat diet alone?*

Consider:

(a) The protein needed.
(b) The calories needed.

NUMBER WORK.

QUERRY: A. *What is the cost and quantity of food required per day for one man, selecting from Table V?*

1. What would be the necessary amount of

each article and the price in each of the following bills of fare for *one day*: Beef shoulder, salmon, butter, milk, potatoes, oat meal, bread and sugar?

2. Beef sirloin, bread, potatoes and butter?

3. Ham, chicken, butter, potatoes beans, bread?

4. Milk, eggs, potatoes, oatmeal, rice, sugar, butter?

5. Mackerel, mutton, sweet potatoes, green corn, bread, butter?

6. Turkey, eggs, oatmeal, sugar, milk, onions, cabbage, turnips, bread, butter?

7. Sausage, bread, butter, cheese, beans, rice, tomatoes, apples?

8. Oysters, veal, milk, bread, butter, oatmeal, sugar?

9. Cod, beef (round), cornmeal, bread, butter, potatoes?

10. Eggs, ham, milk, sweet potatoes, tomatoes, bread, butter, sugar?

11. Which food costs the more in the market, the albuminous or the starchy?

12. One pound of butter yields about the required *calories* needed for a man per day; how much butter would it require to furnish the *protein?*

13. One pound of cheese yields about the required amount of *protein* for a man per day; how much would it take to yield the required number of *calories?*

14. How much milk, alone, would it take to supply the daily dietary of one man?

15. To what extent would a man's diet be wrong who should live upon round steak, only?

16. If a man were to eat six ounces of sirloin steak, only, at each of three meals, what and how much would his diet lack?

17. Judged by the food materials contained, and the price per pound, which is the cheaper food, pork or beef?

18. Which is the cheaper food, sausage or fish?

19. Which is the cheaper food, oatmeal or cornmeal?

20. Which is the cheaper, cornmeal or wheat flour?

21. Which is the cheaper food, eggs or sirloin beef?

22. Which is the cheaper food, milk or mutton?

23. Which is the cheaper food, beans or potatoes?

24. Which is the cheaper food, fish or oysters?

25. Which is the cheaper food, ham or fresh pork?

26. In the bill of fare given above, what is the entire weight of the food consumed?

27. The weight of the albuminous food equals what part of the whole?

28. The weight of the starchy food equals what part of the whole?

29. What is the cost of the bill of fare for one day?

30. What would be the cost, at the same rate, for a family of five for one week? For one year?

31. The cost of the meat equals what part of the whole cost in the given bills of fare?

32. The cost of the milk equals what part of the whole cost?

33. The cost of the bread and butter equals what part of the whole cost?

34. If boarders were to pay $4.50 per week, for food costing as much as that in any of the foregoing bills of fare, how much would be left, after paying for the food, for profits and expenses?

NOTE.—The pupils should actually weigh and measure out the exact quantities calculated in some of the foregoing bills of fare and thus get an accurate idea of the necessary daily dietary of an average man. It will be interesting to compare the actual amounts, as measured, with the pupils' preconceived notions as to the quantity needed.

FINAL QUERIES:

1. *What rule can you make to guide in the selection and purchase of food?*
Consider:
   (a) The percentage of refuse. (The waste.)
   (b) The relation of the amount of nutriment to the market price.
   (c) The proportion of the elements contained in it which the body needs.

2. *Is the most healthful food the most expensive ?*

3. *What constitutes the cheapest food ?*

4. *What constitutes the best food ?*

REPRESENTATIVE EXPRESSION.

1. *Drawing.*

 (a) Draw a 10-inch square to represent a pound of sirloin beef; upon the base of this, represent by another square, the proportion of nutritive material.

 (b) Represent by a 10-inch square, the calories in 1 lb. of beef, shoulder ; upon the same figure represent the calories in 1 lb. of rice.

 (c) Draw a 10-inch square to represent the calories in 1 lb. of oatmeal; upon this draw figures to represent the calories in a pound of each of the other starchy foods given in the tables.

XXV.

WORK AND ENERGY. MACHINES.

GENERAL OBSERVATIONS.

Make a careful study of those operations in life which have for their purpose the performance of what is called work.

QUERIES:

1. *What is the essential thing accomplished in each case observed ?*

Consider, for example :

- (a) The moving of a pile of earth by means of shovels.
- (b) The elevation of bricks and mortar to the top of a wall.
- (c) The lifting of water from a well.
- (d) The lifting of a building by means of a jack-screw.
- (e) The splitting of a log with a wedge.
- (f) The cutting of wood.
- (g) The swaying of a tree in the wind. The floating of a log in water.
- (h) The turning of a water wheel.
- (i) The movement of the piston in the engine.
- (j) The support and movements of the animal body.

2. *What constitute the essentials of work performed ?*

Consider :

(a) The resistance to the force applied.
(b) The distance or space through which the body offering the resistance is moved.
(c) The relation of the amount of *force* applied to the amount of *resistance* overcome.
(d) The *distance* through which the *force* moves compared with the distance through which the resisting body moves.

3. *By what means is force applied to the body offering resistance ?*

Consider :

(a) Each of the examples cited under (1),
(b) The use of the wheels, belts, pulleys, shafts, levers, cog-wheels, and the muscles and bones in the animal body.

NOTE.—Any contrivance used in directing and applying force to some resistance may be called a *machine*. In mechanics the resistance to be overcome is often called the *weight*. The force applied is called the *power*. These terms will be used hereafter according to these meanings.

4. *What are the most important uses of machines ?*

In all the cases studied where machines are used, consider:

(a) As modes of utilizing certain forces in nature, i. e., wind and water, for example.

(b) The direction power moves compared with the direction the weight moves.

(c) The distance the power moves compared with the distance the weight moves.

(d) The absolute value of the power compared with the absolute value of the weight; i. e., the two compared, pound for pound.

5. *When a given amount of power is used through a given distance, as, for example, 1 lb. of power used through 1 foot, how may its equivalent in work appear?*

Study work of some kind that is being done and consider:

(a) The distance through which the weight moves.

(b) The absolute value of the weight moved.

EXPERIMENT: *Equipment.* Two "nickels," (each new, weighs 5 grams), a flat one-foot rule and a small triangular prism upon the edge of which the rule may be balanced. Call the rule a *lever* and the edge upon which it rests a *fulcrum.*

Balance the rule upon the fulcrum and place the two "nickels" on opposite sides of the fulcrum and at equal distances from it. As the ends of the rule are moved up and down alternately, measure carefully the distance traversed by each "nickel." Use two "nickels" as the weight. At what point on the ruler can you place one "nickel" so that it will balance the two? How may they be placed so that 1 "nickel" will balance the three?

Measure carefully the distance the power and the weight move in each case as the rule is moved up and down.

Call the three "nickels," in the last experiment, the weight; when they move $\frac{1}{2}$ inch, how far does the one "nickel" as power move? Call the one "nickel" the weight and the three "nickels" the power; what possible advantage might this arrangement be in machinery?

6. *What are the points of importance to be considered in a lever ?*

Consider :

(a) The point where the power is applied.
(b) The point where the lever is applied to the weight.
(c) The position of the fulcrum.
(d) The shape of the lever—straight or curved.

NOTE.—The distance from the *fulcrum* to the point where the power is applied is called the *power arm.* The distance from the *fulcrum* to the weight is called the *weight arm.* This is true when the power and weight act at *right angles* to a straight bar.

Consider:

(e) What the power and weight arms are in a bent or S-shaped lever.

(f). The relative position which these three points may have in the lever. Observe workmen moving stone or other weights.

(g) In the experiment under (5) the product of the number expressing the length of the *weight arm* by the number expressing the *weight* as compared with the product of the number expressing the length of the *power arm* by the number expressing the *power.*

NOTE.—Procure a stout, stiff stick three or four feet in length and mark it off in units—feet and inches or, better, centimeters. Screw into this stick at various points small hooks capable of supporting considerable weight. Fill a small pail with sand and carefully weigh it. By placing the fulcrum at different points, by means of a small spring balance find out the amount of power necessary to balance the weight.

When the *fulcrum* is between the power and weight it is said to be a lever of the *first class;* when the *weight* is between the fulcrum and power, a lever of the *second class;* when the *power* is between the fulcrum and weight, a lever of the *third class.*

(h) The advantages of each class of lever. Note when and where each is used.

7. *What relationship is there between the windlass or wheel and axle used in lifting weights, water from a well for example, and the lever.*

Consider:

(a) The center of the axle or axis and the fulcrum of a lever.
(b) The weight arm.
(c) The power arm.
(d) The class of lever.
(e) The arms of the lever when the handle of the windlass is at different points of the circuit.
(f) Under what conditions a machine in the form of a windlass is superior to the simple straight lever.

EXPERIMENT: *Equipment.* Cut from a pine board ½ inch in thickness two wheels, one having a diameter of 8 inches and the other with a diameter of 4 inches. Fasten the two wheels together with small screws or nails so that their centers exactly coincide and mount them on an axle. The wheels should be slightly grooved. Prepare two small vessels of sand.

Wrap a string around the smaller wheel, as a pulley, and attach it to a pail of sand the weight of which is known; in a similar manner, suspend a pail by a string from the larger wheel and determine what weight is necessary to balance the other pail. Recall what was learned under the lever.

Consider :
(a) The relative length of the diameters.
(b) The relative weight of the two pails of sand.
(c) The relative distance traversed by the pails when the wheels are turned.

NOTE.—Make a careful study of cogwheels that may be found in certain machinery. The "works" of an old clock make an instructive piece of apparatus for the purpose. Note the relative speed of the wheels that turn upon each other; the distance the circumference of each moves, and the relation of the power to the weight.

8. *What advantage is gained, when men, instead of lifting it up directly, slide a box or roll a barrel up a slanting plank when loading it into a wagon ?*

Consider:
(a) The relation of the slant of the plank to the ease with which the work is done.
(b) The relation of the slant of the plank to its length.
(c) The relation of the length of the plank to the *vertical* distance the weight is lifted.
(d) What is gained by decreasing the slant or pitch of the plank; what is lost.

EXPERIMENT: *Equipment.* Procure two smooth boards about two feet long and six inches in width. Fasten these together by a hinge at one end and bend one back upon another as in closing a book. Polish the outer surface of one board by giving it two or three coats of shellac varnish, rubbing the surface down with fine sandpaper after each application, when dry, except the last. By placing the boards upon a table the one with a polished surface may be inclined and supported by a small block at any angle. The surface of the board when arranged at a slant constitutes an inclined plane. Screw a small pulley into the upper end of the inclined plane. Support the plane at a given angle, for example, so that the height equals one-half the length of the plane. Attach a weight, having a smooth surface, to a cord and place it on the plane. Pass the cord over the pulley and suspend from the end a small pail which may be loaded with sand.

Consider:

(a) The weight required to just balance the block on the plane.

(b) Make the slant of the plane so that the vertical height equals ¼ the length: what weight is required to establish a balance.

(c) What law, as to the power required to lift a given weight, seems to be established by the relation of the length of the inclined plane to the vertical height.

(d) The importance of securing good grades for streets and roads. (See Number Work.)

(e) Why, in hilly countries, roads wind around the hill as they ascend towards the top.

9. *What relationship between the inclined plane and the wedge?*

Observe the different and the peculiar conditions under which the wedge is used by workmen.

Consider:

(a) The way the power is applied.

(b) The distance the weight is to be moved.

(c) The amount of work that is accomplished through the use of the wedge.

(d) The principle involved in the form of an ax; a knife; a nail; other tools.

10. *By what means is the power applied which is used through a bolt and nut to hold two timbers together.*

Observe the various conditions under which bolts with nuts are used. Observe the thread of a screw or a bolt upon which the nut moves. Also the thread in the nut.

Where the screw is used consider:

(a) The distance through which the weight is to be moved.

(b) The relative amount of weight to be moved.

(c) How the power is applied to the bolt or nut.

EXPERIMENT. From a sheet of paper cut a rectangle 6 inches long and 1 inch wide. Cut this in two along one of the diagonals. Beginning with the wide end, roll this triangular piece of paper around a lead pencil, keeping the edge adjacent to the right angle at right angles to the axis of the pencil.

Consider:

(a) The relation of the paper before being rolled to an inclined plane.

(b) The relation of the slanting edge, when rolled, to a screw or the thread of the nut or bolt.

(c) The relation of the thread on a bolt to a wedge ; note the mode of applying the power in each case.

(d) Where the screw might be used to better advantages than the wedge or inclined plane.

(e) The various forms and modifications of the screw.

(f) The *vertical* distance traversed by the bolt or nut with each complete turn of either.

11. *Under what circumstances do workmen make use of pulleys in performing work?*

Make a careful study of this mode of lifting weights.

Consider :

(a) The amount of the weight to be lifted.
(b) The distance the weight moves.
(c) The direction the weight moves.
(d) The distance the power moves.
(e) The relative velocity of the power and weight.
(f) Whether other machines could be substituted for the pulley; the lever; the wheel and axle; the inclined plane; the wedge; the screw.
(g) The advantages and disadvantages of the pulley.
(h) The circumstances when several pulleys are used.
(i) The use of movable pulleys; of fixed pulleys.
(j) The use of two or more pulleys in one block.

EXPERIMENTS: *Equipment.* A strong cord a few feet in length. Single pulleys that may be screwed into some support or otherwise fastened to it. Small blocks containing two or three pulleys each. These may be purchased very cheaply at any hardware store. Two small pails containing sand for weights with some means of weighing the same.

A. Fasten a single pulley to its support and pass a cord over it and balance the weights from the ends. Compare the weights when they exactly balance. Consider any advantage that may arise from this machine.

B. Fasten one end of the cord to a hook in the support and pass the other end through a movable pulley, that is, one not fixed to any support. Suspend a known weight from the pulley and by means of a spring balance attached to the other end of the string, find what power is required to lift the weight.

Consider:

    (a) Why the power and weight vary, in this arrangement, from the relationship found in (A).

    (b) The number of cords that support the weight in (A). The number that support it in (B).

    (c) The relative distance traversed by the power and weight.

C. By means of fixed and movable blocks, arrange the cord so that it passes over several pulleys between the weight and power.

Consider:

    (a) The number of parts of the cord on each side of the pulleys.

    (b) The relation of the power to the weight moved.

    (c) The relative distance traversed by the power and weight.

12. *In the various machines that have been studied, has there been any actual creation of power ?*

Consider :

(a) Whether, in any instance, through the application of one pound of power moving a given distance, more than one pound of weight has been moved an equal distance in the same time.

(b) Whether one pound of power, moving a given distance, has moved a one-pound weight through a greater distance.

(c) Whether one pound of power has in any case moved a one-pound weight more swiftly than it, itself, moved.

(d) How a gain in power or the creation of power should show itself in work done.

13. *Does a machine transmit to the weight, without loss, all the power that is applied?*

Consider:

(a) The bearings of wheels.

(b) The movement of the lever upon the fulcrum.

(c) The movement of the weight on the inclined plane.

(d) The use of oil and other lubricants.

(e) The various forms of bearings; ball bearings, etc.

NOTE.—The resistance which a moving body meets with from a surface over which it moves, either *rolling* or *sliding*, is called *friction.*

14. *In the various forms of machines that have been studied, in which parts has friction been essential to perfect operation? In what parts is it an impediment, or non-essential?*

Consider:
  (a) The movement of a railroad train upon the track.
  (b) The belt upon the pulley. Cog wheels
  (c) The screw; the wedge; the inclined plane; the lever.

15. *What determines the amount of friction?*

Consider:
  (a) That between two soft bodies; between two hard bodies.
  (b) That between two bodies of the same material; of different material.
  (c) Its relation to the extent of surface of the body.

Remove the supporting block from the inclined plane (see [8] above) so that the upper board lies in a horizontal plane. Place upon it a brick and, by means of a cord over the end of the pulley, hang a weight just sufficient to move it. What does the weight measure? Try this with the brick on its side, then on its edge, then on its end.

  (d) Its relation to the weight of the body.

Repeat the experiment given under (c) using two or three bricks.

    (e) Its relation to the character of the surface; note the surfaces of various bearings in machinery.

16. *By what means is work accomplished by the animal body ?*

OBSERVATION: Note the problems that animals have to solve which require the application, direction, and expenditure of energy. Study *locomotion*, in various animals, the human being included; also, other movements; how the habitual position of the body is maintained.

Consider:

    (a) What part of the work of the body is performed by levers.

    (b) The location of fulcra in the bodies with skeletons.

    (c) The levers concerned in holding the human body erect.

    (d) The levers concerned in walking in the human body.

    (e) The levers concerned in the movements of the arms, at the shoulder; the elbow; the wrist; the fingers.

    (f) The levers concerned in the head movements; movements of the jaw. (See any physiology for a description of a curious pulley used in moving the lower jaw downward.)

(g) What levers are so arranged so as to gain power at the expense of velocity or distance.

(h) Those so arranged as to gain velocity or distance at the expense of power.

(i) The levers in the bodies of animals that walk on four legs.

(j) The advantages and disadvantages in the arrangement and pull of the muscles.

(k) How opposite movements, like flexion and extension, are accomplished.

17. *How are the muscles joined to the bones and the bones to each other, so that the body may work as a series of strong levers?*

OBSERVATION: Procure at a butcher-shop the lower part of a sheep's leg, including a joint and a small part of the muscle or lean meat attached. By pulling the muscle, study the direction and range of the movement at the joint.

Consider:

(a) Where the muscle is inserted (attached) and how it is joined. The gristly end of the muscle is called the tendon. The lean meat constitutes the body of the muscle. The white sheets and fibers of tissue are called connective tissue.

(b) The mechanism of the joint. With a sharp knife cut through the tough layers of connective tissue and open the joint.

(c) The sticky fluid inside the joint called the synovial fluid, or synovia.

(d) The cords (ligaments) that bind the ends of the bones together. Try, by pulling, to break one of the ligaments or to tear it away from the bone.

(e) The ends of the bone, smooth with the soft gristly pads of tissue, called *cartilage*. Cut away a thin slice with a sharp knife and examine it.

(f) The friction at the joint; how reduced. Compare it with the bearings of the best machine you can find.

(g) The bone itself, with its closely investing tissue called the periosteum. The periosteum carries the blood vessels that are concerned in the nourishment of the bone.

(h) The spongy character of the bones at the end; find this by splitting the bone. The purpose of the spongy and enlarged ends.

(i) The compact bone in the shaft and the cavity inside containing the marrow or medulla.

(j) Small openings in the bone showing how it is penetrated by blood vessels.

NOTE.—If possible, examine a thin slice of bone, properly prepared under a microscope.

18. *How are movements performed by animals that are not provided with a bony skeleton?*

OBSERVATION: Make a study of such animals as the grasshopper, cricket, butterfly and other insects. Also, the earthworm.

Consider:
- (a) The arrangement of levers.
- (b) The relative number of levers needed to perform the necessary movements.
- (c) The flight of insects as compared with the flight of birds.
- (d) The movements of the earthworm as compared with that of a snake.
- (e) The different points of the lever in each case.

19. *In what respects does the animal body resemble a machine?*

Consider:
- (a) The application of power.
- (b) The transmission of power.
- (c) The character of the work done.
- (d) The source of power.
- (e) The waste of power through friction.

20. *Does the human machine really create power?*

Consider:
- (a) The likeness of the food eaten to the fuel supplied to the furnace.
- (b) The air supplied to the body compared with that supplied to a furnace.

   (c) The real importance of having sufficient
       quantity of good food and pure air.
   (d) The evidence that even thinking is
       through the usage of the physical
       machine.
   (e) The real immediate source of the work
       power, both mental and physical, in
       the animal body.

NUMBER WORK.

QUERIES :

A. *What relation does the work performed
bear to the energy expended in the use of various kinds of machines?*

1. In shoveling earth, how must a laborer
hold his shovel as a lever so that, while it
remains on the shovel, the earth may move
four times the distance of the power ?

2. In supporting a stone weighing 1000 lbs.
with a lever of the first class, how must it be
arranged so that 100 lbs. power will do the
work?

3. In (2) how far will the power move in
lifting the stone one foot.

4. The axis of a windlass is six inches in
diameter and the crank is two feet long ; how
much power must be applied at the end of the
crank to balance a 25 lb. bucket of water ?

5. In (4) will it require the same power at
all points of the circle described by the handle?

6. In (4) how far would the end of the crank
move in lifting the bucket 30 feet ?

7. In changing the grade of a road from 75 feet ascent per mile to 50 feet, what saving in power would be attained?

8. For every mile at the first grade in (7), how long would the road have to be at the second grade to make the same ascent?

9. In bolting two timbers together, how much pressure may be exerted, if the threads of the screw are one-fourth inch apart, and a power of 50 lbs. is applied to the end of a wrench 18 inches long, allowing one-fourth for friction?

10. If there are 11 threads to the inch, how far would the power travel, if applied to a lever five feet long, in lifting a weight one foot.

11. In lifting a capstone weighing 2400 lbs. to its place, a block containing three movable pulleys was used; with one end of the rope fastened to the fixed block of pulleys, how much power was required to balance it?

12. In lifting the stone in (11) 50 feet, how far would the power move?

B. *What is the work value of some of the more important machines as compared with hand labor?*

13. The cotton crop of the United States for 1894 was about 9,500,000 bales of 400 lbs. each; to clean the seeds from one lb. by hand required one man working one day; to clean this crop of its seeds in 60 days if done by hand would represent the work of how many men?

14. In cleaning 300 lbs. of cotton per day, the cotton gin represents how much hand labor?

15. In 1894 the wheat crop in the United States covered about 35,000,000 acres; by hand one man could cut about four acres: how many men would have been required to cut the crop in the working days of one month?

16. Cutting the crop at the rate of 20 acres per day, how many machines would be required to cut the crop in the same time?

17. How many men, each bearing 150 lbs., would be required to carry the load of a single freight train of 20 cars each carrying 25,000 lbs?

18. Visit some of the factories in your neighborhood; the planing mill, iron mill, woolen mill, shoe shops, tailor shops, and gather data from which to calculate the value of machines in terms of human work power.

REPRESENTATIVE EXPRESSION.

1. *Drawing.*

A. Make a drawing of each of the machines that have been studied as you have seen it at work.

(a) The lever—the various forms.
(b) The wheel and axle or windlass.
(c) The inclined plane.
(d) The screw.
(e) The wedge.
(f) The pulley: single, fixed and movable; pulleys in blocks.

B. Make a drawing, showing in a diagram, how the human body is moved by levers.

XXVI.

EQUILIBRIUM OF BODIES. CENTER OF GRAVITY.

OBSERVATION: In turning an object over with a lever notice the shape of the body that is most easily moved. Observe the form of various structures that are built with a view to stability; the shape of towers and derricks. Observe the way vessels are ballasted or read descriptions of how it is done. The stability of a load of sand compared with a load of hay.

QUERIES:

1. *Under what conditions do bodies stand well; that is, what are the conditions of stability?*

Consider:
- (a) The base.
- (b) The height.
- (c) The shape.
- (d) The distribution of the matter in the body; that is, whether it is of uniform density throughout.

NOTE.—Everyone, in handling bodies, has noticed the downward pull that seems to be exerted upon them. The tendency of an unsupported body to approach the earth is called *attraction;* the force of the downward pull is the *force of attraction.* It has been shown that bodies possess an attraction for each other and the law is generally stated that "Every particle of matter in the universe has an attraction for every other particle." The name given to this attractive force is *gravitation.* The attractive force between the earth and the bodies on its surface is called *gravity.* In the *weight* of a body we have the measure of the pull of the earth upon it; that is, the measure of the force of gravity. The attractive force varies *directly* as the *mass*, that is, the quantity of matter which the body contains, and *inversely as the square of the distance* through which it acts.

2. *How is the force of gravity applied to a body?*

Observe some body made up of minute grains, a fine sandstone, for example.

Consider:

    (a) The line which it travels as it falls to the earth. This line is called the *vertical.* If extended upward, what point would it reach? If extended downward? Compare this line with a *plumb-line.*

    (b) The line traversed by each grain of sand in the falling stone.

    (c) What relation these lines have to each other.

    (d) How the individual grains in the stone would fall if their cohesion to each other was destroyed.

    (e) Turn the stone on another side; consider the lines the grains would now describe in falling.

(f) The location of a point or grain within the stone about which all these lines of force are equally distributed. This point is called the *center of gravity*.

NOTE.—Every body may be considered as being made up of very many exceedingly small particles called *molecules*. The force of gravity acts upon each one of these and the total of the attractive force for the molecules is equal to the force exerted upon the entire body.

3. *How may the center of gravity of a body be found?*

Suspend the body by one point and consider:

(a) The path through the body that would be described by a plumb line passing through the point of support. Suspend the body by another point not found in the line described in (a).

(b) The path marked by a plumb line passing through the point of support in the second position.

(c) Consider the point where the two lines intersect. Try balancing the body with respect to this point.

EXPERIMENTS: By means of a plumb line held in front of various bodies when suspended as in (a) and (b), find the center of gravity. Consider where it would be in a *cube;* a square of *sheet-iron* or *tin;* in an inch board, *trapezoidal* in shape; in a *ring;* in a *triangle;* in a *pyramid;* in a *cone;* in a *solid sphere;* in a *hollow sphere;* in a *book;* in a *cylinder.*

4. *How does the position of the center of gravity change when bodies are being overturned?*

NOTE.—The path described by the center of gravity as a body falls to the earth, or as it would fall, is called the *line of direction.*

Using, in the beginning, a regular body as a cube, consider:

(a) How far it may be tipped without being turned over on another side.

(b) The *line of direction* at the point where the cube tips over to another side.

(c) Very carefully, the path described by the *center of gravity* as the cube is tipped to another side.

(d) Which way a body falls when tipped, when the line of direction falls *within the base.*

(e) Which way it falls when tipped so that the line of direction falls *outside the base.*

(f) In the same way, study the stability of a *cone* in the various positions in which it may be placed.

NOTE.—The cone may be made to illustrate the

states of equilibrium : 1st, *Stable equilibrium*, when standing on its base. 2d, *Unstable equilibrium*, when standing on its apex. 3d, *Indifferent or neutral equilibrium*, when lying on its side. To distinguish these three states of equilibrium it is important to notice *the path described by the center of gravity when the bodies are being tipped.*

(g) The state of equilibrium of a sphere.

(h) Why the pyramid on its side is in a different state from the cone in the same position.

(i) When a body is changed from a stable to an unstable state, the change in the position of the center of gravity.

(j) The change when the body moves from an unstable to a stable state.

(k) General considerations : Why a ball rolls down hill. Why water runs down hill. Why the air stays with the earth. Why smoke rises some times, and at other times sinks, as it leaves the chimney. Why a gun aimed at a distant target is always pointed obliquely upward. Why it is possible to make a stone slide further on smooth ice than it can be thrown through the air. Stick a pin half-way into a cork ; stick a small penknife obliquely downward into the cork on either side and balance on the pin. Explain. Read a description of the famous leaning tower of Pisa.

Explain why it is difficult to walk on stilts; explain how it is possible.

REPRESENTATIVE EXPRESSION.

1. *Drawing.*

  (a) Make a sketch, showing the way the center of gravity may be determined.

  (b) Make a sketch showing how the force of gravity acts upon each particle in a body.

  (c) Make a sketch showing why a ball rolls down hill.

  (d) Make a sketch of a body so balanced that the center of gravity lies lower than the base.

XXVII.

THE PENDULUM.

OBSERVATIONS : Make a study of the forces which cause bodies to move along lines not vertical; of movements that are to and fro; how is the force applied? Notice the pendulum of different sized clocks. Also, the swinging or vibration of all bodies suspended from a point, such as chandeliers, ropes, chains, etc. If possible, examine the wheelwork in a clock and study the use of the pendulum. Observe the substitute for a pendulum in a watch.

NOTE.—A complete swing of a pendulum, from one side over and back again to the starting point, is called a double or a *complete oscillation* or *vibration*. A single swing in either direction is called a *simple* or *single oscillation* or *vibration*. The distance from the lowest point in the arc described by the pendulum is called the *amplitude of vibration*. It is measured in degrees by the angle formed at the point of suspension. The complete period of oscillation is the time required for the pendulum to make a complete oscillation. What is usually called the *time* of vibration is the time of a *single vibration*.

QUERIES:

1. *Under what conditions does the time of vibration change?*

EXPERIMENTS:

A. Suspend from a small bracket by means of a light fine thread a bullet or some other weight. Cause it to swing through a very *small* arc and carefully note the number of vibrations per minute. A protractor may be so attached to the bracket that the pendulum will swing in front of it and the amplitude may be measured. By small amounts increase the amplitude and again find the number of vibrations in a minute.

Consider:

    (a) The length of time of each vibration.

    (b) Within what amplitude is the period the same.

    (c) Whether the increase in *amplitude* causes a corresponding increase of *period*.

B. Vary the length of the pendulum and, as before, take the time of vibration.

Consider:

    (a) The relative period of two pendulums, the length of one being four times that of the other.

    (b) The relative period when one is nine times the length of the other.

    (c) The relative period of vibration of two pendulums, one being four inches and the other sixteen inches long.

    (d) The length of a pendulum that vibrates seconds.

(e) The length of a pendulum that will vibrate half seconds.

C. Prepare balls of the same size of wood, cork, lead, other substances. Suspend by threads of equal length and consider :

(a) The relative time of vibration.

2. *What determines the real length of a pendulum when considered as to the period of vibration?*

EXPERIMENTS:

A. Make four pendulums of wood that have the same apparent length, of one foot or more. Make one in the shape of a cylinder, two cone shaped and one spindle form. Suspend these four by a very short thread, one of the cones being inverted; also suspend with them a bullet on a thread having the same length as the other four. Start them all to swinging at the same moment.

Consider:

(a) Which is the shortest; which is the longest.

B. Procure a small board three or four inches wide and about a yard long. By means of a small staple driven into one end suspend it upon a wire so that it will swing edgewise as a pendulum. Upon the same wire, adjust a string and bullet pendulum that will vibrate in the same time. At a point on the board just covered by the bullet when suspended make a mark and through this bore a hole. Suspend the board by running the wire through the hole.

Consider:

(a) The time of vibration from the new point of suspension.

NOTE.—This point found in the pendulum in (B) is called the *center of oscillation*. Notice the effect upon the time of vibration by making the center of oscillation the point of suspension.. The distance between the two points (oscillation and suspension) constitutes the *real length* of the pendulum. Find the real length of each given in (A) above.

C. Find the relation of the *center of gravity* to the *center of oscillation* in the pendulum.

3. *What is the force that causes the pendulum to swing?*

4. *What does the regularity of the swing indicate concerning that force?*

5. *Since gravity pulls vertically downward, how does the pendulum acquire a lateral movement?*

Place two large sized marbles close together, and with a third marble strike them *both* squarely. Note the direction that each of the two takes and compare their direction with the direction of the force which struck them. It will be seen that the single line of force which was exerted against the two marbles by the one, has now been divided into *two lines;* the movements of the two marbles indicate the direction of the two forces. In similar manner consider the *single* downward pull of gravity on the pendulum divided into two; what are the directions of the two forces? Which one moves the pendulum?

6. *What forces bring a pendulum to rest?*

NUMBER WORK.

QUERY : *What relation is there between the length of the pendulum and its period of vibration?*

1. Make three pendulums, 4, 16 and 64 units in length ; compare their times of vibration.

2. What is the relation of the number expressing the time of vibration to the number expressing the length of the pendulum ?

3. Construct two pendulums so that one shall vibrate three times as fast as the other.

REPRESENTATIVE EXPRESSION.

1. *Drawing.*
   (a) Make a sketch showing the way a pendulum regulates the movement of a clock.
   (b) Make a drawing showing the relation of the center of gravity to the center of oscillation.
   (c) Make a sketch showing a complete vibration, single vibration and amplitude of vibration.

XXVIII.

VIBRATIONS IN MATTER. SOUND.

OBSERVATIONS: Make a careful study of the conditions that seem always to be present when different sounds are produced. Study the mechanism and material of a bell. Suspend a small steel rod by a light thread attached to one end. Tap it with something and hold a sheet of paper against one end. Hold the paper against the edge of a bell that has been struck. Put a small amount of water into a light glass bowl or china basin. Lightly tap the edge of the bowl and note the surface of the water. Cause a tuning fork to vibrate and quickly dip the end into a tumbler of water. Hold the end against the teeth. Hold the vibrating fork so that it barely touches the tip of the nose.

Examine a steam whistle and note the material used.

Note the course of the air through an ordinary toy whistle.

Examine various stringed instruments; mandolin, guitar, violin, piano and banjo. Compare the various modes of producing musical sounds with the different conditions that produce merely noise. Notice the conditions under which loud, soft, clear, muffled, high and low tones are produced.

Carefully observe the conditions under which sound travels.

The length of time required for sound to travel a given distance. Observe the puffs of steam from a locomotive some distance away and note the time that elapses before the sound is heard. Place the ear against a telegraph pole and listen to the singing wire when the wind blows. If possible, visit a railroad track; while some one strikes the rail with a stone or hammer, observe the sound at different distances. Try a similar experiment with a wire or board fence.

QUERIES:

1. *What is the relation of motion to sound?*

EXPERIMENTS:

A. Clamp a steel knitting needle in a small vise or drive it into a solid block of wood. Pull the end to one side and start the wire vibrating.

Consider:

   (a) The same facts relating to vibration that were learned under the pendulum —amplitude, complete and single vibration, and period of vibration.

   (b) The essential difference between the vibration of the wire and that of the pendulum.

(c) The effect on the sound by varying the amplitude.

(d) The effect produced by using a second needle shorter than the first: 1st, upon the period; 2d, upon the sound produced.

B. Procure a light dry board one meter or more in length and stretch a cord from one end to the other, fastening the ends to nails, or, better, to wooden keys, which may be turned to tighten or slacken the string. Waxed silk may be used, but fine wire, preferably piano wire, is much better. Fine autoharp wire on small spools may be purchased for a few cents. Make three bridges of the same height and place two under the wire, one near either end. Pluck the cord and

Consider:

(a) The swinging movement of the cord. Note the amplitude and the period.

(b) The effect on the sound of changing the amplitude. Compare with the wire in (A).

Use the third bridge at different points between the other two. It should be but the merest fraction higher than the others.

(c) The *period* of each of the two segments compared with that of the entire cord.

(d) The effect upon the sound of dividing the cord.

C. Loosen one end of the cord from the nail

or key and suspend from it a weight of eight
or ten pounds. It is more satisfactory if a
small pulley is screwed into the end of the
board over which the cord or wire may be
stretched.

Consider:

(a) The effect upon the amplitude by varying the weight on the cord.

(b) If autoharp wire is used vary the
weight so as to produce all the tones
in the scale.

(c) The effect upon the *period* and the
tone of changing the weight.

D. Stretch a *heavier wire*, i. e., of larger
diameter, in a similar manner across the board
and test as directed in the foregoing experiments. Note the effect upon the tone.

E. Pluck the string as before and, while it is
vibrating, touch lightly with the edge of a
sheet of paper.

Consider:

(a) The effect upon the sound.

(b) The effect upon the vibration.

Reflecting upon the foregoing experiments,
Consider:

(a) What it is that determines the *pitch*
of a tone.

(b) What it is that determines the *loud-
ness* or *volume* of tone.

(c) What it is that determines the *quality* of tone.

(d) What it is that determines the *period* of vibration.

(e) What it is that determines the *amplitude.*

(f) What it is that is determined by the *material* in the vibrating string.

(g) What property of a substance is most favorable to the production of a tone.

F. Secure a pane of glass ten or twelve inches square. Balance it on its side upon a block of wood about one inch square. Procure a glass tube three-fourths of an inch in diameter and about two feet or more in length, and supporting it upright in one hand with one end standing on the pane over the block, rub it up and down with a flannel cloth that has been dusted with powdered rosin. Note the character of sounds produced. Sprinkle a light layer of fine dry sand upon the pane.

Consider:

(a) The movement of the sand and what this indicates.

(b) The direction the sand takes.

(c) What is indicated by the lines of sand that are formed.

(d) Why the lines and movements vary with the character of the sound.

(e) The character of the sounds when the sand assumes symmetrical forms.

(f) The character of the sounds when the sand becomes scattered.

(g) What inference may be drawn from (e) and (f) concerning the difference between musical tones and mere noise.

(h) Draw a violin bow over the edge of the pane at various points—holding the latter by the glass rod as before —and note the arrangement of the sand grains.

NOTE.—The lines along which the sand grains gather are called the nodes of the vibrating plate. Repeat experiment (B) and by touching the vibrating cord lightly at different points with the edge of a visiting card, observe whether *nodes* are formed in the string. Hold a vibrating tuning fork near the ear and slowly turn it around. What does the variation in the sound indicate?

G. Connect a small rubber tube a few feet long with a gas jet. Into the end of the tube insert a short piece of glass tubing, the outer end of which is drawn out to form a small nozzle or tip. Light the gas at this tip and, holding it upright lower over the flame, which should not be too strong, a glass tube a yard or more in length with an inside diameter of about one inch. If properly done a tone will be produced which may be varied by means discoverable by the pupil. Try tubes of different sizes.

Consider:

(a) The cause of vibration in this experiment.

(b) What it is that vibrates.

(c) Why the length or diameter of the tube affects the tone.

(d) The mechanism of an organ pipe.

(e) How the pipes are varied to produce the different notes.

NOTE.—The following table shows the number of vibrations per second of each tone in the octave below middle C, and also the relations of the numbers in any octave. It is given as a matter of reference:

TABLE VI.

C_2	D_2	E_2	F_2	G_2	A_2	B_2	C_3
1	$\frac{9}{8}$	$\frac{5}{4}$	$\frac{4}{3}$	$\frac{3}{2}$	$\frac{5}{3}$	$\frac{15}{8}$	2
128	144	160	170	192	214	240	256

2. *How does sound travel?*

NOTE.—In order to comprehend this, it is necessary to understand the nature of an *undulation*. In experiment (A) consider what must be the effect upon the air as the wire springs forward and back. In the former movement the air immediately in front of the wire is compressed or condensed; in the latter movement the air behind the wire is somewhat rarefied. The condensation and rarefaction constitute a wave. As a succession of these waves break upon the ear drum, by means of the mechanism of the ear and its nerve connection, the sensation of sound is derived through the appropriate nerve center.

Consider:

(a) How the second wave i. e., a condensation and rarefaction, is produced in advance of the first one.

(b) How the *wave motion* can be transmitted without the air itself moving beyond the limits of the single wave.

(c) How the *form* of a wave of water moves; whether the water moves.

(d) How condensations and rarefactions, i. e., waves, must be produced in an iron bar and other solids when they are struck ; how these are communicated to the air.

NOTE.—Everyone has noticed that time elapses before the sound from the blow, given at some distance, is heard. At freezing temperature, sound travels through the air at 1090 feet per second. For every degree Fahr. above freezing, 1.12 feet per second may be added.

(e) How the character of the sound of a ringing bell on a rapidly approaching locomotive changes; how the sound changes after the bell has passed. Picture the sound waves in the air in each instance.

(f) Strike a call bell and quickly move it alternately toward and away from the ear. Picture the air waves in each case.

3. *How does the intensity of sound vary?* Consider:

(a) A sound, as that of a bell, emanating from a center.

(b) What shape the sound waves must assume around the center.

(c) The area of that part of a wave which would strike a surface four feet square at a distance of ten feet.

(d) How much surface this area of sound wave would cover at a distance of twenty feet.

(e) What ratio would express the intensity per square foot in the two positions.

4. *What determines the direction that sound travels ?*

Consider :

(a) When no obstruction is interposed between the ear and the source of the sound.

(b) The meaning of echoes.

(c) Why, in an empty hall, it is more difficult to hear a speaker's voice than in the same room when an audience is present.

EXPERIMENT: Procure two concave mirrors eight or ten inches in diameter. Mount these so they will face each other about ten feet apart, and in the focus of one suspend a watch. Find the focus by allowing a beam of sunshine to fall upon the mirror and noting where it is reflected to a point. Insert the end of a small funnel in a rubber tube about two feet long and hold the mouth of the funnel in the focus of the second mirror and facing it. Put the end of the rubber tube to the ear and listen for the ticking of the watch.

Consider:

 (a) Why the ticking can be heard only when the funnel is at the focus.

 (b) What the course of the sound waves must be as they pass from the watch to the ear.

 (c) The use of the rubber tube that is attached to the funnel.

5. *Why can one be heard so much farther through a speaking tube than through the open air?*

Consider:

 (a) The motion of the air in the tube.

 (b) The effect of the column of air being confined on the sides.

 (c) The conditions under which speaking tubes are used.

6. *How is the sound of the human voice produced?*

OBSERVATION: Place the finger upon that part of the throat called Adam's apple. Make the different vowel sounds, varying the pitch and force. Note the movements. Procure from a butcher the lungs, windpipe and larynx of a sheep or calf.

Consider:

 (a) The cartilaginous rings adapting the

wind pipe to the function of an air passage.

(b) The enlarged upper end called the larynx or voice box.

(c) The membranes stretched across it— the so-called vocal cords.

NOTE.—From a good physiology, learn how the muscles are attached and how the tension of the "cords" modifies the tone.

(d) How voice is modified by tongue, teeth, cheeks and lips to produce speech.

7. *How are the sound waves transmitted to the brain by the ear?*

Consider:

(a) The external ear in the human being and other animals.

(b) Its use in the human being and other animals; as a means of expression.

NOTE.—By means of a large model, if possible, otherwise by good pictures, show the structure and explain the function of the internal parts of the ear.

(c) How the wave motion is received by the ear.

(d) How it is transmitted through the middle ear.

(e) How it is transmitted through the internal ear.

(f) The auditory nerve: its root in the brain.

(g) The absolute dissimilarity between the *sound wave in the air* and the *idea of sound* as it exists in consciousness.

8. *How are various sounds modified and for what purpose?*

Observe the size and shape of the different *cases* that are a part of many musical instruments. Note the sound of the strings when the guitar case, for example, is wrapped in a cloth. Note the effect upon the voice of speaking before an empty barrel or box. Study the arrangement of the sounding board in a piano.

Consider in each instance:

(a) The arrangement of the box or case with respect to the strings.

(b) The openings into the box.

(c) The kind and character of material in the case.

(d) The part that air probably plays.

(e) How resonant tones are produced by the human voice.

NOTE.—Read in any good text-book in physics or in scientific journals, descriptions of the telephone and phonograph. If possible, these instruments should be studied while in practical operation, noting the various connections. The points developed in the foregoing lessons will enable the pupils to understand the principles upon which the instruments operate, but the details are rather too complicated for this work.

NUMBER WORK.

QUERIES :

A. *What is the relation of pitch to the length of string ?*

1. In experiment (A) call the note given by the greatest length of wire *Do;* what length will give the octave above ?

2. Find the lengths that will give *Mi* and *Sol.*

3. In experiment (B) find the ratio of the length of string which gives low *Do* to the length required for each of the other notes above in the same octave.

B. *What is the relation of pitch to the tension of the string ?*

4. Call the note given by a certain tension in (B) *Do;* find what weight is necessary to give the tone *Sol* on the string ; the tone *Do* above.

5. Find the ratio between the tension which gives *Do* and that required to give each of the tones of the scale in the same octave.

C. *How does the intensity of sound vary with distance ?*

6. A person is standing 50 feet from a sounding bell ; what change in intensity if he were to move 50 feet farther away ?

7. If a person standing 90 feet from a whistle were to move up to a distance of 30 feet from it, what would be the relative intensity ?

D. *How rapidly does sound travel?*

8. At a temperature of 70° (See Note, Query 2) how long would it be after seeing the lightning flash before the thunder would be heard a mile away?

9. If 8 seconds elapse after seeing the flash of a gun before the report is heard, what is the distance to the gun, the temperature being 75°?

10. Refer to *Table VI* and calculate the length of the sound wave which gives each tone of the scale when the temperature is 70°.

SUGGESTION. When the note *Do* is made by 128 vibrations per second, it is evident that these must be found within the distance that the sound travels in that time.

11. How far is the reflecting surface from the observer when, at a temperature of 85°, an echo is heard in ½ a second?

12. A cliff ¼ mile distant from an observer will return the echo in what time?

REPRESENTATIVE EXPRESSION.

1. *Drawing.*

(a) A vibrating wire, showing *double* and *single* vibration and amplitude.

(b) Of a cord showing nodes.

(c) Of a bell in vibration showing what nodes must be formed.

(d) Of the glass plate (See Exp. F) showing the various figures formed by the sand.

(e) A tuning fork in vibration, showing the condensation and rarefaction of an air wave.

(f) The voice box or larynx.

(g) The parts of the human ear.

XXIX.

ASTRONOMY.

OBSERVATION : The slant of the sun's rays at noon. Use the skiameter. The points of sunrise and sunset. The length of day and night measured between sunrise and sunset. The daily, weekly and monthly changes in slant, in points of sunrise and sunset and of day's length.

QUERIES :

1. *If the earth were really flat, as it seems to be, what difference would there be in present appearances?*

Consider :

(a) The time of sunrise for people on different parts of the surface.

(b) The time of sunset.

NOTE.—Telegraphic communication now makes it possible for us to read in the daily papers of an event that has taken place in Europe on the same day, but, according to our clocks, at an *earlier* hour than that at which the event occurred. That is, we may read at 8 or 9 o'clock a. m. about what is said to have occurred at 12, noon.

Consider :

(c) What the clocks tell us about the sun's position.

(d) The position of the sun, as seen from three places, directly under its daily path, at one of which it is about 6 a. m., and the other 12 noon, and the third about 6 p. m.

(e) The position of the last place named with respect to the first and second places mentioned in (d).

(f) At what other places might observers be located who would see the sun on the horizon when it appeared at the zenith in the second place mentioned in (d).

2. *If the sun were really smaller than the earth, as it seems to be, and if the earth were flat, would there be any change in present appearances?*

Consider:

(a) The forenoon on different parts of the flat earth as compared with the afternoon.

(b) What the real facts are concerning forenoon and afternoon.

NOTE.—The sun is about 864,000 miles in diameter; the earth is about 8,000 miles.

Consider :

(c) Which of the three observers, mentioned in (d) above, can look along the *shortest* line to the sun.

NOTE.—A line that is perpendicular to the *plane*

of the horizon is called a *vertical line.* What is the relation of vertical lines to each other?

(d) The relation to each other of the *shortest* lines to the sun from the three observers referred to in (c) above.

(e) For which observer the line is vertical.

(f) For which the line is oblique.

(g) The direction of the *shortest* lines to the sun from other observers between the three mentioned.

(h) The relation of these lines to the *sur- face of the earth..*

(i) What their relation would be to the surface if the earth were flat.

(j) The effect upon their relation to the surface, the latter being curved.

(k) The relation of the lines to the earth which strike the extreme edge of the lighted area.

(l) What proofs there are that the surface of the earth is curved.

(m) The possible supposition that will sat- isfactorily account for the obliquity of the sun's rays.

3. *How can the northward and southward*

movement of the sun on the meridian in the course of a year be explained?   Also, the changing of the points of sunrise and sunset?

Consider:

- (a) The probable appearances if the north pole of the earth moved with a tipping motion six months toward the sun and six months away from it.

- (b) The probable appearances if the earth were pivoted on the south pole and had a wabbling motion like that of a dying top.

- (c) The north star being a fixed star, what its apparent motion would be in both cases above mentioned.

- (d) The fact that certain constellations appear yearly in the same place in the sky.

- (e) What conditions, besides revolution, are necessary to cause the change of seasons.

NUMBER WORK.

QUERIES:

A. *What is the size of the earth as compared with that of the sun?*

1. Find the ratio of the diameter of the earth to that of the sun?   (See Note above).

2. If the diameter of the sun appears to be one foot to you at noon, what would the diameter of the earth appear to be if you were on the sun?

3. If the diameter of the earth were represented by a line one inch long, by what length would you have to represent the diameter of the sun?

4. Representing the earth and sun as in (3) how far apart would they have to be placed to preserve the proper ratio in the distance between them? (The earth's distance from the sun may be taken as 96 million miles).

5. If the sun were a hollow shell, how many earths could be contained within it? (The contents of a sphere = the diameter cubed × .5236).

6. A cannon ball moves about 2000 feet per second; at this rate, how long would it take to traverse the sun's diameter?

7. How long to traverse the earth's diameter?

8. At the rate of 1000 miles in 24 hours, how long would it take a railroad train to traverse the sun's diameter? The earth's diameter?

9. At this rate, how long would it require to go from the earth to the sun?

10. Light travels 186000 miles a second;

how long does it take the light from the sun to reach the earth?

11. Suppose the sun revolved around the earth once in 24 hours; how far would it travel? How far per second?

12. How many miles does the earth move in its orbit in one year? How far does it travel per day? In one hour? In one minute? In a second?

13. The sun being regarded as stationary, how far does a point on the equator have to travel in 24 hours? How far in a minute? In one second?

14. What is the size of the spot on the earth's surface that receives, at any one moment, vertical rays from the sun?

B. *How has the distribution of sunshine varied since December?*

15. The area cast by a beam of sunshine, as represented by the skiameter, on January 21st, is what part of the area covered by the same beam on the corresponding date in February? In March?

16. Compare the relative intensities of heat and light for the three months.

17. The beam of sunshine that fell upon 20 acres of ground in January (at the above dates) falls upon how much ground on the same date in February? On the same date in March?

REPRESENTATIVE EXPRESSION.

1. *Drawing.*

   (a) Make a drawing which will illustrate what sunrise, sunset, forenoon and afternoon would be like if the earth were flat and the sun smaller than the earth, as appearances would indicate.

   (b) Make a drawing showing why some rays from the sun are oblique as related to the earth.

   (c) Make diagram of the sun six inches in diameter and one of the earth of proper proportions. Indicate how far apart they should be.

   (d) Make a diagram showing how the sun may appear on the horizon to one observer and in the zenith to another at the same time.

   (e) Draw a diagram required to illustrate problem 14, under Number Work, above.

   (f) By a series of rectangles, show by observation and measurement made with the skiameter the distribution of a given beam of sunshine during January, February and March, about the 21st of each month.

(g) Make a diagram showing the relative positions of the earth and sun in January, February and March.

2. *Painting.*

(a) A landscape carefully portraying the characteristic colors of the season.

(b) Showing cloud coloration, at sunrise and sunset.

XXX.

A STUDY OF LIGHT.

OBSERVATIONS: Make a general survey of nature with a view to finding out the various things that are affected by light and also the ways in which their light relations are formed.

QUERIES:

1. *By what means do members of the animal kingdom take advantage of light?*

Consider:

(a) The eyes.

(b) The position of the eyes in the different animals; for example, in the human being; the fish; the various kinds of birds; the various kinds of quadrupeds.

(c) The eyes of animals of nocturnal habits; owls, bats, cats, moles and other midnight marauders; is their sense of sight important.

(d) The habits of animals without eyes, as for example the earthworm.

(e) What experiences would not be possible, were it not for our relationship to light, as to color, distance, etc.

2. *How do plants establish their relationship with light?*

Consider:

(a) The color of the tender growing parts that are exposed to the light.
(b) The color of the parts that are not exposed to light.
(c) The color changes that occur in tender growing parts that are usually exposed when they are deprived of light. For further development of this *query* see the *queries* under the heads of *Germination*, and *Bud and Leaf Development*.

3. *How do people manage to make the most of their relationship to light; that is, how is that relationship established and preserved?*

Consider:

(a) The position of the eyes.
(b) The advantage of two eyes. Close one eye and note the relative accuracy in judging distance with but one eye.
(c) The number, size and position of windows in the houses.
(d) The modes of artificial lighting that are employed.
(e) The best position from which an object may be seen.

EXPERIMENT: Look at some object lying on that side which is between you and the sun. Change your position so as to view it with your back to the sun, and note the difference in the clearness of vision.

Again, facing a window, try to read from a printed page. Now turn the back to the window, note the relative ease of feeling in the eyes. In the same way try to read by facing a lamp and by turning from it, allowing the light to fall upon the page from above and behind.

4. *Why are we able to see in certain positions better than in others?*

Consider:

    (a) If light may be too strong to enable us to see clearly.

    (b) If light may be too weak.

    (c) How the brilliancy of the light changes: with the time of day, the degree of cloudiness, the direction we turn the eyes, whether towards or away from the sun, whether towards dark surfaces or light ones, etc.

    (d) How the eyes are enabled to get the right amount of light to secure clear vision.

OBSERVATION: Let each pupil examine closely the external structure and appearance of his neighbor's eyes. Note the movements of the lids as the eyes are turned towards or away from the window or some strong source of light. The round dark spot in the eye is really an opening into the interior of the eyeball and it is called the *pupil* of the eye. Note the size of this pupil when the eye is turned away from

the window towards a black board or a black
sheet of paper or cloth. Let the head be quickly turned so that the eye will face the window
and note the rapid change in the size of the
pupil. After facing a window for some time,
note the size of the pupil, then turn quickly towards a dark corner of the room and study the
change in the size of the opening. The size of
the pupil is regulated by a light proof curtain
called the *iris*, whose movements are controlled
by muscles independent of our will, and which
are, therefore, said to be involuntary.

In attempting to read or to see objects when
facing a light, consider:

(e) The strength of the light which comes
to the eye from the book.

(f) The strength of the light coming to
the eye through the window.

(g) The effect of the weaker light upon
the size of the pupil; the effect of the
stronger light upon it; the effect of the
two acting upon the pupil at once; how
the nerves and muscles controlling the
iris would show the effects.

(h) The importance of receiving the proper
amount of light. For example, note
what change in your power to see
clearly when you leave a dark room
and suddenly come into the presence
of a bright light. Also note the
change in your power to see when
these conditions are just reversed.

(i) What these observations tell about the power of the eye to use light and to adjust itself to it.

(j) How extreme and constant changes in the quantity of light would likely affect the *sensitiveness* of the eye.

(k) Whether we should seek to increase or to diminish the sensitiveness of the eye.

5. *What are the causes which operate to make a variation in the intensity of light?*

To answer this, consider:

(a) How light reaches the eye from a luminous point.

(b) Why it is that a lighted lamp or gas jet may be seen from all parts of a room.

(c) How the light must proceed outwards from such a center to fill the entire room. This is called the *radiation* of light.

(d) What it is that determines the *volume* of light that shall enter the eye.

(e) If the light mentioned in (b) were reduced to a luminous point, the *shape* of the volume of light that would enter each eye.

(f) What determines the shape of the cross section of light that enters the eye.

(g) Select a single point in some non-luminous body, as a book, and consider how the light which reveals this point must reach the eye of the observer, and the eyes of different observers at the same time.

(h) If a surface be conceived as being made up of a great number of minute points, consider how the surface, as a whole, is revealed to observers.

NOTE.—A great deal of the confusion which usually arises in the minds of pupils in the study of light comes from the notion that each single minute point is revealed to the observer by means of a *single line of light* instead of by means of a *cone of light*, the base of which is at the pupil of the eye and the apex of which is at the point. Such a cone may be called a *pencil* of light. Since what we see may be considered to be revealed to us, by countless cones of light which come from an innumerable number of points which make up ,the surface seen, it is well to pause to reflect how wonderful this becomes when we take in at a single glance the broad sweep of a landscape of perhaps hundreds of square miles. Each one of the myriad cones performs its wonderful work and through it by means of additional parts of the eye, to be studied a little later, the whole world of color is opened to us.

(i) How the quantity of light, as represented by the number of lines the cone would contain, would diminish as the eye is removed from the point observed. Example: Suppose one man stands five feet and another ten feet from a point, what would be the relative intensity of the light received from it by the two observers? (See Number Work and Representative Expression.)

EXPERIMENT: To find the relative intensity of two lights proceed as follows: Prepare two blocks of paraffin one and one-half inches square by one-half inch thick. Mount these blocks face to face with a small sheet of black paper between them. The paper may be trimmed down to the size of the blocks which may be held in position by a string wrapped around them. To measure the relative power of two lights say a candle and a lamp, place the blocks between them with the opposite faces towards the light. Now standing so as to see the edges of the blocks, vary the position of the lights until the same degree of shade in the two blocks indicates that the intensity of light received from one source is the same as that received from the other. Compare the distances of the light from the blocks and calculate the relative intensity. The instrument here described is called a *photometer*. By this means compare a candle with a kerosene lamp. A lamp with a gas jet. A gas jet with an electric light.

NOTE.—A *standard candle* burns **120** grains of sperm per hour.

6. *How is it possible to see bodies which do*

not of themselves emit light; i. e., bodies that are non-luminous.

Consider the conditions under which bodies are visible:

- (a) The presence of light from some luminous source which falls upon the body.
- (b) The path between the body and the eye.
- (c) The effect of so placing the body that no light will fall upon it.
- (d) The effect upon its visibility of placing some obstruction to the light between the body and the eye.
- (e) What must be the path of light from its source to the eye which makes any non-luminous body visible.

OBSERVATION: Note the path traversed by a band of light from the sun that enters a room through a window. Observe the character of the path marked by the light. Consider whether the *light itself* is visible. What makes it, at least, seem to be visible?

7. *How does a beam of sunshine thus entering an apartment make objects more clearly visible, although it does not directly fall upon them?*

EXPERIMENTS:

A. Place a mirror in the path of a beam or pencil of light and by means of dust from a blackboard eraser observe the path of the light after it leaves the mirror. Light having its path broken and its direction changed by some object like the mirror is said to be *reflected.* That part of the beam of light approaching the mirror is called the *incident beam* and that part proceeding from the mirror is called the *reflected beam.* Note the relative brightness or intensity of the incident and reflected beams and try to account for any differences.

B. For the mirror used in A, substitute a sheet of white paper and note the effect upon the reflected beam. Consider the effect upon the visibility of objects in different parts of the room. Note the area that seems to be covered by the reflected beam from the paper and compare it with that which was covered by the reflected beam from the mirror. Observe the character of the surface of each and account for the difference in reflection. Substitute for the sheet of paper various other surfaces and study the results.

Light reflected, as from a mirror, is said to be *regularly* reflected; when reflected, as from the paper or any surface not polished, it is said to be *irregularly* reflected or *diffused.* Consider how one is enabled to see objects in a room that is in a part of the house opposite to that upon which the sun shines.

8. *What determines the direction taken by the reflected beam?*

Consider:

> (a) The direction of the incident ray. Refer to experiment A, (7) above. Vary the slant of the incident ray and note the change in the reflected ray.

NOTE.—A line perpendicular to the reflecting surface at the point of incidence is called a *normal*. The angle formed by the incident ray and the normal is called the *angle of incidence;* the angle formed by the reflected ray and the normal is called the *angle of reflection.* Consider the relation of these angles to each other and devise means to *prove* what it is.

> (b) As the angle of incidence varies, note the angle of reflection. Consider the plane of these angles.

9. *Under what conditions is an image formed?*

NOTE.—In attempting to answer this query, the pupil should hold clearly in mind what has been previously learned. *First*, that a point is revealed to us by means of a *cone* of light reaching the eye. *Second*, that an object is revealed by a large number of cones coming from a corresponding number of points which make up the surface of the object. *Third*, that each point appears at the *apex of the cone*. *Fourth*, that light travels in straight lines, when passing through a uniform medium, and objects are seen in the direction of the cone of light as it enters the eye.

EXPERIMENTS :

A. Admit through a screen a small pencil of sunlight and allow it to fall upon the surface of a plane mirror.   Very carefully consider:

(a) The size and shape of the spot of light that is formed upon the mirror.

(b) The size and shape of the spot of light which appears upon the wall at the end of the reflected ray. The relative size of these two spots.

(c) The appearance of the incident and reflected beams when their paths are made visible by means of dust or smoke.

(d) The relation of the lines of light which compose the pencil as it *approaches* the mirror; their relation as they leave the mirror.

(e) What the mirror has done to the pencil of light.

(f) Compare carefully the reflected pencil from a *mirror* with the same pencil when it is reflected from a sheet of white paper; from a piece of rough wood.

B.   Select a single point of some object, the corner of a book, for example, and fix the eye upon it.   Picture to yourself the *cone or pencil of light* which reveals this point to you.   Now interpose a mirror between your eye and the point, and change your position so that you can see the *image* of the same point in the *mirror*.   Recalling what was actually seen to be the result of placing a mirror in the path of a pencil of light (see experiment **A**), consider.

(a) How the cone or pencil of light which revealed the points when you occupied the *first position* must now be changed by the mirror.

(b) Where the image appears with respect to the surface of the mirror. To understand this refer to the third point in the note under query 9.

(c) Where the image appears with respect to the object. See the fourth point in the note under query 9. Try to picture (1) That part of the cone of light between the *point* and the *mirror;* (2) That part of the cone that lies between the *mirror* and the *eye;* (3) That part of the cone which lies between the *mirror* and the *image* of the point. Compare (1) and (3).

(d) Devise some means of proving what the relation of the distance of the image from the mirror must be to the distance of the object from the mirror.

10. *What is the effect upon the image when the surface of the mirror is curved ?*

Experiments :

A. Procure a small lamp reflector which may be obtained at any lamp store for fifteen or twenty cents. As described in experiment

A, query 7, admit a beam of sunshine and note the direction and shape of the part that is reflected from the mirror. When the rays of the *incident* beam are *parallel*, the point to which they are reflected from the *concave* surface is called *the focus* of the mirror. If the incident light is a pencil the reflected rays will be brought to a *focus*, but not quite to *the focus of the mirror*. Measure the distance of the focus from the surface of the mirror. In the case of the concave mirror the *normal*, referred to above, is a *radius* of the sphere of which the mirror is a part. A normal to the *convex* surface is the radius *extended*.

B. Mount a short piece of candle upon a small block of wood. Light it, and by holding it at different distances from the concave surface

Consider:

(a) The position of the image.

(b) The attitude of the image—erect or inverted.

(c) The size of the image as compared with the object.

(d) The position of the (object as the different images are formed), with respect to the focus, and the center of curvature, i. e., the point at the center of the sphere of which the mirror is a part.

(e) The essential difference between an image which is seen apparently *be-*

hind the mirror and one which actually appears in *front* of the mirror and may be caught upon a sheet of white paper. The former are called *virtual* and the latter *real* images.

(f) The number of *real* images that may be formed by a concave mirror. The number of virtual images.

(g) In a similar manner study the images formed by the convex surface of the mirror.

NOTE.—In seeking for an explanation of the formation of images, there is but one thing to consider which has not already been studied in the direct seeing of objects, namely, that the *cone or pencil of light from the given point is broken at the surface of the mirror.* When the mirror is plane, the cone is thus made to enter the eye from a new direction and the *image* of the point appears at the apex of the cone, the *basal portion* of which lies between the eye and the mirror. In the case of the *concave* mirror, under conditions already observed, the rays are so reflected as to come to a point *in front* of the mirror; consequently, the *image* of the point appears at that place where the rays are brought to a focus. It should be clearly understood (1) that, if rays of light regularly diverging from a real point, by any means, may be made to regularly *converge* to a point again, the *image* of the real point will appear at the latter place; and, (2), when a cone of light proceeding from a real point is broken by a plane mirror and is made thereby to enter the eye from a new direction, the image of the point will appear where the rays which enter the eye, would converge to a point if produced in straight lines through the mirror. What is true of a single point is true of every point in the surface of any object; hence, the exact reproduction of that object in the form of an image.

11. *How are the images produced which are formed by a lens?*

Compare a lens with a mirror, using for the former a small magnifying glass.

Consider:

(a) The surface.
(b) The shape.
(c) The material of which it is made.
(d) What becomes of the light that strikes its surface.

EXPERIMENTS :

A. Mount the lens in some way so that it will face a well lighted object, such as a tree which may be seen through a window. Behind the lens hold a white sheet of paper or cardboard at such a distance that an *image* of the object will appear on the screen. Compare this image with those formed by the three kinds of mirrors already studied and also with the object: (1) size; (2) attitude; (3) position.

Remembering, now, that the *image* of a point always appears at the *apex of a cone of light*, just as the *real* point appears at the apex of a corresponding cone,

Consider :

(e) How cones of light must proceed from

the numerous points in the object to the face of the lens.

(f) What must happen to the diverging lines of these *incident* cones as they emerge on the opposite side of the lens.

B. With the lens mounted as before, use a lighted candle as an object. Place the candle at a given distance from the lens and then so place the screen that it will receive the image. Compare the size of the object and image. Can the object be placed so that the image formed will be of the same size? Of half the size? Of twice the size? Compare the distance of the object from the lens with the distance of the image in each of the above instances. Can you write a proportion which will express the relation between the size and distance of the object and the size and distance of the image ?

C. Place the lens in the path of a small pencil or cone of light admitted through a very small opening in the window shade. Make the path of the light visible by means of dust or smoke and note how the rays of *incident* light dispose themselves as they pass through the lens.

12. *Why is the image inverted ?*

Consider :

(a) A cone of light reaching the lens from the extreme upper point of the object.

(b) Since the *image* of that point appears

in the extreme lower part of the image, picture how the cone must proceed as it *emerges* from the lens.

(c) Select and study cones of light from other points in the object and, from the attitude of the image, infer the course of the emerging cones.

13. *What part does image making play in seeing; how are the images formed?*

OBSERVATION:

With but very little trouble, the pupils may procure from a butcher a few eyes that have been carefully removed from the heads of slaughtered sheep or cattle. Note the muscles and the connective tissue that hold the eye ball in place and also the *optic nerve* that protrudes from the rear part of the ball. With pointed scissors cut the ball in two in the middle in a plane at right angles to its axis. Note and carefully remove the glairy substance, the *vitreous humor*, found within. The delicate pinkish *retina*, which may be traced as radiating from the inner end of the optic nerve may be seen on the inside of the posterior portion. In front, just behind the *iris*, will be found a somewhat spherical transparent body called the *crystalline lens*. If this be carefully removed from a fresh eye, it may be mounted upon a pin-point, and, if used as the lens in the preceding experiment, a small image may be produced by it upon a properly placed screen. Note the distance between this lens and the screen when the image is formed, and compare with the depth, from front to back, of the eyeball.

In the act of seeing, the function of the lens is to form an image of the object upon the retina. Without the clearly defined image on the retina, vision is blurred, or impossible. Without the crystalline lens light may be distinguished from darkness, but not objects in detail.

Out of this wonderful miniature which the lens forms upon the retina, the mind constructs all the myriad details of a landscape, it may be, covering hundreds of square miles of area.

14. *How does the crystalline lens bring the images of objects at various distances into the one plane of the retina?*

EXPERIMENT :

A. Using the magnifying glass as a lens, and a sheet of paper as a screen, find the effect of varying the distance *between the object and the lens.*

Consider:

    (a) How the position of the image changes as the object is brought nearer to the lens; as it is moved away from the lens.

    (b) With the object in a fixed position, note the effect upon the image if the screen is jarred or shaken.

    (c) The effect upon the appearance of the image if the object is jarred or shaken.

B. If possible, procure another lens whose surface is either more or less convex than that of the first one.

Consider :

    (d) The effect of increasing the convexity upon the position of the image.

NOTE.—The crystalline lens is elastic, and it is held in a thin, tough, transparent sac, called a capsule, which is a little thicker in front than at the back and which, under ordinary conditions, compresses or *flattens* the lens somewhat. By the contraction of certain delicate muscles which connect the capsule to one of the coats of the eyeball, the tension of the capsule may be slightly slackened which allows the lens to become more convex.

Consider :

    (e) In which condition the lens is adapted for distant objects; in which, for near objects.

    (f) The position most likely to strain or tire the eyes. Of course, when work is done by muscles, fatigue is the certain result. Refer to the note above for a hint in working out this point. The normal reading distance for type of this size is about fifteen inches.

    (g) In view of what was observed under *Experiment A*, above, give the real reason why it is injurious to read when the body is moving, as, for example, on a railroad train.

NOTE.—It sometimes happens that the eyeball is too *flat* from front to back and the image of objects in a normal position, say for reading, does not fall upon the retina, but beyond it; it likewise occurs in other instances that the eyeball is too much elongated and the images fall short of the retina.   In view of what has been said, (*see 13, Observation.*)

Consider:

(h) Which is the short sighted eye; i. e., the one which requires objects to be brought very near.

(i) Which is the far sighted eye.

OBSERVATION: Find out how the sight of people changes as they grow old; do they become near or far sighted?   Examine the spectacles of an elderly person and explain how they help to fix the image upon the retina, instead of in front or behind it.

Examine the glasses of some nearsighted person and compare with those used by far-sighted persons. Give reasons for the difference. It should be remembered that as people grow old all the tissues of the body lose their elasticity and the crystalline lens tends to remain in a flattened shape.   Consider the effect this will have upon the sight.

15. *What is the property of the glass which makes it useful in aiding the sight, and in the formation of images?*

Under *reflection of light,* it was found that

light travels in *straight lines* as long as the *medium* remains the same; we shall now note the effect when the medium changes.

EXPERIMENTS:

A. Procure a large square-sided bottle made of clear glass. Fill this with water which should not be *too clear*. As before described, admit through a small opening a pencil of light and allow it to fall upon the side of the bottle of water. Study the path of the light through the water and compare its direction with that of the pencil on either side of the bottle.

Consider:

(a) The path of the pencil through the bottle when it enters at right angles to the side.

(b) The path when the pencil enters the bottle of water at an oblique angle.

(c) The effect of changing the size of the angle.

(d) Picture a *normal*, within the bottle, erected at the foot of the beam of light as it enters: does the beam deviate from the path outside the bottle towards or away from the normal?

(e) In a similar manner erect a *normal* at the foot of the beam as it *emerges* on the opposite side of the bottle: as compared with its course through the bottle, is the beam bent towards or away from the normal?

Note.—Rays of light bent from their course by *passing* from one transparent medium to another are said to be *refracted*. Compare the direction of the bending, with respect to the *normal*, when passing from a rarer to a denser medium, with the direction when passing from a denser to a rarer medium. For example, from the air into the water, and from the water into the air again, as in Experiment A.

(f) How the light strikes the surface of a lens; are any rays normal to its surface?

(g) Judging from what was seen in the experiment with the bottle, how the lines of light must be refracted at the incident surface of the lens. Remember that a normal to a curved surface is a radius, or a radius extended, of the sphere of which the surface is a part.

(h) How the rays must be refracted at the *point of emergence.*

(i) Whether the combined effect of the refraction at the two surfaces is to cause the rays to converge or to diverge.

(j) From the fact that an image is formed, what inference may be made as to the relative direction of the emergent rays.

B.   Hold the lens in the path of the pencil of light admitted through the window: note the direction of the emergent rays and consider why an image is formed when a cone of light *from any* point falls upon the lens.

C.   Procure a small triangular prism and

allow the beam of light admitted through the window to fall upon the surface. Find the surface from which it emerges, and examine the emergent rays.

Consider:

(a) The direction.

(b) The relation of the rays to each other as compared with their relation before entering the prism.

(c) Count the different colors noted in the spot found on the opposite wall when the emergent light falls upon it.

NOTE.—The band of colored light thus formed by the prism is called the *spectrum*. The prism has the power to refract the ray of white light so that it is separated into colored rays. Allow the spectrum to fall upon some white surface and note the colors given to it. The part with the *red* color sends the *red* light to the eye, the part colored *green* sends *green* light to the eye, and so on. The color of an object, therefore, depends upon what?

D. Let the light that passes through the prism fall upon a concave mirror or pass through the lens used above. Note the color when the rays are all brought together at the focus. What does this show as to the nature and composition of white light?

E. Place a stick or a pencil in a glass of water and view it from different positions

Consider:

(a) Why it seems to be broken.

(b) The effect of placing the stick at different angles in the water.

(c) Why the bottom of the tumbler seems to change its position when you look into the water at a very oblique angle.

F. Place a penny or a small pebble in the bottom of a tin cup. Hold it up so that it is just out of the line of vision as the eye looks across the edge of the vessel.

Cautiously add water, and explain why the object appears to change its position.

NOTE.—To explain these various appearances it is only necessary to recall what has been learned before, namely: (1), An object, as a point, is seen at the apex of a cone of light. (2), The *image* of the point is seen at the apex of either a *real* or an *apparent* cone of light. (3), The image is seen in a direction which is determined by the direction of that part of the *reflected* or, as in this case, the *refracted* cone which enters the eye.

Consider:

(a) In looking into a pool of water, do you see the images of the fishes, pebbles, etc., or the real objects?

(b) In looking through window glass, do we see the objects or their images?

(c) The relative position of the observer, the sun and the rainbow. Here the bow is formed partly by *reflection* and partly by *refraction*. The light enters the upper part of the drops on the side next the observer: it is reflected from the *inner surface* of the opposite side of the drop, and in passing out of the lower part is refracted, the rays being separated as in the case of the prism. Different drops at different heights give different colored rays to the eye. Study the spectrum on the wall and try to explain the order of colors seen in the rainbow. For fuller description, see any elementary work on physics.

(d) What effect is produced apparently upon the position of the sun and moon, at the times of rising and setting, by the fact that the light enters and passes through the atmosphere in reaching the eye of the observer.

(e) The possible explanations that may be suggested for the formation of halos about the sun and moon.

16. *Why does a lens magnify an object?*

Keep the points mentioned in the note under F well in mind and consider:

(a) Whether in looking through a lens, you see an *object* or its *image*.

(b) Picture two cones of light, one from a point in each extremity of the image to the eye.

(c) That the direction of the basal portions of the cones, i. e., the portions between the lens and the eye, determine the position of the two points in the image.

(d) What must be the positions of the *real* cones of light between the lens and the corresponding points in the object.

NOTE.—To find the magnifying power of the lens, make two parallel lines one-half an inch long and an inch or two apart. Place the lens over *one* and look through the lens with *one* eye keeping the other open. By carefully moving the head the two lines may be made to coincide and the length of the object may be then compared with its image.

NUMBER WORK.

QUERIES:

A. *How does the intensity of light vary with the distance?*

1. Find the relative intensity of light for two persons, one of whom is seated 3 feet from a lamp and the other 9 feet.

2. Using the skiameter, find the relative intensity of light at 8 a. m. and 12 noon.

3. If an electric light have a brilliancy equal to 2000 candle power at a distance of 30 feet, what will be the brilliancy at the end of a city block 600 feet away?

4. A lamp of 3 candle power is 1 yard from the photometer and a gas jet is 9 feet away; both give the same shade to the photometer; what is the candle power of the gas light? (See experiment under 5 above).

5. The earth is 96 millions of miles from the sun; Mercury 35 millions; Venus, 66 mil-

lions; Mars, 139 millions; Jupiter, 476 millions; Saturn, 872 millions; Uranus, 1753 millions; Neptune, 2746 millions; calling the intensity of light received by the earth from the sun 1, calculate the intensity for each of the other planets.

6. If a lens magnifies 10 diameters, how many times does it magnify the size of the object?

7. Demonstrate why an image must appear as far behind a plane mirror as the object is in front of it.

REPRESENTATIVE EXPRESSION.

1. *Drawing.*

   (a) Represent the cone of light which reveals a given point in an object to the eye.

   (b) Show how a plane mirror breaks a cone of light.

   (c) Show how the image of a point is made to appear behind the plane mirror.

   (d) By a series of drawings, show how a cone of light may be reflected from a concave mirror.

   (e) By a series of drawings, show where the images may be formed by a concave mirror.

   (f) Show where the image is formed by a convex mirror.

   (g) By a series of drawings, show where images may be formed by a lens.

Show the relative size of object and image.

(h) Show the appearance of a stick "broken" when placed in a tumbler of water.

(i) Show, by representing cones of light, why images are inverted by lenses and mirrors.

(j) Draw diagrams showing the form of the near and the far sighted eyes.

2. *Painting.*

(a) Represent, as nearly as possible, the colors in the spectrum.

(b) Try to represent a rainbow after careful observation.

XXXI.

STUDY OF WOOD.

OBSERVATIONS: The pupils should make an examination of the woods used in various parts of buildings, in furniture and woodenware of all kinds. If properly conducted, this study will naturally lead to a consideration of those features of structure which determine the selection of the wood for each particular place and the structure, in turn, will be explained through a study of the mode of growth.

Visit lumber yards, saw-mills and planing-mills, furniture factories and any other wood-working establishments within reach. Visit a forest, that the various trees may be studied, and, if possible, let the pupils observe the history of lumber (or at least some part of it), from the time it is felled in the forest until it is found in the finished product. Use pictures of logging scenes in the great forest areas.

QUERIES:

1. *What properties of wood influence the selection for different uses?*

Consider:

(a) Lightness.
(b) Strength.
(c) Elasticity.

(d) Hardness.   Smoothness.
(e) Toughness.
(f) Brittleness.
(g) Color.   Grain.
(h) Durability—indoors and outdoors.

Learn the names of the different kinds, each of which possesses at least one of these properties; find out in what places each kind has a general use.

2.   *What is the relative strength of different kinds of woods?*

EXPERIMENTS: Split from different kinds of wood pieces two feet long which may be shaved down with the grain to sticks having a cross-section one-half inch on each edge. Support the ends, so that a weight may be hung from the middle of the stick.   For a weight, use a small pail which may be loaded with sand. Having suspended the pail as directed, add sand gradually until the stick breaks; the weight of pail and sand will show the breaking point. Repeat this experiment, using sticks of different length, and note the result. (See Number Work.)

At the same time the elasticity or bending of the stick may be measured.   Lay a rule or a straight-edge on top of the stick and measure the distance the stick bows downward before it breaks.   It is evident that for a fair test the sticks should not be cross-grained.

Try sticks having different form in cross-section; e. g., instead of half-inch square, try one one-fourth inch thick and one inch wide. Test the strength and elasticity of such a stick when on its edge and when on its side. (See Number Work.)

Try sticks of the same kind of wood but different sizes; e. g., one, one-half inch square and another one inch square, etc. Compare results.

3. *How is wood cut in order to show the "grain" as seen in the "finish" of buildings and in furniture?*

If possible, at this point in the study visit some wood-working establishment.

Procure a small trunk or a large-sized branch of the oak and make several sections.

Consider how many of these may be made to advantage in wood-working:

    (a) How the sections may be made with respect to the central pith—longitudinal.

    (b) How the sections may be made with respect to the grain—transverse.

    (c) Which of these sections are used in the woodwork about you in the building and furniture.

    (d) Which sections are least used.

4. *What peculiarities in growth give rise to the different appearances of surface?*

Consider:

    (a) The appearance of the end of a tree-trunk or large branch.

(b) The ringed appearance.

(c) The varied texture as shown in different parts of the rings.

(d) The lines of hard tissue radiating from the pith. These are called *medullary rays*.

(e) The difference between the substance in the medullary rays and that in the adjacent wood fibres. Test with a pen-knife.

When the log is cut into boards, those cut from the sides tangent to the rings are said to be *tangential* sections. A board cut along the line of a radius is a *radial* section.

In "quartered" or "quarter-sawed" oak, the log is first divided into four quarters and then the boards are cut *alternately from each face of the quarter*. Consider,

(f) Why the quarter-sawed lumber is much used when a handsome finish is desired. What peculiarities of growth does the manufacturer take advantage of in using quarter-sawed wood?

(g) Why quarter-sawed lumber is more expensive than that cut in other ways.

5.   *What peculiarities of growth give rise to the twisted and gnarled appearance in some woods?   What is the origin of knots?*

OBSERVATION: Make an examination of various tree-trunks, noting any irregularities which appear on the surface. Split, or saw lengthwise, through a small trunk, or branch, where a limb grows from its side and note the appearance of the fibre. Examine trees that have lost their branches by accident or in pruning. If possible, examine some tree which has been pruned and note the effect of cutting off the branches at different lengths from the trunk.

Consider:

    (a) What is likely to happen to a tree at the point where it loses a branch.

    (b) What happens when the branch is cut off at some distance from the trunk.

    (c) What happens when the branch is cut off at the surface of the trunk.

    (d) The relation of a knot to a branch.

An examination of a growing branch in the spring shows the sappy layer of new wood lying between the bark and the wood. Thus, year after year, ring by ring, the tree is built up around the central pith which in the older trunks and branches nearly, or quite, disappears. The inner wood is therefore encased in a thin shell of living substance, and while this is unbroken the wood is safely kept. But, if at any point, the living layer is broken, as through the loss of a limb, wrenched off it may be by a storm, or if entrance to the wood is made by the stroke of an ax, access is at once given to heat and moisture and decay sets in. It is interesting to observe how promptly the tree begins to repair the damage by wrapping a new layer over the wound. Sometimes the wound is healed over and the tree suffers but little damage, but quite frequently the decay penetrates the central part and destroys the heart wood, and the comparatively thin outer shell alone remains. The inner wood is practically dead but remains much the same, it may be, for centuries, provided the outer layer of living matter is undisturbed.

6. *How does it happen that the pith is not always found in the center of the tree, as may be seen by looking at the end of a log or stump?*

Examine a number of stumps, note their surroundings, the points of the compass and

Consider:

    (a) If each ring is continuous around the pith.

    (b) How the pith becomes gradually removed from the central axis.

    (c) At what time it was nearest the center.

    (d) Whether the pith at different periods occupied relatively different positions with regard to the center.

    (e) What possible influences tended to thicken the rings on one side and make them thin on the other; proximity of trees; points of compass, prevailing wind, etc.

    (f) If the pith is in a corresponding position in all the stumps in the same neighborhood.

(g) The position of the pith in horizontal branches.

(h) A possible reason why some rings are thicker than others.

(i) Since the tree grows in height as well as in thickness, consider what the real form of an entire ring must be.

(j) Study the shape and relative dimensions of the trunk as adaptations to the strain that is exerted upon it when the wind blows.

7. *How is the surface of wood finished in furniture and various parts of buildings?*

Visit, if possible, a furniture factory and observe the methods of turning, planing and the smoothing of the raw surface; then the process of filling, varnishing and polishing. Pupils will find it interesting to prepare specimens of various sections for a permanent collection. Use the plane, then sand paper; after filling and varnishing, polish with pumice stone and oil. A small supply may be obtained for a trifling cost from any dealer in paints and oils.

Consider:

(a) The character of the woods selected for finishing work.

(b) What properties must be kept in mind in making the selection.

REPRESENTATIVE EXPRESSION.

1. *Drawing.*

(a) Showing the structure seen in the

various sections that may be made in a stick or tree.

(b) Cross - sections showing the forms of lumber used for different purposes; i. e., joists, posts, boards, shingles, etc.

(c) Some of the effects in ornamentation that may be secured in wood carving.

2. *Painting*.

(a) Sections showing heart wood, sap wood and layers of bark.

(b) The effects of various modes of finishing wood.

NUMBER WORK.

QUERIES:

A. *How much water does green wood contain?*

1. Weigh a piece of fresh lumber, of convenient size, dry until the weight becomes practically stationary, and calculate the amount of water it contained.

2. What part of the volume of the wood is the volume of water that it contained?

3. Accurately measure the width of a board of "green" lumber, and dry until it no longer loses weight; the lateral shrinkage equals what part of the original width?

B. *How does the stiffness of wood vary with its condition and its dimensions?* (Follow the suggestion and *Query* 2, above.)

4. Measure the downward deflection of a stick when a given weight is suspended from the middle and the supports are, say, 1 foot apart. Now place the supports 18 inches apart and under the same weight measure the deflection. Place the supports 2 feet and then 3 feet apart and measure the deflection in each case. Proceed in this manner until you can show the relation of the amount of deflection to the distance between the supports.

4. With the supports a given distance apart, say 2 feet, find the ratio of the deflection to different loads; that is, double, triple and quadruple the load and compare the deflections.

6. Place the sticks in water until soaked and repeat the experiments suggested in (4); find the ratio between the two sets of results thus obtained.

C. *How is the stiffness related to the cross-section?*

7. Prepare clear straight-grained sticks of different kinds of wood each about 3 feet long and 1 inch wide and ½ an inch thick. Under a given weight (not sufficient to break the stick) find the ratio of the deflection when they are placed flatwise to that when on the edge.

8. Find the ratio between the stiffness of a stick (as indicated by the deflections) ½ an inch wide and ½ an inch thick to a stick 1 inch wide and ½ an inch thick.

9. What is the effect upon the stiffness of doubling the *width?*

10. Place the second stick, mentioned in (8), on its edge and compare the deflections, under the same conditions with those of the first stick.

11. What is the effect, upon the stiffness, of doubling the *thickness?*

12. If the joists supporting a floor are required to be 2x10 inches, what would have to be their thickness if their length were to be doubled?

13. If joists to bear a given load must be 3x12 inches, what would be their necessary thickness if the load were to be doubled?

14. What would have to be the width of the joists in each of the foregoing cases, if they were to lie flatwise?

15. By determining the deflections under the same conditions, find the ratio of oak to white pine in stiffness; of oak to ash; of pine to ash; of pine to poplar; of poplar to bass wood, etc., etc.

D. *How do various kinds of wood differ in strength, and how does the form of the cross-section affect the supporting power of a stick?*

16. Prepare sticks as suggested in the foregoing problems; find the ratio of the weights at the breaking points of the sticks; that is, the supporting power of sticks.

(a) When placed flatwise and on the edge.

(b) When the supports are at different distances.

(c) Sticks of the same size but different kinds of wood.

17. What properties of wood should be combined in timber used for joists? What woods are suitable?

18. What properties should be combined in wood used for floors? For doors? For window sashes? For weather boarding? What properties combined in "British Oak" have made England's navy famous? What properties make oak suitable for spokes in wheels?

19. In what position in joists are knots most injurious? The least injurious? Give a reason for both.

20. To support a given weight, which would be the more expensive for joists, oak or pine? Pine or hemlock?

E. *What are some of the constituents of wood?*

EXPERIMENTS: Perform the necessary experimental work in this connection in accordance with the general suggestions found in *Chapter VIII*, page 76, *et seq.*

21. What is the ratio of the weight of the ash to the weight of the dry wood in the specimens used in the foregoing problems?

22. What is the ratio of ash, by weight, between the same weights of different kinds of wood?

23. Does the relative weight of the ash seem to depend upon the relative weight of the wood? That is, do the heavier woods have more or less ash than the same weight of the lighter woods?

REPRESENTATIVE EXPRESSION.

1. *Drawing.*

  (a) Draw diagrams showing the relative stiffness of different kinds of wood under the same conditions.

  (b) Draw diagrams showing the relative amount of deflection of the same stick under different loads.

  (c) Draw diagrams showing the relative amount of deflection in different lengths of the same stick.

  (d) Draw diagrams showing the amount of deflection in a stick when lying flatwise and when lying on its edge. (See problem 16.)

  (e) Draw diagrams, showing the relative amount of water in green lumber.

  (f) Draw a diagram showing the relative amount of ash, dry solid and organic matter in different kinds of wood.

  (g) Given a beam having a cross-section of 1 square foot; draw a diagram showing what its cross-section should be in order to have the greatest supporting strength. Examine the iron work of bridges, noting the cross-sections of the supporting iron work.

XXXII.

THE STUDY OF A FOSSIL.

OBSERVATION : Make a careful search about coal yards in the blocks of soft coal for traces of forms having plant-like structure. Miners and other workers in coal often find such forms, and, not infrequently, they acquire an interesting collection. If requested, they are usually glad to place such collections at the disposition of school children, and are very willing to save any specimens they may find.

Examine the rocks about the coal strata, if there is any opportunity, and collect odd forms. The fossil fern is often found in the coal regions, and by means of it an instructive view of the past may be obtained.

In limestone regions, various forms of fossil animals may be found, and through these there may be interesting studies of times long past.

QUERIES:

1. *What evidence is presented by the fossil plant—the fern, for example—that it was once a living thing?*

Consider it in its likeness to present forms:

(a) The general appearance and contour of the leaf.

(b) Ribs and veins.

(c) The margin.
(d) The stem.
(e) The color.
(f) The *substance* of the fossil.

2.   *What conditions must have prevailed at the time, if the fossil was once a living fern?*

Consider, in view of what is known of ferns at the present time:

(a) The question of heat; the probable range of temperature, the possible range of temperature, the most probable source of the heat.

(b) The question of light; the most probable source of light.

(c) The question of moisture; the quantity of moisture, the form of the moisture —rain, dew, frost, fogs, &c.—the source of the moisture.

(d) The question of seasons; change of seasons, the most probable cause of the seasons and their changes.

(e) The question of soil; the source of the soil.

(f) The character of the surface—bare or covered with vegetation—level or hilly.

(g) The question of streams, lakes, oceans.

(h) The general appearance of the earth at the time in which the fossil fern lived. Compare its probable appearance then with that of the present.

3. *Under what conditions did the fern become a fossil?*

OBSERVATION: Observe the fate of plants which live and perish at the present time. Are there those which you·believe may in due time become fossils? What is the fate of the majority of the plants which perish at the present time? · By what means are plants which perish buried beneath the surface? Observe the work of wind and water in this direction.

Consider :

(a) Whether the forces which buried the fern were violent or gentle; note the condition of the fossil fern leaf.

(b) Could it have been so well preserved if it had been buried by the wind?

(c) If it had fallen into a current of water, would it have been so well preserved?

(d) The chances that it may have fallen into standing water. Observe the action of back water when streams are at flood height. Almost any stream formed by a heavy shower will show this on a small scale.

(e) The character of the material in which the fern leaf is imbedded. Grind a small portion of this in water.

(f) Could this have been deposited in a swift current?

(g) The conditions under which it may have buried the fern leaf.

4. *What changes took place in the fern leaf after it was covered with silt?*

Consider:

(a) Whether it decayed.

(b) Whether any of the original substance remains. Look for evidences of carbon or charcoal.

(c) How it was possible for the exact form of the fern to be preserved.

(d) Was the material which covered the fern violently disturbed afterward?

(e) The thickness of the material deposited on top of the fern. Find, if possible, the height of the hill in which the fern was found. Is there evidence of the work of water?

(f) The length of time necessary to cover the fern to the depth at which it was found.

OBSERVATION: Procure from a lake, stream, or pond, a jar of water; allow it to stand for several days and note the amount of sediment at the bottom. If possible, calculate the amount of sediment to the gallon of water. Consider what becomes of this sediment that is thus held in suspension, how slowly it forms a layer on the bottom. Consider the length of time that would be necessary to build a hill like that which covered the fern. Procure a vessel holding 1 gallon or more and fill two-thirds full of water. Stir in the water a quart or more of

sand and silt and when about half-settled drop
into it a few leaves, twigs, etc., slightly weight-
ed. When the water is clear, pour off and dry
the sediment. The imprint of the leaves, etc.,
may then be obtained in the dried mud. As
the object thus buried decays, fine silt takes its
place, which, when hardened into stone, becomes
a *cast;* when the rock is split and the cast is
removed it leaves an *imprint;* when the form
of the object is preserved by material that is
deposited from a *chemical solution* it is called a
petrifaction; sometimes some of the original
substance, as *carbon*, remains, and this is also
called a fossil. Thus the term fossil, applied to
any of these four forms, is variously used.

5. *How was the fern leaf again brought to
the surface?*

Consider:

    (a) The various forces now at work chang-
ing the surface of the earth—wind,
water, frost, plants, animals.

    (b) Which of these agencies has done the
most toward removing the material
piled on top of the fern?

    (c) The work of streams, the rate at
which they cut their valleys.

    (d) The relative length, probably, of the
building and wearing periods which
followed the burial of the fern leaf.

NOTE.—It is said that the basin of the Mississippi
river is being worn down at the rate of one foot in five

thousand years. This will give a faint idea of the length of time taken to wear down the hill which once covered the fern. This is but a small part of the earth's history.

6. *What must be the history of a fossil animal like the coral, or some of the shell fish, frequently found in limestone?*

Consider:

(a) Where corals and the smaller shell fish grow at the present time.

(b) The surroundings of the animal when alive—ocean or lake or river.

(c) The various life conditions of these animals; the temperature, the light and the food they require.

(d) The various life conditions that probably surrounded the ancient forms.

(e) The probable appearance of the world in that remote time.

(f) The changes that have taken place since the fossil was alive; its death, its dropping to the bottom of the sea, its burial to a great depth in silt, the hardening of this to a rock, the removal of the ocean, the upheaval of the rock as dry land, its wearing down, or upheaval, which brought the fossil to the surface.

7. *What are the conditions to-day which are favorable to fossilizing animals that die?*

Consider:

    (a) The various forms of insect life; what is their fate?

    (b) The, various forms that have bony skeletons. What parts of these are most likely to become fossilized? What will prevent their becoming fossilized?

    (c) The various forms of life found in water which are most likely to become fossilized. Compare the chances of the fish, the craw-fish, the turtle, the snail.

    (d) The conditions under which the tracks of various animals may become fossilized; those of the shore birds, the earth worms and the animals that live in the marshes.

8. *What knowledge of the earth may be gained through the study of its fossils?*

Consider:

    (a) The climate of those ancient times; the age of the earth; the changes that have taken place in the earth.

    (b) The character of the forces that have been concerned in earth-building.

REPRESENTATIVE EXPRESSION.

1. *Drawing.* (a) Sketch the tracery made by leaves, etc., in clay and mud.

2. *Painting.* (a) A landscape showing conditions under which plants and animals may become fossilized.

XXXIII.

STUDY OF STONES.

OBSERVATIONS: Examine the various buildings in your vicinity, and procure samples of all the stones that are used in the construction. If possible, gather specimens of the rock which underlies the soil. Gather specimens of loose fragments which may be found on the surface or in the soil. Gather samples of the rock used in street paving.

QUERIES:

1. *What properties of the stones found in your neighborhood have led to their use in buildings and elsewhere?*

Consider:

    (a) Hardness. (See Scale of Hardness.)
    (b) Color.
    (c) Luster.
    (d) Transparency.
    (e) Ease with which it can be worked.
    (f) Solubility.
    (g) Fusibility.
    (h) Weight.
    (i) Chemical composition.

EXPERIMENT: Procure samples of stones weighing a pound or more, and about the same size, which are used in various ways in construction, as street-paving, house-building, flagging, etc. Dry in the sun, or in an oven, until the weight becomes constant. Soak the stones for a day in water; wipe dry and weigh again.

Consider:

    (a) The meaning of any difference of weight observed.

    (b) The effect of the result upon the choice of stone for different purposes.

    (c) By what forces the various stones would be most affected.

    (See Number Work.)

As a guide to be used in the examination of minerals with a view to learning something of their properties, the following outline is given. In the study of any specimen, it is not necessary to apply any tests except those needed in the determination of those properties which appear to give the mineral its distinctive character.

SYNOPSIS OF TESTS TO AID IN THE STUDY OF THE PROPERTIES OF MINERALS.

This table has been compiled from various sources for the sake of convenience in classroom work. A manual such as Crosby's, or Dana's, should also be used by the pupil.

I. MATERIALS AND APPARATUS.

A. Physical Tests.— Small balances with weights to one centigram. A beaker or tum-

bler.   A flat file.   Glass with ground and plain
surfaces.   A small pair of pliers for breaking
off fragments.   A small mortar and pestle;
many minerals can be powdered by grinding up
a fragment between two pieces of glass.

B.   Chemical Tests.—Bunsen burner, or
alcohol lamp or large candle. Blowpipe. Piece
of charcoal two or three inches square and of
same thickness. Three inches platinum wire
No. 27 fused into a small glass tube for handle.
Steel (or better, platinum-tipped) forceps. Small
magnet.   About 2 oz. each of carbonate of soda,
borax, salt of phosphorus, cobalt solution, and
hydrochloric acid.   Open and closed glass tubes
3 in. long, ¼ in. diameter.   One or two test-
tubes.   A few strips each of red and blue litmus
paper.

II.   PHYSICAL PROPERTIES.

A.   Structure.

1. Cleavage. (*a*) Perfect. (*b*) Imperfect.
2. Fracture. (*a*) Conchoidal — breaking
with concavities; shell-like surfaces. (*b*) Even,
smooth. (*c*) Uneven. (*d*) Hackly. (*e*) Splin-
tery.

B. Form.

1. External.

(*Usually can be determined only by examination of large specimens.*)

Botryoidal—Surface grape-like.

Mammillary—Same but larger.

Tufaceous — Porous mineral incrustations formed from solutions.

Concretionary—Rounded masses.

Geode—Hollow concretion.

Stalactitic—Hanging from under surface of a rock, cone-shaped.

Stalagmitic—Formed on floors of caverns from dripping water.

Stratified—Deposited in layers.

2. Internal.

Granular—Coarse or fine—Small crystals.

Compact—Crystals invisible to unaided eye. Crystalline.

Foliated—In layers.

Fibrous—Thread-like.

Columnar—Stout, fibrous.

Amorphous—Without crystallization.

C. Scale of Hardness.

1. Talc,
2. Gypsum,

Very Soft: can be scratched with finger nail, or very easily with a knife.

3. Calcite,
4. Fluorite,

Soft: cannot be scratched with finger nail, but easily scratched with a knife.

5. Apatite,
6. Orthoclase,

Hard: not easily scratched with a knife; scratches glass.

7. Quartz,
8. Topaz, } *Very Hard:* { Cannot be scratched with a knife ; scratches glass. Scratches quartz.

9. Corundum,
10. Diamond, } *Adamantine:* { Scratched by the diamond and itself. Not scratched by any other mineral.

D. Tenacity.

1. Brittle—Breaks easily.

2. Malleable—Flattens into thin sheet under hammer.

3. Sectile—May be cut into thin slices.

4. Flexible—Retains its form when bent.

5. Elastic—Comes back to original form when bent.

E. Lustre, or Glance.

1. *Metallic,* as in metals.

2. *Non-Metallic:* { Vitreous, as in glass. Pearly, as in pearl and mica. Resinous, as in sulphur, sphalerite, resins. Pitchy, as in cannel coal. Silky or satiny, as in satin spar. Greasy or waxy, as in serpentine. Dull, as in chalk.

F. Streak.

Color of powder; may be obtained by rubbing the mineral over the surface of a piece of ground glass or over a file.

G. Diaphaneity.

1. Transparent.   Semi-transparent.
2. Translucent.   Sub-translucent.
3. Opaque.

H. Specific Gravity.   (Ratio to the weight of an equal bulk of water.)

1. Weigh in air.
2. Weigh in water.
3. Specific gravity = weight in air ÷ loss of weight in water.

III.   CHEMICAL PROPERTIES.

A. Solubility.   (Soluble or insoluble).

1. In water; touch to tip of tongue.
2. In acid; (observe this order in testing: dilute and concentrated, cold and hot).

Dissolves, (*a*) With effervescence.   (*b*) Without effervescence.   (*c*) Gelatinizes.

NOTE.—Sulphuric and nitric acids may be needed.

B. Fusibility.   (Fusible or Infusible).

(1.) NOTE.—B. B. = before blowpipe.   O. F. = oxidizing (outer) flame.   R. F. = reducing (inner) flame.

(*a*) Hold small splinter of mineral in forceps in both O. F. and R. F.

(*b*) Same, B. B.   (*c*) Same, with *infusible* minerals, moistened with cobalt solution; alumina turns *blue;* zinc oxide, *green;* magnesia, *flesh red.*

(2.) *Heat mineral* (powdered, generally) *on charcoal without soda.* Use both O. F. and R. F.

(*a*) Note fusibility; decrepitation; intumescence; odors; coating around mineral on charcoal.

(*b*) Test heated product for magnetism by using a small magnet.

(*c*) Powder heated product on silver coin, and moisten; dark stain indicates sulphur.

(*d*) Moisten heated product, and test with litmus paper; *alkalies turn red litmus paper blue; acids turn blue litmus paper red.*

(3.) *Heat mineral* (powdered) *on charcoal with soda.*

(*a*) Repeat observations under (2): note coatings; *yellow* when hot, *white* when cold, zinc; *brown*, silver; *yellow*, lead.

(*b*) Note if metallic globule is found.

(4.) *Heating in Borax or Salt of Phosphorus Bead.**

(*a*) Note color of bead, hot and cold. Color indications: *green*, copper; *yellow* or *brown*, iron; *amethyst*, manganese; silica *effervesces* in soda, leaves *skeleton* in phosphorus.

(*b*) Flame colors, wherever noticed, indicate elements as follows: *yellow*, soda; *violet*, potash; *orange*, lime; *purplish red*, lithia; *red*, strontia; *yellowish green*, baryta; *green*, copper; *blue*, chloride of copper; *bluish green*, phosphates.

*To make the bead: turn a small loop on end of platinum wire; cleanse by holding in flame until the latter becomes colorless; while hot, dip loop into the borax and fuse in the flame; repeat until a clear globule is obtained. Heat a minute piece of mineral in the bead.

(5.) *Heat powdered mineral in closed tube.*

(*a*) Note fusibility; sublimation; condensation of vapor in upper end of tube.

(*b*) Test vapor and water with litmus paper.

(6.) *Heat powdered mineral in open tube.*

(*a*) Note odors; sublimation.

(*b*)Test vapors with litmus paper.

2. *Is there any evidence concerning the origin or history of the rocks or minerals under consideration?*

Consider, first:

The possibilities of water as an agent.
   (a) Solubility.
   (b) The evidences of deposition from solution.
   (c) The fineness of grain or texture.
   (d) The evidences of stratification.

EXPERIMENTS: *Solution and crystallization.* Procure any substances that may be within reach, and test for solubility. Among such substances that are interesting in this respect are chloride of ammonium, carbonate of soda, nitrate of soda, common salt, copper sulphate, iron sulphate, prussiate of potash, bichromate of potash and alum. An ounce or two of each, which may be purchased at any drug-store, will be sufficient.

Prepare several tumblers, or beakers, of perfectly clear water, either distilled or filtered. Use about 150 or 200 cubic centimeters. Thin copper or tin vessels are, in some respects, better than tumblers. Wrap the vessels with layers of flannel, or thin asbestos paper, and provide covers of the same material. The water, and the substances used, should be the temperature of the room. Having determined this with a thermometer, add a given weight (ten grams will be sufficient), of the substance, *finely pulverized*, to the water, stir with the thermometer, and note the temperature as solution proceeds. What do the results mean? Refer to *Chapters XVIII and XIX.* Results are well shown if 10 grams of the substance and 150 cubic centimeters of water are used. Consider what the variation in results obtained with the different substances means.

Repeat the experiment with water 10°, 20° and 30° higher temperature for the purpose of comparing the different amounts dissolved.

Set the solutions where they will be free from dust and from disturbance and observe the formation of crystals. If a string, with a knot at the end, be suspended in the solution, sometimes a single large crystal will form about it; at least, a cluster of crystals may be obtained. The crystals may be more quickly obtained if the substances are dissolved in hot water nearly to the point of saturation.

(e) The rate at which the crystals form.

(f) Their size and shape. (See Number Work.)

Sorting and Stratification. General Observation. After a rain, note the arrangement of the gravel, sand, silt and fine mud, that have been moved by the surface water. When one streamlet or brook enters another, or where it enters a quiet pool, note the distribution of the material that has been carried in the water. Cut down through the deposited materials and look for layers or strata. What determines the order of distribution? Stir into a Mason jar, filled with water, a mixture of the materials moved by rain—sand, gravel and silt. Allow the mixture to settle and observe the position of the materials. Account for the sorting of the materials. Contrast what is observed here with the process and the results obtained under crystallization.

Consider:

(a) Whether these experiments give any hint as to the history of any rocks or minerals that you find in the vicinity.

(b) The signs of stratification shown in the rocks.

(c) The angle of the strata with the horizontal; i. e., the dip of the strata.

Consider, second:

The possibilities of heat in rock formation.

EXPERIMENT: Melt one or two ounces of roll sulphur in a small porcelain evaporating dish and allow it to cool gradually. When a crust has formed on the surface, break through it and pour out the liquid that remains, and examine the inside for crystals. These are formed by fusion. Compare with the process of solution.

Examine any rocks that may be found for crystals. Test for solubility and fusibility. Is there any evidence as to how they were formed?

3. *What are the natural conditions afforded in the earth for the formation of crystals from solution?*

Consider:

(a) The solvents: water, acids.
(b) The source of soluble matters.
(c) The conditions for natural filtration.
(d) The natural conditions for crystal formation; receptacle for the solution; the chances for supersaturation; absence of disturbance.

Read any good book on geology on the subject of stalactites, stalagmites, calcite, bog iron ore, gypsum, etc.

4. *What are the natural conditions afforded in the earth for the formation of crystals by fusion?*

Consider :

(a) Volcanic regions.
(b) The evidence afforded by hot springs.

Read, in a work on geology, the story of marble, and granite.

5. *Under what conditions were the crystals*

formed, which, in the laboratory, are practically infusible, and insoluble?

Read the history of the quartz family.

6. *What evidence do the rocks show concerning their relations to living things?* (See chapter on the study of the fossil.)

Consider:

(a) The fragments of shells, etc., that are sometimes found in limestone.

(b) The fossil forms found in coal.

(c) The filling up of marshes by plant-life.

Read, in a book on geology, the story of limestone, and the story of coal. (See Le Conte's Geology, for the history of bog iron ore.)

7. *What evidence may be gathered at the present time, respecting the stratification of rock materials?*

OBSERVATIONS: Note the general appearance, the clearness or muddiness, of any stream, or lake, or small pool of water. After a rain, and the streams become swollen with surface water, consider what the muddiness means.

EXPERIMENTS: With a clean, clear tumbler, dip up a quantity of water from the stream or pool to be studied. Look through it toward the light. Better still, fill a tall, clear glass jar with the water, and place it on a white sheet of paper, and look down through it. Fill a two-quart Mason jar with the water, protect from dust, and set away where it may be quiet.

After some time, a week, perhaps, examine the bottom of the jar for sediment. Draw off the clear water—a siphon is most convenient for this—until but a few ounces of water remain. Thoroughly rinse all the silt with this water, into a small evaporating dish, and evaporate, at a low temperature, to dryness. If enough dry solid to be weighed is not obtained thus, repeat the experiment until a sufficient quantity is gathered, then weigh, and calculate the amount per cubic foot, per cubic yard, etc. (See Number Work.)

In the same way, test the water of a small stream, or of a river, when in ordinary condition, and when muddied by a rain, for the amount of silt that is carried per cubic foot of water. In very small streams, the water may be deflected through a pipe, and actually measured. In larger streams, the rate of flow may be approximately determined, by observing the distance that a chip floats in a given time— taking the average of a number of observations— and by estimating from actual measurements of depth, the area of a cross-section of the stream-bed. In streams of small or moderate size, the measurement may be made as follows: With a board of sufficient length, construct a dam across the stream; on the upper edge of the board, cut a rectangular notch, say, two inches deep, and of sufficient length to allow all the water to flow through it. Arrange the board so that the water shall flow evenly over the edge. The quantity of flow may be calculated thus: Suppose the water is one inch deep in a notch that is 2 feet long, and that the rate of the current in the stream is 100 feet in a minute. The quantity of water in this case would be $2\times100\times\frac{1}{12}=16.6$ cubic feet per minute.

After making some of these observations, read the introductory chapter in F. H. King's book on *The Soil*, especially that part devoted to "Water and Its Work." (See Number Work.)

Consider:

    (a) What becomes of these sediments in the waters.

    (b) The shores and mouths of streams.

    (c) The bottom of pools and lakes.

Read the story of the great deltas, and find out why deltas are not formed at the mouths of *all* streams. Almost any roadside system of brooklets will show the reason.

8. *What evidence may be collected as to the sources of the sediments found in water?*

Consider:

    (a) The small gullies cut out of the surface by every rain-storm.

    (b) The large and small land-slides that occur upon almost every hillside during wet weather, and especially in springtime, when the frost leaves the ground.

(c) The up-rooting of trees on hillsides, and the projecting rocks in cliffs.

(d) The pebbles and stones in the streams and on the shores of lakes and pools.

(e) The correspondence that appears be· tween the strata that lie with edges exposed, in the hills on opposite sides of a stream.

In a book on geology, read on the subject of erosion and transportation. See F. H. King's *The Soil.*

9. *What evidence is there concerning the part that the atmosphere plays in the wearing and transportation of rock material?*

OBSERVATIONS: In dry weather, note the clouds of dust that are being continuously lifted by the wind. Observe the increased transparency of the atmosphere after a rain. If possible, examine the shelving rocks in a cliff, and observe the fine dust, worn from the rocks, that collects in cavities, that have themselves been made mainly by the eroding effect of the atmosphere.

With a brush and a piece of paper, collect from walls that have been built for some years the rock dust that has been loosened by weathering.

In the winter time, after a fresh fall of snow, collect the snow that has fallen on a square meter of surface, not going deep enough to take any of the dirt from the surface of the ground, and melt it. Evaporate and note the sediment that remains. Weigh this and calculate the amount per square mile.

After the snow has lain for several days, repeat the experiment and note the accumulations of materials.

Consider:

(a) The source of the materials found in the snow.

(b) By tests, given on preceding pages, the nature of the materials.

10. *What evidence is there that plants are concerned in the disintegration of rocks?*

OBSERVATIONS: Note the behavior of the roots of those plants that grow about rock ledges, and that clamber over rocky cliffs. Examine an old wall that for a long time has been covered with vines. In this connection, also,

Consider:

(a) The result of the freezing of water that finds its way into rock crevices.

(b) The part probably played by burrowing animals, as the earth-worm, in the work of erosion.

(c) The growth of mosses and lichens upon rocks.

NUMBER WORK.

QUERIES:

A. *How do stones vary in their power to*

absorb water? Use the results obtained by the experiments under Query (1).

1. What part of its dry weight, is the weight of the water absorbed by the following: limestone, granite, slate, sandstone, shale, marble, brick, cement.

2. Arrange a table which will show the relative absorbing power of the different materials suggested in (1), allowing 1 to represent the stone which absorbs the least.

3. Compare the results obtained, thus: the water absorbed by the limestone, equals what per cent. of that absorbed by the brick? By the granite? By the sandstone, etc., etc.? What bearing do these results have upon the usefulness of the stones for constructive purposes?

B. *What is the relative amount of energy, as heat, used in dissolving various substances? Use the results obtained under Query (2).*

4. Arrange in a table, the substances used in the experiments, according to the amount of heat consumed in their solution, representing by 1 the substance which lowers the temperature of the water least.

5. Compare the results obtained with each other, thus: the amount of heat used in the solution of the salt, equals what per cent. of that consumed in the solution of the alum? the carbonate of soda, etc., etc.? What inference may be made from these results, respecting the nature of the different substances?

C. *What is the amount of sediment held in suspension in lakes and streams? Use the results obtained by the experiments under Query* (7).

6. Find the quantity of silt per cubic foot, in the given stream or lake.

7. From the average of several observations, calculate the amount of sediment transported by a given stream in one year.

8. From the average of several observations, calculate the thickness of the layer of silt, which would be on the bottom of the lake if all in suspension were deposited.

9. If the surface of the ground were cut away, by erosion, to a depth of $\frac{1}{8}$ of an inch, how many cubic feet of soil would be carried from an acre? From a square mile? Give each result in the form of a cube.

10. Using the data obtained under *Query 9*, estimate the quantity of dust that settled from the atmosphere, per square mile, in the given time.

11. For the relation of mineral matters to plant growth see chapter on *Wood*.

REPRESENTATIVE EXPRESSION.

1. *Modeling.*
   (a) The forms of various crystals that may be found.
   (b) If possible, visit brick-yards to observe the process of brick-making.

2. *Drawing.*
  (a) The forms of crystals.
  (b) The forms of stalactites, stalagmites, etc.
  (c) The face of a cliff, and, in general, the landscape, showing how the contour and relief are related to the order in which rocks of different kinds are placed.

3. *Painting.*
  (a) Stones, giving characteristic colors.
  (b) The landscape, showing the coloration due to rocks and soil.
  (c) The landscape, showing variation of color of plants growing in different soils.

XXXIV.

METEOROLOGY FOR THE WINTER MONTHS.

QUERIES:

A. *What are the temperature conditions for the winter months?*

1. What is the average temperature for each winter month?

2. Compare the rate of change in the winter months with that of the fall, month by month.

3. Compare the greatest extremes of temperature noted in the winter months and compare with the autumn months.

4. Compare the greatest *daily* extremes for the different months.

B. *What are the cloud conditions during the winter?*

5. What is the ratio of the cloudy days to the clear days during the winter months? Compare with the fall months?

6. The clear days are what per cent. of the whole in each month? During the fall?

C. *What is the relation of the rainfall to the cloudiness?*

7. The rainfall for each month averages how much for each rainy day: i. e., for each day having at least .01 inch of rainfall?

8. What is the average rainfall for each cloudy day?

9. Compare the foregoing averages with the same for the fall months and establish the relative *rain value* of clouds in the two seasons.

10. Compare the number of rainy days with the number of cloudy days in each month?

11. What is the ratio of the rainy days to the cloudy days in the entire season? In the fall?

12. The rainfall for each month averages how much per day during the winter? During the fall?

13. The rainfall for each season averages how much for each day?

D. *What is the relation of the precipitation in rain to that which falls as snow?*

14. Compare the snowfall, in inches, with the depth of rain.

15. Allowing ten inches of snow to equal one inch of rain, find out ratio between the precipitation by rain and snow.

REPRESENTATIVE EXPRESSION.

1. DRAWING.

    (a) Represent the depth of rainfall for each month, and for the season, by drawing a black band upon white cardboard, as many inches long as there were inches of rainfall.

2. By lines, show the relation of the precipitation in snow to that as rain.

XXXV.

STUDIES OF THE LANDSCAPE.

With the gradual approach of spring, careful and extended observation and study should be given to the changing aspects of the landscape. If a detailed record of all the influences at work be kept, it will greatly increase the interest in the picture, and add much to its intelligibility. Pupils will find it interesting to select some part of the landscape each day and represent it in water colors. If these paintings be pasted side by side, after the fashion of a calendar, the pupils will be able to build up, month by month, a beautiful pictorial history of the year in color. Proceeding with the study of the landscape as a whole, there should be, also, a study of its details or parts. "From the whole to the parts" does *not* mean, however, from the whole to the *fragments*, but to the *smaller related wholes*. The study of each detail should tell its own story, and this should be a chapter in the whole. Among the interesting stories which may be written up with brush, pencil and pen, during the spring, may be mentioned,

1. The changes of the landscape as a whole.

2. The story of the plant which sprouts from root or stem.

3. The story of the seedling from seed to flower and seed.

4. The story of the bud and leaf.

5. The succession of plants on the same area as the season advances.

6. The story of the plant's adaptation to soil, heat, light and moisture.

When these stories are bound together, or placed side by side, they form an attractive volume.

QUERIES:

1. *What are the sources of color in the winter landscape?*

Consider:

    (a) The ground.
    (b) Vegetation—trees, shrubs, etc.
    (c) Rocks and soil.
    (d) Water.
    (e) The sky; the effects at different times a day.
    (f) The various colors—drab, brown, etc.
    (g) The domains of nature that furnish the colors of winter.

2. *What are the sources of landscape colors in the spring?*

Consider:

    (a) Where the first changes of color are seen. Compare this with the location of the first touches of autumn coloration.

(b) The relation of the earliest spring coloration to streams and bodies of water.

(c) The shades of color through which the landscape passes from spring to summer.

(d) How the spring shades are contrasted with those in autumn as winter approaches.

(e) The domains of nature that furnish the most brilliant coloring. Compare with winter.

3. *What features in the landscape have enabled plants to colonize themselves?*

NOTE.—It is interesting to observe how certain plants, pond lilies and rushes, for example, attempt to adapt themselves to the trying extremes of soil, water and air in the different seasons.

Consider:

(a) The water; its surface, the mud at the bottom of ponds, etc.

(b) The shores within the reach of high and low water.

(c) The marshy areas.

(d) The dry uplands; different slopes; meadows.

(e) The woodlands.

(f) Sandy areas; rocks and cliffs.

4. *By what means do plants adapt themselves to the various areas and to the trying extremes of temperature, drought and moisture?*

Consider:

- (a) Those plants that drop their leaves each year.
- (b) Those coming from seed each year—annuals.
- (c) Those with thickened root or underground stems—biennials and perennials.
- (d) Those with runners, ascending, climbing and upright stems.
- (e) The leaves of plants which grow in different areas. (See lesson on development of leaves.) In the water; in marshes; in sunshine; in shade, etc.

5. *Do plants within a given area support or hinder each other's growth?*

Consider:

- (a) Plants of the same kind: e. g., ragweed, smart-weed, plaintain, dandelion, cinque-foil, docks, etc.
- (b) Plants of different kinds: e. g., a tree with the various plants which grow about it or upon it; the tendency of certain plants, the chick-weed, for example, to cluster close to the trunk on the ground; the moss area which extends over perhaps only one side of the tree and up to a certain height; the area of lichens extending further up the trunk and on the branches.

(c) The colonization of one plant upon another, the latter furnishing the living substance for the former: e. g., the dodder.

(d) The relation between a vine and the plant supporting it.

(e) The colonization of fungi about and upon dead plants.

(f) The colonization of mosses and lichens upon rocks and elsewhere.

6. *Do plant colonies encroach upon each other, migrate, or become extinct?*

Consider:

(a) The effect upon the undergrowth of an accidental clearing, such as the falling of a tree, in a forest.

(b) Under what conditions grass makes its way. Study the boundaries of grass plots and determine whether it is spreading or not. Search for the reasons.

(c) The effect upon plants when a marsh is drained.

(d) The succession of plant colonies which covers an area, in the various stages through which it passes, from a wet swamp to dry land covered with fine pasturage: rushes, flags, sedges, weeds, etc.

(e) The succession of plants as a dry area becomes converted into a marsh.

7. *Do plant colonies succeed each other in the same area according to the seasons?*

Consider :

(a) An area devoted to early spring flowers—the spring beauty, for example.

(b) An area devoted to phlox, wild geranium, trillium, etc.

(c) An area devoted to golden rod, asters, etc.

(d) The plants which precede and follow each of the foregoing.

(e) Areas which differ physically—wet, dry, high, low, etc.

8. *In what centers, in the landscape, and in what order, do the different forms of animal life appear in the spring?*

NOTE: Keep a record of temperature of air, soil, water, etc.

Consider:

(a) The streams and bodies of water; in the water; on the shore.

(b) The swamps.

(c) The woodlands; on the ground; in the trees.

(d) The soil.

(e) Whether the earliest forms come from the egg, from the hibernating state, or from other parts of the country.

9. *What inducements do the different features of a country present, which favor colonization among animals?*

Consider:

(a) The water: as a source of food; as a means of protection and shelter; as a medium for support and locomotion; as a means of nesting.

(b) The shore areas: between low and high water; sand banks; marshes and swamps; each as a source of food supply, means of protection, etc., as in (a) above.

(c) The drier lowlands: the soil; the long grass, weeds, etc., each considered as in (a) above.

(d) The uplands, hills, cliffs, etc., each considered as in (a) above.

(e) The woodlands: the loam; the leaves; the old logs; the hollow trees; the dead trees, etc., each considered as in (a) above.

10. *By what means do the different forms of animal life adapt themselves to the special features of their surroundings?*

It is interesting to consider in this study, that any given area must present, at least, as many different *aspects* as there are different living forms subsisting within it. As an illustration, a tree may be taken as a center of colonization for certain birds. Still further, the *trunk* of the tree may be taken as a subordinate center, which supports a host of living things, each kind of which corresponds to some particular aspect. Thus, as the tree increases in diameter, its older layers of dead bark break into irregular cracks, which become the haunts of many insects. Attracted by the insects, the bark becomes a center of interest for the little brown creeper, which catches many of them while .it works its way *up* the trunk. But it doubtless overlooks a goodly number, which can be more readily found by the nut hatch, which makes its way *down* the tree.

Again, the sap of the tree has its attractions, which has brought forth a race of sap-suckers, for whom it exists as a special food supply. When the tree-trunk dies, it becomes infested by various kinds of larvæ, that burrow under the bark and in the wood. It is this aspect that rejoices the heart of the red-headed woodpecker, who holds, in this narrow realm, almost a monopoly.

Occasionally, a limb is torn from the tree by a storm, or other accident, and decay sets in and eats its way into the trunk. But the golden-winged woodpeckers, as they dig the soft material out, and make a capacious lodging for their nestlings, might well consider this aspect of the tree-trunk an expression of special providence in their behalf.

Thus, an object which presents so few differences of feature as the tree-trunk, is varied enough in its aspects to support, mainly, at least six species of woodpeckers, to say nothing of the brown creeper, and other birds, that have thought it worth while to cultivate the power to climb, for the sake of those aspects which the woodpeckers consider beneath their notice. The many sides of the tree-trunk which are thus presented to living things, may each be very narrow, and the existing differences may be slight. They cannot be regarded as trivial, however, when one considers the countless numbers of living beings that each one supports.

The intelligibility of this topic will be much enhanced, if each peculiarity of structure and form is tested by the notion that it is a *concession*, (that is, a yielding to a demand,) which the living thing has made to some special feature of the surroundings, which requires that some function be performed in a certain way. Thus, the fin of a fish, as a structure concerned in locomotion, is a concession to the properties of water, which requires that locomotion through it shall be performed in a definite way. The wings of a bird are, in like manner, a concession, that is, a yielding to the demands of the atmosphere, which the latter imposes upon those living things that propose to move through it. See NATURE STUDY AND RELATED SUBJECTS, *Chapter VII.* Also, *The Elements of Organic Evolution*, by David Star Jordan, THE ARENA, May, 1898.

In accordance with the foregoing suggestions, Consider:

  (a) The various adaptations shown by animals that live in the water: for

movement, locomotion, food-getting,
defense, offense, flight, etc.

(b) Adaptations of the animals that live
mostly on land, but seek their food in
water.

(c) Adaptations of those taking food on
land, but seeking safety in the water. (See The Study of a Frog.)

(d) Adaptations of those that take food
from the water, but seek safety on
the land.

(e) Adaptations of those living in the soil;
of those living in decaying wood,
under stones, etc. (See The Study
of the Earth-worm.)

(f) Adaptations of birds, and other animals, living mainly on the surface of
the ground.

(g) Adaptations of those that burrow, or
live in cliffs, etc.

(h) Adaptations of those that colonize in
woodlands; in the tree tops; in the
underbrush; in long grass, etc. Birds,
bumble-bees and field-mice all nest on
the ground; how do animals having
such different structures, find convenience in habits so similar?

11. *What are the most important sources of
the change constantly taking place in the landscape?*
Consider:

(a) The transient changes; the effects of

sunshine and clouds; the morning and evening tints of the sky; reflections from sheets of water, woodlands, hill-sides, etc.

(b) Seasonal; the changes due to vegetation; the earlier and later growths; the blossoms, etc.

(c) The effects due to fertile and barren areas.

(d) The effects of a rainy period; of a dry period; of a high wind.

(e) Those changes which more profoundly and more permanently affect the land-scape.

NUMBER WORK.

1. Find the quantity of water in the soil, about the grass roots, at the earliest signs of growth. (See Directions for these measurements, page 47.)

2. Take the temperature of the air at different times of day, and compare with that of the soil.

3. Observe the extremes of temperature of the soil and air, on cloudy days, and during the night.

4. Calculate the rainfall in cubic feet, barrels, etc., for given areas; e. g., the roots of a tree; a field of grain; a meadow, etc.

5. Calculate, from observations made with the skiameter, the relative intensity of sunshine upon a given area, for the different months.

6. Find the ratio of sunshine to cloudiness, during the spring months.

7. Find the ratio between the length of day and the length of night, during the spring months.

REPRESENTATIVE EXPRESSION.

1. *Drawing.*

(a) Profiles taken in different directions across the landscape, showing slopes, structure as far as it is possible to determine it by observation.

(b) Maps, drawn or modelled, showing courses of streams, marsh areas, woodlands, etc.

2. *Painting.* (For data to accompany the paintings, see Number Work.)

(a) Continue daily landscape sketches, which will show, through color, the gradual advent of spring.

(b) A series of sketches, at least once a week, showing the opening of different kinds of buds.

(c) A series of paintings, showing the development of a plant, from the root to the seed; as, for example, the dandelion, dock, burdock, thistle, etc.

(d) A series of paintings, showing the story of a plant from seed to seed.

XXXVI.

SPRING STUDIES. ANIMAL LIFE.

GENERAL OBSERVATIONS: Keep a sharp lookout for the earliest signs of spring that are evident in the reappearance and activity in animal life. Bear well in mind the points studied in Chapter XIV which relate to the preparation of animals for winter. Make a calendar which will show the dates and the order in which the various forms of life appear.

QUERIES:

1. *What surroundings seem to present the most favorable conditions for the early appearance of animals in the spring?*

Consider:

(a) The ponds and streams: look among leaves, etc., at the bottom and along the shores. Take the temperature of the water.

(b) The earth: look under stones, old logs, in newly-turned-up ground. Take the temperature of the soil.

(c) The air: look for the earliest appearance of gnats or mosquitoes, and other insects in the air. Take the maximum and minimum temperature of the air each day.

(d) Trees and other plants: look about the bark and in the earth about the roots; especially, as the tree starts its early growths.

2. *What forms of animal life are best able to make an early appearance in the spring?*

Procure a net, with a long handle, and use it for a dredge in the ponds. A dipper, made of tin, and having a *fine* wire cloth bottom, fitted to a long handle, is useful in dredging. With this, many forms of aquatic life and insect larvæ may be found. These may be kept under observation in glass jars or aquaria.

Consider:

(a) The forms found in the water: fishes, crawfishes, tadpoles, water beetles and other aquatic insects.

(b) The shore life: frogs, turtles, wading birds.

(c) The land forms: earth-worms, insects; mammals—gophers, squirrels, chipmunks, field mice,. etc.; snakes and birds.

(d) Whether the earliest forms are migratory or hibernating in winter habits.

3. *Upon what features of their surroundings do the early forms depend?*

Consider:

(a) Food—animal and vegetable.

(b) Temperature and moisture.
(c) Condition of the soil: its temperature.
(d) The condition of vegetation.
(e) The simultaneous appearance of other forms of animal life.

4. *How do animals suit themselves to the surrounding conditions?*

Those conditions upon which the animal (or plant) depends for its life, and for all the details of living make up what is called its *environment*. It is well to consider to what extent a group of animals, of different kinds, *living within the same area*, have a common interest in the *same environment*. For example, a field-mouse, a snake, a bird, an earth-worm and an insect, may be found within the same meadow or pasture. Does each really have the same lively interest in the same features of this environment? Again, wood-peckers, robins, snipe, quail, bob-o-links and bitterns may be found within the same area, and they are all birds; do they each really depend upon the same environment? Select any rather small area, and, making a list of the various living forms found within it,

Consider :

(a) The dependence of each upon direct sunshine.
(b) The dependence of each upon air.
(c) The relation of each to the surface of the earth; to the soil beneath the surface.

(d) The relation of each to water.

(e) The relation of each to temperature.

(f) The food supply of each.

(g) In establishing and preserving these relationships, to what extent the different forms are brought into conflict: how conflicts are avoided.

(h) The conflicts of animals with others of their kind, compared with their conflicts with animals of a different type.

(i) The incentives to community life.

(j) The incentives which lead to isolation of individuals.

5. *To what extent may a correspondence be traced between details of structure and features of environment?*

In this study it is well to bear in mind that *all forms* of animal life in the process of living have the *same problems* to solve. Thus, no matter where or how the animal lives, there must be a bodily income of nutritive matter which makes up the bodily substance; this constitutes the food supply. There must also be another source of income from the atmosphere —*the oxygen*—and the process by which this gas is obtained is the essential thing in respiration. This unites with the bodily substance, resulting in heat and the freeing of energy, which is directed in various ways as work power. (See Lesson XI, page 95, *et seq.*) The tissues, torn down by oxygen, then exist as waste products, which must be thrown off; this is accomplished, partly by the process of respiration and partly by the kidneys, in the higher animals, and by means of the surface covering of the body. The distribution of the digested food, the gathering up and conveyance of the wastes to the different points of discharge is the essential function of the machinery of circulation, whether that be simple or complex. The automatic control of the various working parts of the animal, or their direction by its will, proceeds from another center of structure, which is composed, in the higher forms, of the nervous tissues of the body. And, finally, there is, in each case, a provision for a continuation of the species through some process of reproduction. In the exercise of these really fundamental functions of life, animals have assumed every conceivable form, that not a cubic foot of space may remain unoccupied. To hold their own, they have adopted every possible mode of movement, every hue of color, every manner of concealment, defense and attack. Whether the animal is but a minute, jelly-like speck, showing no distinct organs of any kind, or whether it is the highly complex being that man is, it cannot escape these common problems. It can only vary, and possibly improve, in its method of solving them.

The study of animals, therefore, resolves itself into finding definite answers to a very few specific questions, as follows:

(1.) Its nutrition: food getting, digestion and assimilation.

(2.) The development of its energy or work power: respiration.

(3.) The direction of its energy and its control: the movements and sensibility.

(4.) The conveyance and distribution of materials within the body: the circulation.

(5.) The riddance of waste materials: excretion.

(6.) Its relations to other forms: social life, concealment, defense. attack.

A. In the study of food-getting,

Consider:

    (a) How the place where the food is found —water, land or air—affects the form and structure of the body.

    (b) To what extent the kind of food gives form and character to the body as a whole.

    (c) How it affects the mode of movement.

    (d) How it affects the form and use of the limbs.

    (e) How it affects the way in which the body is supported by the limbs.

    (f) How the kind of food and the way it is obtained affects the shape of the head; the shape, size, direction and the movement of the jaws.

    (g) Where the *mechanical* part of digestion occurs: that is, that part that in

many animals is performed chiefly by
the teeth.

(h) The different kinds of teeth needed in
food-getting, and the use of each kind.

(i) Does food-getting affect the position of
the eyes.

(j) How the tongue assists in food-getting.

(k) How the food supply affects the habits
of the animal at different seasons.

B. In the study of respiration,
Consider:

(a) The surroundings which favor lung
structure.

(b) The conditions which enable the animal to use its skin as a respiratory
surface.

(c) The conditions under which the gill
structure is found.

(d) The conditions favoring the air-tube
structure, as in insect life.

(e) The form of the body adapted to lung
structure; the relation of the lungs to
the digestive tract; the respiratory
muscles and their movements in
breathing.

(f) The structure and form of the body
when gills are present.

In this study, the pupils should carefully examine the lungs of a sheep, or calf, or of some
other mammal. The lungs of a bird may be
examined when it is being dressed for the

table. It will also be of great interest to examine the lung of a frog, comparing its simpler form with that of the mammal and bird; also, the lungs of a snake, one being rudimentary and the other long and narrow to suit the shape of the body. The pupils should learn something of the size, position and outline of their own lungs. A slide showing a section of the lung viewed through a microscope is exceedingly instructive. The importance of the respiratory function is implied in the relatively large surface that is set apart for this purpose in the various animals studied. In the human lungs, the lung area—that is, the area that would be covered if all the small air sacs were cut open and spread out—has been estimated to be 2,600 square feet. (Refer to Chapter XII, page 107.) Some idea of the lightness and delicacy of the lung tissue may be gained by inflating the lungs by blowing in through a tube inserted in the windpipe or a bronchial tube. Consider the use of the cartilage rings in the tubes.

C. In the study of movements,

Consider:

    (a) Those made in food-getting—locomotion and prehension.

    (b) The three-fold work of the muscles: that of merely supporting the body in its upright position, that of moving the body from place to place, and that of simply moving various parts.

(c) The relative importance of these three uses in different animals. Compare, in this respect, the fish and earth-worm with the bird, the horse, and man.

(d) The movements concerned in prehension in man, the monkey, the squirrel, the cat, the dog, the horse, the cow, the earth-worm, the fish.

(e) How the form of the body varies according to the movements.

(f) The offensive and defensive movements.

(g) The life of an animal that is fixed compared with the life of one having powers of locomotion.

(h) The relation of locomotion to intelligence.

It is interesting to note that in man the problem of supporting the body is given over almost entirely to one pair of limbs, and that the other pair has developed the greatest prehensile power. As one moves along the line of animal life and finds the fore-limbs sharing more and more the function of support, the problem of prehension, to a corresponding degree, is assumed by other parts of the body, as the jaws, lips, teeth, tongue, etc. In the fish, from the nature of the medium in which it lives, both the problems of support and prehension are removed from the limbs, and they have been reduced almost to insignificance; the problem of locomotion is solved chiefly by the curious development of the tail fin.

D. In the study of the circulation,
Consider:

(a) The heart-beats, as they may be observed by counting the pulse-beats. Note the variation when sitting, standing, and after exercise.

(b) The pulse-beats in different animals.

(c) If possible, the blood-flow should be witnessed by means of a microscope, as it takes place in the external gills of a very young tadpole; in the tadpole's tail, or in the web of a frog's foot. The circulation may also be seen in the body and legs of a very young spider.

(d) Procure from a butcher, the heart ot a sheep; cleanse it in cold water. If it is necessary to preserve the specimen for any length of time, it may be placed in salt water, to which a small amount of alum has been added. The heart and lungs may be procured together, and the course of the circulation between them may be readily studied. To dissect the heart, it is, perhaps, simplest to begin at the lower end, or apex. One inch from the point, make a transverse section. Note the double cavity, and the wall separating them. Consider, also, the difference in the thickness of the walls of the two cavities—what this means in work that is done. By carefully slitting the two chambers upward, the internal valvular arrangement is easily seen. Note the opening leading from each of the lower chambers, which are called ventricles, into the upper chambers, which are called auricles. Compare the thickness of the walls of the two auricles. Compare these two chambers with the ventricles. The blood passes from the right auricle into the right ventricle; thence to the lungs; thence, through the left auricle into the left ventricle, and then into the aorta. Spread over the outside of the heart, are some of the vessels concerned in its nourishment. Compare the tissue found in the walls of the heart, with lean meat. Compare the tissue in the valves, with the thin covering of the heart. Note, in the walls of the ventricles, the small elevations called papillæ, to which the valve-cords are attached. The heart is, in reality, a hollow muscle, which, by contracting, diminishes its cavity, thus forcing the blood out into the arteries and veins.

As a reference, use any good physiology for a further description.

E. In the study of excretion, that is, the mode by which the body gets rid of its waste material,

Consider:

(a) What was said, in Lesson XII, about the excretion of carbonic acid gas from the lungs.

(b) What is thrown off from the body through the skin; the perspiration.

(c) How perspiration differs from pure water. Test with litmus paper. Evaporate a drop on clean glass.

(d) The third organ of excretion, the kidneys. Specimens of sheep's kidneys may be obtained from the butcher, and their gross structure is readily understood. .Note the fleshy outer part, which is permeated through and through with minute blood-vessels, called capillaries, through the walls of which the waste material escapes into the cavity of the kidney, called its pelvis; from this cavity, the waste, in solution, is carried outside the body.

F. In the study of the animal's relations to other forms,

Consider:

(a) The social habits—whether they live singly, in pairs, or in communities.

(b) The marks by which they seem to be

rendered attractive to each other—
the colors.

(c) The colors which seem to be designed
as a means of concealment.

(d) The defensive structures: spines, shells,
hairs or bristles, offensive odors or
secretions.

(e) Means of offense: teeth, claws, beaks,
heels, &c.

G. In accordance with the foregoing suggestions, make a study of the life of a frog.

Consider:

(a) The character of the surface upon which
he lives, and his mode of movement;
the structure and character of his
legs.

(b) Whether he walks or runs, and his
resting position; compare the structure
of the fore and hind limbs.

(c) The color of the body; the color of his
surroundings.

(d) The relation of the under side to the
surface; the color of the under side.

(e) His movements on the surface and in
the water; the form of the body, the
relative length of the legs, the foot
structure, the protection of the eyes,
absence of projecting ears.

(f) The character of the food; the mouth
structure, and movements of the
tongue.

(g) Whether the food is masticated; the structure of the jaws and teeth.

(h) His food lives on land; adapted to breathe by lungs.

(i) Escapes some of his enemies by taking to water; his skin acts also in the capacity of lungs.

(j) Does not migrate; hibernates in mud; skin acts as lungs.

(k) Blood partially ærated through the skin; spends his time in damp situations. The respiratory surface is always a thin, moist membrane.

(l) True ribs and diaphragm absent; note the throat movements in breathing.

(m) No parental care for the young; eggs laid in water, in great quantities. Count a small mass of eggs, and weigh them; by weighing, then estimate the number of eggs laid by a frog.

(n) Tadpoles live in water; provided with gills; tail for swimming.

(o) Tadpoles vegetable feeders; alimentary canal relatively longer than in the frog.

(p) Adult frog betakes himself to land; acquires legs and lungs; loses tail.

(q) Compare the toad with the frog, in accordance with the foregoing outline.

H. In a similar manner, make a study of the earth-worm.

Consider:

(a) How it pushes its way through the earth; its spindle-shaped body.

(b) How it habitually pushes with the same end; Compare the shape of this one end with the other.

(c) For a greater part of its time it is surrounded by the equal influences of the soil; a cross section of its body is circular.

(d) Sometimes it rests and moves on the surface, air above and soil beneath, with the force of gravity acting downward, along cross diameters of its body; it has a distinct upper and under side, and section of its body is not an exact circle, but somewhat elliptical.

(e) Small burrows, supplied with a limited amount of air; it has a large exposure of breathing surface, that is the skin of the entire body.

(f) In mid-day, in cloudless weather, the surface is heated by the sun; it can safely come to the surface only on damp, cloudy days, or at night. A breathing surface must be kept moist.

(g) Its burrow protects it on all sides; its movements are slow and cautious; its skin is thin; a breathing surface must not only be moist, it must be delicate.

(h) Its burrows are dark, and it comes to

the surface regularly only at night; it is blind; searches for food without leaving its burrow entirely.

(i) In the day time it lies near the surface, probably for the sake of pure air; this brings it within the reach of birds.

(j) The body is supported by the walls of the burrow, and flexibility is of great importance; there is no skeleton, and the muscles are arranged in two sets, circular and longitudinal.

NOTE. Study the movements of a worm upon the surface; note the alternate contraction and relaxation of the two sets of muscles. The contraction of the longitudinal muscles tends to shorten the body from both ends. By rubbing the sides of the body with the finger-tips, it is easy to discover the spines, or setæ, which are thrust out as the body elongates; these, by pointing backward, give fixed hold to the front, and the hind end is, therefore, pulled up. Compare the movement of the worm with that of a snake; the latter depends somewhat upon his ribs in moving.

(k) The food of the worm is decaying vegetation, sometimes mingled with soil; the worm is provided with a strong gizzard, which takes the place of teeth.

(l) Its entire life is passed in surroundings which change but little; the worm shows no special changes in form or structure.

(m) Its food, for a long period, is unavailable; migration impossible; it hibernates.

6. *What relation does the work of the earthworm bear to the life of plants, and the condition of the soil?*

Consider:

(a) The effect of the soil being made porous about the roots of plants, admitting the air and water.

(b) The effect of the lower layers of the soil being brought to the surface.

OBSERVATION: Measure off, in various places, small squares, a yard or more in size; carefully clear this of all castings that may be found upon it. At the end of twenty-four hours, gather the fresh castings that have been brought to the surface; thoroughly dry these, and weigh them; by means of a cubical box, find the volume. Calculate the amount of earth thus brought to the surface, that would be found upon an acre.

(c) In the same way, make a study of other animals, as they appear in the spring; birds; those which live in the trees, as the woodpeckers; those which find their food in the ground, as the robins; those which make their home in marshes, as the heron and bittern; those that find their living in the streams and ponds, as the ducks; those that take their food in the water, as the gulls. The crawfish, finding its food in the water, making its home at the bottom of the streams; the turtles, living partly on land, and partly in water; the insects, living in the ground, under stones, logs and rubbish; those that live about the trees, under the bark, and on the leaves; those that spend much of their time on the wing, in the air, and visiting flowers.

7. *From what sources does animal life make its appearance in the spring?*

Consider:

   (a) The ponds and streams; using a dredge net, procure the larvæ of insects from the water, which may be preserved in jars until the transformation takes place.
   (b) Observe the cocoons that have been preserved through the winter; note the time and the temperature at which the transformation into the perfect insect takes place.
   (c) Observe the transformation of the various grubs that may be found in the ground.
   (d) The return of the birds; their problems, mating, nesting, laying eggs, care of the young.

(e) The reappearance of the aquatic forms of life; the fish, crawfish, turtle, water beetle, and the larvæ of insects.

8. *What relationships may be observed between insects and plants in the spring?*

Consider:

(a) The work upon the leaves, the formation of galls, the leaf-rollers, the leaf-miners.

(b) The stings on the stems, which are thereby transformed into irregular forms.

(c) The borers, working under the bark, in the trunks of the trees.

(d) Those that live in the ground, about the roots of the plant.

(e) How the plant is used for food.

(f) How it is used as a nesting place.

(g) How it is used as a depository for eggs.

(h) How it becomes transformed to feed the young larvæ.

NUMBER WORK.

QUERIES:

A. *What temperature is necessary to support animal life in the spring?*

1. What is the temperature of the water during the week when the first crawfishes appear?

2. What is the average temperature of the air?

3. What is the average temperature of the soil when the earth-worms first appear?

4. What is the average temperature of the air noticed at the first appearance of insects?

5. What is the temperature of the air when the moths leave the cocoons?

B. *What is the ratio of land to water life?*

1. How many different forms of animal life can you find in the water?

2. How many different forms of animal life can you find on the land?

3. What is the ratio of the number of animals found on land to the number found in water?

4. How many different kinds of animals live partly on land and partly in water?

5. How many different kinds live in water, but procure their food on land? How many live on land but procure their food in the water?

6. Of all the different kinds of animals observed, what part lives upon vegetable food? What part lives upon animal food?

7. What part of the entire number of animals observed breathe by lungs?

8. What part of the entire number observed are adapted for breathing in water?

NOTE.—For problems relating to respiration, see Page 109.

C. *The circulation of the blood?*

1. What is the average number of heart-

beats per minute? Find this by counting the pulse-beats in the wrist.

2. Compare the number of heart-beats per minute when sitting with the number taken when standing; compare these with the number when walking.

3. Run 100 yards, and again count the pulse-beats.

4. At each pulse-beat the heart discharges six ounces of blood; how many ounces are discharged by this organ in one hour? In a day?

5. By what per cent. is its work increased when one changes from a sitting to a standing position?

6. By what part is its work increased by running 100 yards?

7. Count the respirations per minute. What is the ratio of the number of respirations to the number of heart-beats per minute?

8. Find increase, if any, of respirations in changing from the sitting to the standing position.

9. In running 100 yards, by what part is the work of respiration increased?

10. After running 100 yards, what is the ratio of the number of respirations to the number of heart-beats per minute.

11. Is the ratio between the respirations and heart-beats the same after exercise that it is when at rest?

12. Following the suggestions on Page 109

find the increase in the volume of air breathed in each respiration after running 100 yards.

D. *The relations of animals and plants.*

1. What part of the number of animals observed seems to be colored with a view to concealment? What part of this number is made conspicuous by its color?

2. What part of the leaves of the oak are in some way used by insects? By what per cent. is the weight of the leaf increased when a gall is formed? Take the average weight of 25 leaves.

3. Compare the number so used of the oak with those similarly used of the maple, of the ash, the boxelder, the willow, the elm.

4. Find the percentage of buds that are stung or otherwise used by insects on various plants.

5. Find the percentage of young twigs that are distorted through insect depredations.

REPRESENTATIVE EXPRESSION.

1. *Drawing.*

   (a) Make a series of drawings showing the various means by which animals defend themselves.

   (b) Make a series of drawings showing the various means used by animals in the prehension of food.

   (c) Make a series of drawings showing the means employed by various animals in locomotion.

(d) Make a series of drawings showing the forms of teeth used by animals in masticating their food.

2. *Painting.*

(a) Make a series of paintings, showing how animals protect themselves by coloration.

(b) Make a sketch of the landscape, showing the spring colors.

XXXVII.

PLANT STUDY.   GERMINATION.

OBSERVATION.   Begin the study of germinating seeds when the plantlets first make their
appearance outdoors.   Even before this, take
the temperature of the soil, as well as that of
the air, daily, that the degree of heat necessary
for sprouting may be approximately determined.   Note the peculiarity of the areas where
the young plants appear earliest: the nature of
the soil; its slope; surface bare or grassy; soil
loose or compact.   Measure off areas for special
observation.

It must be remembered that the seed cannot
realize its aspirations to become a plant unless
it is able to solve certain definite problems by
chosen means that are correspondingly definite.
The study of germination is, therefore, a careful consideration of what the seed has to do,
and an investigation of the way and means it
employs in doing it, as it establishes those relationships with moisture, heat, light, air, etc.,
which enable it to change from an embryo to
a mature plant.

QUERIES:

1. *At what temperature of soil and air do
seeds begin to sprout?*

Select certain typical areas, and
Consider:

(a) The temperature at various levels below the surface, down to a foot or more in depth.

(b) The temperature in wet and dry soils. If possible, make this and the following observations both in daylight and at night—at least after the sun has set.

(c) The temperature of shady and sunny locations.

(d) The temperature of compact and loose soils; of clayey, loamy and sandy soils.

(e) The temperature of grassy and bare ground.

(f) The depth in each case where the temperature becomes constant.

(g) The temperature of the water when the earliest growth of water plants is observed. Compare with temperature of the adjacent soil; with the mud from which they grow.

(h) The temperature of the water when algæ make their earliest appearance.

(i) The kinds of plants that sprout at the lowest temperatures. (See Number Work.)

2. *Do the earliest germinating plants make provision for the uncertainties in temperature of the early season?*

Consider:

(a) The effects of a freeze upon the plant-lets.

(b) The advantages afforded by location.

(c) To what extent the distribution of the plants is affected by the habit of early germination.

(d) The position of the seed-leaves (coty-ledons), above or below the surface.

(e) The position assumed by the leaves at night, or when the temperature is lowered from any cause.

(f) The effects of sunshine, cloudiness and rain upon the position of the leaves.

(g) What later plant habits may depend upon early germination.

(h) Whether early germinating seeds re-quire a long season in which to mature their seeds.

3. *Is the temperature at which the early seeds germinate outdoors the best temperature for their sprouting?*

EXPERIMENT: At or a little before the time when the earliest seeds outdoors begin to sprout, take up a few pots of soil and place them under different conditions of temperature. Some may be placed near a stove or register and others in cooler locations. Make a careful record of the soil and air temperature indoors and out. Keep the moisture conditions as nearly the same as possible. Study and determine, by measurements, the rate of growth under the different conditions. (See Number Work.)

Consider:

    (a) The highest temperature at which growth occurs.

    (b) The lowest temperature.

    (c) The range of temperature within which healthy growth occurs.

4. *By what means does the seed obtain the moisture necessary for germination?*

OBSERVATION: Search for germinating seeds and note the depth at which they are found in the earth.

Consider:

    (a) Whether any germinate while lying on the surface.

    (b) Whether the seeds have any special device for self-planting.

    (c) Whether any are planted too deep for germination.

    (d) What relations must be formed by the young plant which determine its proper depth.

EXPERIMENT: Select a square foot of ground in some area known to be self-seeded by various weeds. Take the soil from the square foot to a depth of 2 inches and place it in a pan under conditions which will be favorable for the germination of any seeds that it may contain. Place the 2 inches of soil found immediately below the first layer into a second pan under conditions as before suggested. In a similar manner arrange two or three successive layers of soil taken at depths of 6, 8 and 10 inches below the surface. Count the number of seeds that germinate in each pan, and in this way determine the depth to which seeds may be planted by natural agencies. The experiment may be extended so as to include a layer of much greater depth, thus determining the maximum depth at which certain seeds may be found. As the young plantlets appear they may be removed, and the number of germinating seeds per square foot may be counted. It is often surprisingly large.

5. *How much moisture in the soil is at the disposal of the germinating seeds?*

Note.—For directions for recording rainfall, see page 29.

Experiment: Take a few cubic inches of earth from various depths, weigh, dry, and calculate the amount of water per cubic foot.

6. *In what way is the rate of absorption and the amount of water absorbed by seeds affected by different temperatures?*

Experiment: Weigh a few grams, each, of corn, beans, morning-glory and other seeds, conveniently obtained, and soak them, for an hour or more, in water with a temperature uniformly about 60°. Try other lots of the same seeds, in water, for the same time, with temperature 20° higher and 20° lower than 60°. Weigh the seeds again, after having dried them with blotting paper, and calculate the quantity of water absorbed at the different temperatures. Note the relative amount of water absorbed by the various kinds of seeds. Find out if seeds absorb all the moisture possible, when germinating in the ground, by planting different kinds in soil with normal moisture and weighing at the first sign of germination.

7. *To what extent is force exerted during the process of absorption?*

Experiments:

A. Fill a bottle, having a neck just large enough to admit the dry seeds, with beans or corn, or some other kind of seeds. Pour upon them all the water the bottle will hold, and, as it is absorbed, add more water. The best way is to completely immerse the bottle, with the seeds, in a larger vessel of water. When they begin to swell, some of the seeds may be made to lie crosswise at the lower end of the neck of the bottle, and thus effectually stop it. The bottle will eventually burst, sometimes with a loud report.

B. Procure two pieces of gas pipe, one, 1½ inch, and the other, small enough to slip easily inside the larger. The pieces may be about 1 foot in length. Screw to one end of each a metal cap, and in the one fitted to the smaller pipe, drill a small hole. A plumber or gas-fitter will prepare the pipes for a trifling sum. Pour into the larger pipe, a given depth, say 3 inches, of beans, the weight of which is known; slip the smaller pipe, cap end first, down upon the seeds. By means of a stiff scantling, arrange a lever so that it will rest across the end of the smaller pipe, as it projects out of the larger, and suspend, from the power end, a known weight. Fill the inner tube with water, which will find its way, through the hole in the cap, down among the seeds, as it is absorbed by them. Note the distance which the inner tube is lifted as the seeds swell, and, by a calculation based upon the ratio between the arms of the lever, determine the weight lifted while the water is being absorbed. Test the lifting power of different kinds of seeds.

C. Half fill a Mason jar with seeds and add enough water having the temperature of the room to start germination. Take the temperature at regular intervals and note the results. What inference may be made from the changes in temperature observed?

8. *Is the germination of seeds dependent upon light?*

Consider:

    (a) The relation which the question of depth has to this query.

    (b) Whether the depth that a seed is planted is determined by its relations to light and moisture.

EXPERIMENT: Place in two jars or shallow pans a layer of cotton or blotting paper, soak it with water, and spread upon this a number of different kinds of seeds. Cover both to prevent loss of water by evaporation and cover one vessel so as to exclude all light. Keep the vessels together to insure a similarity of temperature and

Consider:

    (a) The length of time required to sprout the seeds.

    (b) The percentage of seeds germinating in each case.

9. *Are germinating seeds favored by a circulation of air?*

Consider :

    (a) Whether, at the depth seeds in the soil, when seeds usually germinate, there is air circulation.

    (b) The agencies that tend to keep the soil porous.

    (c) The effect of cultivation; work of worms and insects; roots of plants.

    (d) The agencies tending to bring about a flow of air into the upper layers of the soil, and out again—*earth-breathing*.

    (e) The effect of variation of heat, day and night.

    (f) The effect of variation of air pressure, as indicated by the barometer.

EXPERIMENTS :

A. Arrange two vessels, one, a Mason jar, for example, that may be lightly capped, and the other, a shallow pan, which will freely expose the seeds to the air. In the bottom of each vessel arrange a layer of moist cotton, or blotting paper, as described above, [Query 8, (b) Experiment], and upon each place a variety of seeds. Seal the jar air-tight, but preserve all other conditions most favorable for growth. As before, observe the time necessary for germination, and note the percentage of seeds that sprout in each lot.

B. When satisfied as to the result of Experiment A, remove the cap from the jar, and test the gaseous contents of the jar, by lowering into it a burning splinter, or, better still, a short piece of a candle, fastened to a bent wire. The test should be made before the seeds begin to decay.

10. *Is the presence of air necessary for germination?*

EXPERIMENT : Procure a strong bottle, and fit it with a rubber stopper, perforated with a single hole. Insert a glass tube through the hole, and bend the outer part, which should be several inches long, in the form of a right angle. Arrange a layer of different sorts of seeds, upon wet cotton, at the bottom of the bottle, and, by means of an air-pump connected with the glass tube, exhaust the air as completely as possible, and place under all other conditions necessary for germination. The bottle may be sealed by melting the glass tube, and drawing it apart, between the pump and the stopper, or by connecting the tube with the pump, by a rubber tube, which may be clamped. Observe the changes in the seeds, and note the length of time covered by the experiment.

B. When satisfactory results under A are obtained, test with a lighted splinter, as before directed, the gaseous contents of the bottle.

NOTE. At the suggestion of the author, an air-pump has been prepared, under the direction of Mr. Hays, of the Chicago Normal School, by reversing the valves in an ordinary bicycle pump, which gives about 90 to 95 % vacuum. This pump can be furnished at the very low cost of one dollar, which places it within the reach of every teacher. It is needless to state, that this single piece of apparatus opens up a wide range of interesting experimental work.

11. *Does the germinating seed acquire new material from its surroundings from the beginning?*

Consider:

(a) The change in size and form.

EXPERIMENT: Place a *known weight of dry seeds*, beans, corn, peas, etc., under proper conditions for germination. Divide each kind of seeds into several lots, the weight of each being known, so that they may be examined in succession. When the end of the germ makes its appearance, examine one lot; first, dry them thoroughly, and then weigh; compare with the original weight. Later, as the seeds sprout in the remaining lots, dry and weigh, and compare with the original weight.

(b) At what stage the weight is permanently increased.

(c) The variation among seeds in this respect.

(d) The rate of increase, after the plantlet begins to root itself in the ground.

(e) From what source the plant draws its first food from without.

(f) By what agency the earliest outside food is supplied.

NOTE: An interesting comparison may be made by making the same observations as those suggested above, upon plants that have been grown under covers that entirely exclude the light.

12. *As germination takes place, in what order do the various parts appear, and how are they formed?*

OBSERVATION: Gather a great number of sprouting seeds and young plantlets, that may be found in any waste piece of ground.

Consider:

(a) What parts have appeared in addition to those found in the seeds.

(b) What parts of the original seed continue to develop in the plantlet.

(c) What becomes of the the parts of the

seeds that do not remain as such as the plantlet grows.

The parts of a seed easily recognizable in a large bean, as typical of a large class of seeds, are,

I. The markings on the seed, the *hilum*, or *scar;* the *micropyle, (little gate)* near the hilum.

II. The seed coats: the outer, the *testa;* the inner, the *tegmen.*

III. The two parts into which it is easily separable, the *cotyledons.*

IV. The small stem below the cotyledons, the *hypocotyl.*

V. The small, leafy part above the cotyledons, the *epicotyl.* The seeds with two easily separable parts, as in the case of beans, peas, squash, maple, and many others, are called *dicotyledons. (Adjective, dicotyledonous.)*

Seeds like corn, with but one cotyledon, are called *monocotyledons. (Monocotyledonous.)* Compare this kind of seed, in other respects, with a dicotyledon.

(d) As the seed unfolds, what forms of growth, and what movements are due to efforts to establish its relation with moisture? With the soil?

(e) What forms and movements are due to efforts to establish its relation to the light?

(f) How the plantlet makes its way to the surface of the soil.

(g) How it gets outside of its seed-coats.

(h) The meaning of the sticky substance that is found on the outside of squash, gourd, and some other seeds, when they are moistened. Moisten these seeds and let them germinate on the *surface* of the ground. Note the adherence.

(i) The meaning of the arching of the hypocotyl in the early stages of germination.

(j) The anchorage by the roots.

(k) The effect upon form and direction of growth of the various parts, of planting in different positions.

(l) The most favorable position for the bean; the pea; the grain of corn; the squash.

(m) The causes which determine whether the cotyledons shall appear above ground, or remain below the surface. .

13. *Is there a tendency to form plant colonies?*

Consider:

(a) Whether the seeds found germinating are all of one kind.

(b) Whether the struggle is the greatest between plants of the same kind, or between those of different kinds.

NUMBER WORK.

A. *The Temperature of Germination.*

1. What is the difference between the tem-

perature of the air, maximum, and the temperature of the soil, at the depth of the seeds when they begin to germinate?

2. What is the difference between the temperature of the soil, in the layer where the seeds sprout, and that of a layer 18 inches below the surface? Make these tests in the early days of spring, when germination is first noticed.

3. What is the difference between the temperature of the water in which plants are growing, (maximum in 24 hours,) and the corresponding temperature of the adjacent soil?

4. What is the difference in temperature, between bare and packed earth, and adjacent grassy soil?

B. *The distribution of sunshine; cloudiness; rainfall.*

5. By means of the skiameter; find the area covered by a given beam of noon sunshine, and compare with the area covered a month earlier; the present area covered, is what per cent. of the area covered then?

6. The intensity of noon sunshine, at present, is what per cent. of that a month ago?

7. The cloudiness, the month when germination is studied, bears what ratio to the sunshine?

8. How much water during that month, is secured, per square yard, in rainfall? Per acre? Per square mile?

9. What is the average rainfall, per cloudy day, during the month? Per rainy day? Compare with the winter months.

C. *The best temperature for germination.*

10. What is the difference between the indoor and the outdoor temperature, at which the same seeds germinate?

11. The difference between the highest and the lowest temperature at which the same seeds germinate?

D. *Moisture in germination.*

12. What per cent. of the weight of the soil, within 1 foot of the surface, is water?

13. What per cent. of the volume of the soil, within 1 foot of the surface, is water?

14. How many gallons of water, within 6 inches of the surface, in an acre? How many barrels?

15. How many barrels of water in an acre, in the lower 6 inches of the first foot of depth?

16. The quantity of water in the soil, within 1 foot of the surface, is the equivalent of how much rainfall?

17. By means of the hygrometer and the Tables, (see pages 18–22,) find the amount of water, per cubic foot, that is suspended in the atmosphere.

18. How many barrels of water in the atmosphere, within 50 feet of the surface, over one acre of ground?

19. Dry beans absorb what per cent. of their weight of water, at a temperature of 40° to 50° Fahr.?

20. Dry corn absorbs what per cent. of its

weight of water, at a temperature of 40° to 50° Fahr.?

21. The weight of water absorbed by the corn, equals what per cent. of the weight absorbed by the beans in the same time?

22. The water absorbed by corn and beans, at a temperature of 40° to 50°, equals what per cent. of that absorbed by each, at a temperature of 70° to 80° in the same time?

23. A given quantity of beans will absorb what per cent. of their volume of water, at a favorable temperature for germination?

24. A given quantity of corn will absorb what per cent. of its volume of water, under favorable conditions for germination?

25. A given weight of beans, will lift how many times its own weight, in absorbing water? (See Experiment, under 7).

26. Find the number of times its own weight, a given quantity of corn will lift, in absorbing water.

27. In problems 25 and 26, find by what per cent. the volume of seeds increased, under the weights employed.

E. *Light and air in germination.*

28. Compare the length of time required by seeds to germinate, in the light, with that required by those kept under similar conditions, but in the dark.

29. In the same way, determine the ratios of the times required by seeds which are supplied with air, to those from which it is withdrawn.

F. *The addition of new material through growth.*

30. Weigh a number of selected beans, grains of corn, or other seeds of uniform size; find the average weight of the seeds when *dry*.

31. Plant the seeds: when germination begins, take up a few of the young plantlets, on successive days, and thoroughly dry; weigh, and compare with the weight of the dry seeds.

32. What is the ratio which expresses the amount of new material built up in the plant, in the first, second and third weeks? Take the average of several plants.

G. *The vitality of seeds.*

33. Arrange a known number of seeds, not less than 100 of each kind, upon blotting paper, arranged to afford proper conditions for germination; what per centage of the seeds fail to germinate?

34. Test wheat; if 1.5 bushels are required to sow an acre, allowing for the bad seed, how much should a farmer sow?

35. In the same way, with the other samples, for each bushel of seed needed, find out how much should be used, allowing for seed that will not germinate.

H. *The number of germinating seeds, and their chances for maturing.*

36. Select areas of 1 yard square, in various localities, and count the seeds that germinate on the spot, within a space of 1, 2 and 3 weeks,

in early spring. Pull up the germinating plants, each day, as the count is made. What is the average number per square yard?

37. Select an area of a square yard, in various localities, and each week, count the plantlets that have germinated, but have died, from some cause; what is the percentage of loss?

38. What is the ratio which will express the loss, week by week, during April? During May?

39. After a hard frost, or late freeze, what percentage of a given group of germinating plantlets, is found to be killed?

REPRESENTATIVE EXPRESSION.

1. *Drawing.*

   (a) Begin with the *earliest* seeds found germinating outdoors, and make a serial list of drawings of different plantlets, as they appear. Note, by each specimen represented, the name, if possible, date, temperature of air, temperature of soil, location, exposed or protected, shady or sunny. The *order* of germination, thus represented, will form an interesting plant calendar. Note the varying relative length between the root and stem. Record measurements.

   (b) Depict the problems of germination: select a few large seeds, such as an acorn, castor bean, corn, bean, squash, morning-glory, sunflower, and nasturtium. At the proper, and different stages of germination in each, select specimens, and show by a drawing: (a) How the plant solves its problem of piercing its seed-coat—involving the structure about the micropyle. (b) How the seed solves its problem of .getting moisture. (c) How the seed solves the problem of getting rid of its seed-coat. (d) How the plant solves its problem of forming its relation to light.

2. *Painting.*

(a) Show, by a series of paintings, how and where the plant gradually acquires its colors. Note the relation of the various parts to the light.

(b) Paint a landscape, each week, showing the gradual incoming of the color that bespeaks the renewal of life.

XXXVIII.

PLANT STUDY. DEVELOPMENT OF LEAVES.

OBSERVATIONS: In earliest spring, make careful averages of the results recorded in the *Science Record*, (see page 24). Especially, a careful record of the temperature, soil and air, cloudiness, sunshine and rainfall, is necessary. Note the earliest appearance of the swelling of buds. Refer to the suggestions on pp. 47–50, for soil study, temperature, moisture, and loss by evaporation, and thus find out what stores of moisture and heat the plant draws upon, in opening its buds. Select a tree for special study during the spring.

QUERIES:

1. *What is the order of succession that may be established among plants, with reference to the times of bud unfolding?*

Consider:

    (a) The kinds of trees; make a list, showing the order in which the buds unfold.

    (b) Whether bud unfolding or germination is the earlier in the spring.

    (c) Whether the earliest buds to unfold are leaf buds or flower buds.

2. *Do all the buds formed on the previous year's growth unfold?*

Consider:

(a) The position of those first to unfold.
(b) The position of those last to unfold, or which may not unfold at all.
(c) Whether buds on the older shoots unfold.

As to *activity*, buds may be
  Active; those which unfold, or
  Dormant; those which do not unfold.

As to *position*, buds may be
  Terminal; at the end of the twig, or
  Lateral; arranged along the sides of the branch.

Lateral buds may be
  Axillary; when produced in the axil of the leaf, i. e., the upper angle between the last year's leaf and the branch.

Accessory; buds clustered about the axillary bud.

Adventitious; buds produced irregularly on the branch or trunk. They often form when the other buds are destroyed.

The points on the stem, at which buds are produced, are called the *nodes;* the spaces between the nodes are called internodes.

3. *What precautions are adopted by the young leaflets, in adapting themselves to their new surroundings?*

Consider:

(a) How the surroundings of the leaf change as it emerges from its bud coverings; the new things with which it must establish helpful relations.

(b) The forces from which it needs some protection.

(c) The special problems which the bud has to solve, which develops on an *underground stem or root.* Examples: May-apple, Calumus, Iris, Potato, Onion, Trillium, and those buds from which sprouts grow, on roots of trees. Compare the form assumed by the developing underground bud, with that of the germinating seed. Compare the problems of the two forms.

(d) The meaning of the special manner of folding in the bud, which is exhibited in different leaves.

(e) The wrinkling of the young leaf surface.

(f) The side that is turned sunward as the leaf unfolds.

(g) The position of the unfolding leaf.

(h) The sticky varnish that sometimes appears on the young leaf.

(i) The presence of hairs.

(j) The function of the stipules—i. e., the small leaflets around the base of the petiole.

As to their coverings, buds may be

Scaly; covered with the ordinary bud scales.

Naked; without scales.

Hidden; buried in, or under. the bark.

The manner of the folding of the leaf in the bud, is called its *vernation.* If the margins are rolled *inward,* on the upper side, it is *involute;* if rolled, under side in, *revolute;* if *folded,* upper side in, *conduplicate;* when one half is rolled *within the other, convolute;* when folded as a fan, *plicate,* or *plaited.*

4. *What determines the order in which buds unfold on a branch?*

Consider:

(a) The relative size of the buds.
(b) The order of the buds on the branch, as to size.
(c) What established this order.
(d) The relation to the leaves of the previous year.

5. *Are the dormant buds of any advantage to the plant ?*

Consider:

(a) The effect on dormant buds, of removing all the buds toward the outer end of the branch. Of cutting off the end of the branch.
(b) The possible effects of a hard freeze on the buds that have unfolded.

(c) The use of adventitious buds. (See
2, [c] above).

6. *What are the parts of a bud : what develops from it ?*

Consider

    (a) Its position—its relation to the stem.
    (b) The recognizable parts in a large bud.
    (c) The function of the terminal bud.
    (d) Of a lateral bud.
    (e) The signs which show how much of a branch was developed from a last year's bud.
    (f) The shape of the tree, as determined by the relative development of terminal and lateral buds. (See page 69 *et seq.*)
    (g) Its relation to a seed.
    (h) The relative importance of seeds and buds.
    (i) The relation of buds to roots.

EXPERIMENT: Plant a small branch, cut from a willow, in a moist place, or, immerse one end in a bottle of water, so that some of the buds shall be below the surface. Find out from what places the roots are produced. Whether, or not, they come from the buds; whether, or not, the buds below the surface of the water will develop.

    (j) The effect of light upon the growth of roots. Devise a means of showing the effect.

7.   *What proof is there that a plant's relations to light are established through its leaves?*
Consider:

(a) The color of plants growing in the dark, a cellar, for instance, compared with that of the leaves growing out doors.

(b) The extent to which the other dissimilar conditions may affect the plant referred to in (a), i. e., temperature, circulation of air, moisture, etc.

(c) The growth of plants receiving light on one side only; e. g., plants growing in a window.

(d) The arrangement of leaves on the stem or twig.

NOTE.   The arrangement is *opposite* or *alternate.* In the former, study the arrangement of the *pairs* of leaves.   In the latter, count the number of rows or *ranks* of leaves on the twig.   Starting with one of the lower buds, wind a string upwards around the twig, allowing it to pass through the *nodes.*   What kind of a line is described?   How many buds, (representing ranks), are passed before reaching a bud immediately over the one at the starting point?   The leaf arrangement may be expressed by a *fraction,* whose *numerator* represents the number of turns of the string, and whose *denominator* expresses the number of buds crossed, or the number of *ranks.* Thus, $\frac{3}{5}$ would express three turns of the string, and that the fifth bud stands over the first: The entire fraction represents the angular distance between the ranks; in the example given, it would be $\frac{3}{5}$ of 360°, or 216°. Pupils may readily apply these facts in the examination of any twigs.

    (e) The use of the petiole. Its shape. Its relative length at various points on the twig.

    (f) The position of the leaves as affected by the direction of the twig and by the general form of the tree top.

    (g) The shape of the leaf; the effect of the pointed base or apex.

    (h) The margin; entire, notched, lobed, etc.

    (i) The venation.

    (j) Simple and compound leaves.

    (k) The arrangement in leaf-clusters.

    (l) The thinness or density of the shade cast by a tree; what this tells as to leaf arrangement. Stand beneath the tree in the shade and look towards the sun. Look up through the tree in other directions.

8. *What are the possibilities of sunlight reaching the interior leaves?*

Consider:

    (a) The angle of the sun at different hours.

    (b) The movement of the branches and leaves by the wind.

    (c) The position of the best developed leaves.

    (d) The relation of the largest leaves to the largest buds.

9. *What proof is there that the plant is related to heat through its leaves?*

Consider :

(a) The position of the leaves during the warmest part of the day.

(b) The edge-wise position assumed, habitually, by leaves of certain plants; e. g., the compass plants, as in wild lettuce; also, in sweet clover.

(c) The position of leaves of certain plants on cloudy days or at night time.

(d) The meaning of the wisping of leaves. (See 10, below.)

(e) The position, coverings, foldings, and various shields of the young leaves as they emerge from the bud.

(f) The color of young leaves when emerging from the buds. Place a number of young leaves of different colors in separate tumblers of water, submerging them. Place in a window in sunlight under similar conditions. Take the temperature of the water from time to time. Does this give a hint as to the use of the high coloration of young leaves?

10. *What proof is there that the plant is related to moisture through its leaves?*

Consider:

(a) The wilting and withering of leaves.

(b) The meaning of the funnel-like leaves on the canna, the mosses, Indian corn and other grasses.

(c) The significance of hairs; pour water on a hairy-leaved plant; e. g., the mullein.

(d) The position of leaves on different trees, and on smaller plants, during a rain-storm; do they shed the water away from or towards the trunk? The meaning of this?

(e) The effect of water falling on leaves of different plants: observe the plants whose leaves are wet and those whose leaves shed the water; e. g., the lilac, calladium, nasturtium, oak, maple, willow, mullein, locust, honeysuckle, etc., etc.

NUMBER WORK.

A. *The temperature at which buds develop.*

1. Find the average temperature in the month when the buds begin to develop.

2. Find the difference between the extremes of temperature in the same month.

B. *The percentage of buds that develop.*

3. What percentage of the buds on the last year's growth is dormant?

4. What percentage of the buds on the growth of the year before the last is dormant?

5. What is the highest percentage of dormant buds in any year's growth found upon any tree?

6. What is the lowest percentage of dormant buds, in any year's growth, found on any tree? How do you account for the differences?

7. Find the ratio of the various diameters of the different kind of tree-tops; are the ratios connected in any way with bud development?

8. In what percentage of cases is the terminal bud dormant?

9. Find the ratio of the dormant to the active buds in any one year's growth on the following: willow, poplar, maple, oak, beech, cherry, apple, elm, boxelder and catalpa.

10. Find the average number of buds formed on the last year's growth, on different trees, under practically the same conditions; is there any regularity in the number formed on the same tree on different branches? On different trees of the same kind? Do different trees vary widely in the number of new buds formed?

11. At what temperature of the air and soil do you find that various plants wilt?

12. With what quantity of moisture in the soil, per cubic foot, do plants—Indian corn, for example—begin to wilt?

REPRESENTATIVE EXPRESSION.

1. *Drawing.*

    (a) Select a large bud and carefully draw longitudinal and transverse sections. Enlarge to a scale.

    (b) A sketch of various branches, showing shape of buds, their arrangement, etc.

(c) The details of leaf structure and form.

2. *Painting.*

(a) Sketch of the landscape, twice a week in the lower grades, and oftener in the upper grades, showing the color transformation of the season.

(b) A sketch, once a week, of some tree selected for special study.

(c) A sketch, once a week at least, showing the stages of leaf development.

XXXIX.

A STUDY OF PLANT GROWTH. TRANSPIRATION.

OBSERVATION: The conditions under which leaves wilt and wither. The conditions under which they regain their freshness; the location, nature of soil, time of day, temperature, water in the soil, humidity of the atmosphere, etc.

QUERIES:

1. *What evidence is there that plants lose water through their leaves?*

Consider:

    (a) A fresh leaf compared with a withered one.

EXPERIMENTS:

    (A) Select a small twig bearing a few leaves and enclose it in a wide-mouthed bottle. Properly close the mouth of the bottle about the twig without injury to the latter. This may be done by using cotton, coating it with soft paraffin, if necessary. Support the bottle so that the branch will be as nearly as possible in a normal position. Observe what takes place inside the bottle. Compare the effect of sunshine and shade, night and day.

(B) Secure several small seedling plants of maple, oak, or any other kind having a woody stem. Carefully remove the soil from the roots and weigh the plants. Transplant each one to a wide-mouthed bottle filled with soil. Keep the soil thoroughly wet until growth begins, and then aim to preserve the normal conditions as to light, moisture, temperature, etc. Splitting a cork into halves, and cutting out a groove in each half, to enclose the twig properly, insert it so as to prevent moisture from escaping by any means except through the plant. A little soft paraffin may be needed to enclose the pores of the cork or the opening around the twig.

It is well to use woody plants, as the stems are less liable to injury, but many herbaceous plants will serve the purpose equally well. Among these may be mentioned the sun-flower and pig-weed. The former is interesting because of the enormous amount of water it pumps from the soil in the course of a day.

Measure, as accurately as possible, the leaf surface of each plant. Keep the plants under all the varied conditions by which they have been surrounded in nature. They may be placed in the sunshine, in the shade, and the observations may cover both periods of daylight and darkness. The records for cloudy days may be kept, as well as for those having sunshine.

Weigh the plant and the bottle; note the time; and at the end of a given period of observation, weigh again and account for the difference in weight. After results have been obtained in this manner, it will be interesting to remove the leaves from some of the plants and note the difference. In others, the roots may be removed and the stem and leaves preserved. Compare the results obtained in this experiment with those obtained under Query (4), page 50.

2. *How does the amount of water and other materials in the leaves compare with what we found in autumn?*

Gather and tabulate results, as directed on page 76; also, see Chart 7, page 82. In the course of the spring it is interesting to repeat, each month, the experiments there outlined for the purpose of determining the relative amounts of water, carbon and other materials, at the different stages of development of the leaves.

NUMBER WORK.

QUERIES:

A. *How much water is thrown off by the leaves of plants?*

1. Under experiment (A), weigh the plant carefully, calculate how much water is thrown off into the air during the daylight.

2. Compare the amount thrown off by each plant when in the sunshine with that thrown off during a cloudy or rainy day.

3. The amount of water thrown off during the night equals what part of that thrown off of plants during the day.

4. Estimate the leaf surface of a tree, say, the oak, ash, maple, etc. Do this by counting the leaves on some of the smaller branches; and estimate their area, and then consider what part this branch is of the whole tree.

5. At the rate indicated by the plants in the bottle, how much moisture does an oak tree lift into the air during the hours of sunlight.

NOTE.—It has been estimated that a full-grown oak tree has about 700,000 leaves and that an elm tree has about 1,000,000.

B. *How much water is in the leaves of a tree at any one time?*

6. Weigh a given number of leaves, say, 100 or more, and dry them. What part of the weight of the fresh leaves is the weight of the water? Repeat this experiment, and calculate at different times during the spring.

7. Compare the amount of water found in the oak leaves with that contained in the ash.

8. Compare the amount of water found in the poplar with that found in the maple. What is the ratio of the former to the latter?

9. Secure some plants that grow in the marshes, like the pond lilies, flags, water plantain, arrow-leaf and others. Weigh while fresh, and again after being thoroughly dried. What part of the original weight is water?

10. Compare the amount of dry solid with the amount found in the oak, ash, maple and other trees. Compute the quantity of water in barrels in the leaves of a forest of a given area.

REPRESENTATIVE EXPRESSION

1. *Drawing.*

   (a) Draw a 10-inch square. Allow this to represent the weight of fresh oak leaves. Upon this draw another square representing the amount of water they contain. What does the rest of the original square show?

   (b) Draw a 10-inch square and allow it to represent the original weight of the water plants. Upon this draw a second square, representing the amount of water these contain.

NOTE.—These diagrams may be made up in different colors, if desired.

2. *Painting.*

    (a) Make a painting of the landscape, showing how the presence or absence of water is indicated in the coloration of plants.

    (b) Paint some water areas, dry woodland areas and meadowland.

XL.

METEOROLOGY. SUMMARY FOR THE YEAR.

Near the close of the school year, it is interesting and profitable, to gather up the observations that have been made upon the weather, in the course of the different seasons, with a view to picturing more clearly the varied conditions, often reaching the most trying extremes, under which living things have to make their way in the world.

It is well to obtain from the nearest *Weather Bureau Station*, a summary of the observations made by the office, for the full term of its existence. With these, it is exceedingly interesting to compare the results of single years. A table of such average results, obtained from the Chicago Station, covering a period of about 24 years, is given in TABLE VII.

QUERIES:

1. *How much water may be expected for plants during the growing season, judging by the* AVERAGE *rainfall?*

Select some convenient unit area, and calculate the amount of water which, on an average, it receives for each month. For example, find out, by calculation, how much water falls upon a square foot of ground. This may be done readily, by finding how much water per square foot falls in one inch of rain. Select such a fraction of a square foot, as will bring the extreme quantity of water which falls during any month, within 2 quarts. One-twelfth of a square foot, in a rectangle, 3x4 inches, will be about right. Measure out, in 2-quart Mason jars, the quantity of water which each month brings to the plant during the growing season, and place these jars of water in a row, in the order of the months, and label them with the name of the month, and the quantity of water that each contains.

Consider:

(a) How much a small plant standing upon the given area, receives during the month when it is germinating.

(b) During the month when the stem and leaves are growing.

(c) During the month when it is in bloom.

(d) During the month when the seed is ripening.

(e) The quantity of water received during the entire season.

In another series of jars, measure out the quantity of water which actually fell each month during the past season, and compare the quantity with the average results in the first series of jars. The quantity of water shown in the average, is what Nature promises the plants;

the amount measured out in the jars for a single year shows how her promises are fulfilled.

2. *What is the probable effect of the irregularity of rainfall, upon plants, and living things in general?*

Consider:

(a) The effect of a wet season.
(b) The effect of a dry season.
(c) How irregularities must affect the vigor and size of plants.

3. *How does the rainfall vary with the seasons?*

Consider:

(a) The quantity of water which falls upon a given space, according to suggestions already given, for each season.
(b) The relative importance of rainfall in the different seasons.
(c) In what season are the floods the heaviest.
(d) The influences which contribute to floods.

4. *How does the relation of rainfall to cloudiness vary in the different seasons?*

Find the average rainfall for each month, and for each season, per *cloudy day;* measure out, in a jar of convenient size, the water that falls upon a square foot, on the average, per cloudy day, for each month, and for each season.

Consider:

(a) What may be learned from these measurements as to cloud values, when expressed in rainfall.

(b) The cloud value of different months and seasons.

(c) Also, the relation of rainy days to cloudy days, in the different months and seasons. (Days when .01 of an inch of rain, or more, falls, may be called, for convenience, a rainy day).

(d) The relation of rainy days to rainfall, in each month and season. Find the average rainfall per *rainy day*. Measure out in jars of convenient size, the amount of water which falls upon a square foot per *rainy day*, for each month and each season. Note the variation of the *water value* of *rainy days*.

(e) The water value of rainy days in spring; in summer; in autumn; in winter.

5. *How does the air pressure vary with the rainfall and cloudiness?*

Consider:

(a) The average for each month, and each season.

(b) The correspondence between the extremes of barometer, and the extremes of cloudiness, rainfall, and the number of rainy days.

(c) The extremes of dry, clear weather.

6. *How does the humidity of the air vary with the cloudiness, rainfall. etc.?*

Consider:

(a) The times when the greatest extremes of humidity occurred.

(b) The variation with the months and seasons.

7. *How does the temperature vary with the seasons?*

Consider:

(a) The average for each month, and for each season.

(b) The extremes for each month and season.

(c) The dates of the last frost in spring, and the first frost in autumn.

(d) The average temperature at different stages of plant and animal growth; temperature when seeds germinate; when buds open; when 'frogs' eggs hatch; when snakes appear; when earth-worms show themselves, etc.

8. *What is the prevailing wind for the various months, and for the seasons?*

Consider:

(a) The prevailing wind for the year.

(b) If possible, the part of the whole year that the prevailing wind blows.

   (c) The same facts for each month, and
      season.

   (d) The temperature, barometer, rainfall,
      cloudiness, humidity, that accompany
      the various winds.

9. *How are the storms distributed over the United States in the course of a year?*

Refer to the file of Weather Bureau Maps, and

Consider:

   (a) The tracks pursued by the storms
      across the country: from the N.-W.;
      from the S.-W; from the S. and S.-E.

   (b) The rainfall of each; the changes of
      temperature, clouds, etc.

   (c) The area that has been reached by
      snow, during the year.

   (d) The area that has been reached by
      frost, during the year.

   (e) The areas reached by rain, that caused
      floods.

   (f) The areas of greatest drouths.

   (g) The points of extremely high temper-
      ature; low temperature.

TABLE VII.

Showing the mean annual and the mean monthly summaries of weather observations for 24 years at Chicago, Ill.

Compiled mainly from Records furnished by the Chicago Weather Bureau.

OBSERVATIONS.	Mont'ly Mean	Sept.	Oct.	Nov.	Dec.	Jan.	Feb.	Mar.	Apr.	May	June	July	Aug.
Noon slant of sun's rays ‡Length of day (21st day of month)		42.°	53°	62°	65.°5	62°	53°	42°	30°	22°	18.°5	22°	30°
		12:06	10:48	9:26	8:54	9:26	10:48	12:00	13:26	14:36	16:10	15:33	13:26
Temperature*	49°	64°	52°	38°	30°	24°	27°	34°	46°	56°	67°	72°	71°
Barometer	29.26	29.29	29.29	29.29	29.30	29.28	29.29	29.25	29.22	29.21	29.20	29.24	29.25
Precipitation	Total, 34.55 Av., 2.89	*2.83	*2.93	*2.59	*2.34	*2.15	2.22	2.44	3.08	3.70	3.84	3.48	2.95
Rainy days.† (.01 inch or more)	Total, 131 Av., 10.9	9	10	11	12	12	11	12	11	12	12	10	9
Cloudy days†	Total, 112 Av., 9.3	7	10	13	13	12	10	11	10	9	8	4	5
Partly cloudy†	Total, 142 Av., 11.8	11	11	10	11	12	10	13	12	12	14	13	13
Cloudless†	Total, 110 Av., 9.2	12	10	7	7	7	8	7	8	10	8	13	13
Prevailing winds†	S. W. 75 pr. ct.	S. W.	S. W.	S. W.	S. W.	S. W.	S. W.	N.	N. E.	N. E.	S. W.	S. W.	S. W.
Max. velocity of wind†		60	60	60	60	64	54	68	65	60	72	52	50

*25 years. †September to February 24 years. Other months 23 years. ‡See Nautical Almanac.

NUMBER WORK.

A. *The relative rainfall for different months and seasons, and the relation of yearly rainfall to the annual average.* (See Query [1] above.)

1. What is the ratio of the amount of water which falls upon a given area of ground in the winter season to that on the same area in the spring? The same area in summer? The same area in autumn?

2. What is the ratio of the rainfall of each season, in any given year, with that of the annual average? Find, also, the ratio, month by month; i. e., compare each month of a given year with the annual average of each month.

B. *Relation of rainfall to cloudiness.* (Query [4] above.)

3. Find the ratio of the rainfall per cloudy day in winter to that per cloudy day in spring; in summer; in autumn.

4. Find the ratio of the rainfall per cloudy day in each month with that per cloudy day in June.

5. Find the ratio of rainy days to cloudy days in each season.

6. Find the ratio of rainy days to cloudy days in each month.

7. Find the ratio of the quantity of water which falls on a given area per rainy day, in each season, with that which falls per cloudy in summer. Measure the amounts in bottles.

8. Find the ratio of the quantity of water which falls on a given area in June, per rainy day, with that which falls on the same area in each of the other months. Measure the amounts in bottles.

9. Show by ratios the *water value* of a rainy day in June as compared with that of every other month.

10. Show by ratios the *water value* of a summer day as compared with that of every other season.

11. Show by ratios the *water values* of clouds in different months of the year and in different seasons.

12. Show by ratios the comparative reading of the barometer for the different seasons; for the different months.

13. Show by ratios the comparative humidity for the different seasons.

14. What part of the whole number of storms in a year comes from the gulf? What part comes from the northwest? What part traverses the Atlantic coast?

15. Make an approximate calculation in cubic miles of the rainfall for the Mississippi basin for the year; of the Ohio basin; of the Missouri basin. For further data, see Government Reports on Rainfall, Weather Bureau, Washington, D. C.

16. What part of the whole country was covered by snow during the winter?

17. What per cent. of the total area of the

TABLE VIII.
RAINFALL, EVAPORATION FROM RIVER BASINS AND OUTFLOW OF RIVERS.

Compiled by I. B. Myers from *Government Report for Year 1889, with monthly rainfall average for 18 years.* Results all given in CUBIC MILES.

	OHIO RIVER BASIN.†				MISSOURI RIVER BASIN.				MISSISSIPPI RIVER BASIN.			
	Rainfall	*Possible Evaporat'n	Outflow of River.	Rainfall av. 18 yrs.	Rainfall	Possible Evaporat'n	Outflow of River	Rainfall av. 18 yrs.	Rainfall	Possible Evaporat'n	Outflow of River	Rainfall av. 18 yrs.
January	26.85	5.43	16.69	12.96	4.67	9.11	0.84	6.21	55.95	27.47	18.98	36.00
February	21.70	6.66	17.61	12.58	6.43	13.53	1.23	6.30	58.89	35.87	22.08	36.24
March	16.73	8.84	16.18	12.34	7.44	14.55	1.60	9.55	45.22	43.89	29.57	40.99
April	9.95	16.19	6.87	12.45	20.53	39.67	1.69	16.00	54.06	90.60	28.36	54.00
May	20.98	15.39	8.46	11.91	29.26	37.00	2.04	21.74	98.45	88.12	24.79	60.85
June	15.12	20.75	8.03	15.50	27.60	48.46	2.76	20.79	74.02	112.21	22.90	71.14
July	13.75	19.20	4.16	14.37	19.73	61.23	3.42	20.19	67.78	129.55	21.65	63.74
August	20.61	20.34	2.79	11.90	7.00	49.98	1.26	15.23	52.11	115.72	12.10	51.73
September	11.32	17.70	2.47	10.26	9.92	44.70	0.56	13.71	38.74	101.59	6.08	49.16
October	6.39	14.11	1.44	8.79	14.64	30.82	0.55	11.86	48.07	78.44	4.92	39.16
November	8.90	10.98	1.27	10.64	5.82	25.50	0.70	6.21	37.18	61.70	5.10	34.12
December	7.86	6.09	2.11	11.52	6.97	13.49	0.40	6.74	25.54	33.73	6.18	34.37

*The amount of evaporation possible from a sheet of water. †Area of Ohio Basin 211,280 sq. mi. Annual Rainfall. 43 in. †Area of Missouri Basin 545,240 sq. mi. Annual Rainfall, 17.7 in. †Area of Mississippi Basin, 1,272,000 sq. mi. Annual Rainfall, 28.5 in.

United States fell within the frost line during the year?

18. If the rainfall for the year averaged only in accordance with that which fell during the dryest month, how much would it be? Find, by your geography, some region with such an annual average. Contrast with your own neighborhood.

19. In the same way find what the average annual rainfall would be if it were in accordance with the wettest month. See suggestion under (18).

Refer to Table VIII.

20. Find the ratio of the rainfall to the out-flow of the rivers for each month, and account for the variation.

21. Show by ratios the relative evaporation during the different seasons, and account for the variation.

22. Show by ratios the relation of river out-flow to the basins drained, and account for the difference.

23. For every cubic mile of rainfall in the Ohio basin, how much of a cubic mile of out-flow? Compare with the Missouri basin.

24. Suppose each river were to empty into large tanks, each ½ mile deep and 1 mile wide, how long would each have to be to hold the outflow for a year.

REPRESENTATIVE EXPRESSION.

1. *Drawing.*

    (a) A 10-inch square for each month of the year. Upon this represent the relative amount of clear, cloudy and rainy days. Color the parts with water color or colored paper.

    (b) A 10-inch square for each season; represent the clear, cloudy and rainy days as in (a).

    (c) A 10-inch square for the year; represent the clear, cloudy and rainy days as in (a).

    (d) On a large cardboard show, by broad lines, or bands of colored paper, the depth of rainfall for each month; for each season; for the year.

2. *Painting.*

    (a) The landscape painted during the year should be collected and arranged in a series, showing the history of the year in color.

XLI.

ASTRONOMY. SUMMARY FOR THE YEAR.

At the close of the school year, through a summary of the observations provided for in the preceding lessons, there may be some application of the results obtained to a study of the world as a whole.

From what has already been observed the pupils will be able to consider some additional

QUERIES:

1. *What are the factors to be considered in estimating the value of sunshine?*

Consider:

(a) The distribution as shown by the skia-meter.

(b) The absorptive effect of the atmosphere upon sunshine, and the further modification due to the slant of most of the rays.

(c) The effect of the day's length; keep constantly in mind the ratio of the time during which the earth is both receiving *and* radiating to the time when it is *radiating* only.

The absorptive effect of the atmosphere upon the sunshine traversing it at different angles, is

TABLE IX.

Altitude of the sun	0°	5°	10°	20°	30°	50°	70°	90°
Thickness of the atmosphere in units	35.5	10.2	5.56	2.90	1.99	1.31	1.06	1.00
Am't of sunshine reaching the earth	0.00	0.05	0.20	0.43	0.56	0.69	0.74	0.75

Table X gives approximately the daily duration of sunshine each month, and it enables one to understand how the great length of day compensates for the relatively low altitude of the sun in summer, and it also indicates how the reverse condition, together with an extremely low altitude of the sun, produces the low temperature attained in high latitudes in the winter.

TABLE X.

SHOWING APPROXIMATELY THE DAY'S LENGTH ON THE 21ST DAY OF EACH MONTH.

Compiled from the Nautical Almanac.

	Sept.	Oct.	Nov.	Dec.	Jan.	Feb.	Mar.	April	May	June	July	Aug.
Latitude 0°	12:00′	12:00′	12:00′	12:00′	12:00′	12:00′	12:00′	12:00′	12:00′	12:00′	12:00′	12:00′
Latitude 20°	12:02′	11:28′	11:00′	10:46′	11:00′	11:28′	12:02′	12:36′	13:00′	13:14′	13:00′	12:36′
Latitude 30°	12:02′	11:12′	10:24′	10:04′	10:24′	11:12′	12:02′	12:56′	13:38′	13:56′	13:40′	12:56′
Latitude 42°	12:06′	10:48′	9:26′	8:54′	9:26′	10:48′	12:06′	13:26′	14:36′	15:04′	14:36′	13:26′
Latitude 50°	12:08′	10:18′	8:34′	7:50′	8:34′	10:18′	12:08′	13:58′	15:28′	16:10′	15:28′	13:58′
Latitude 60°	12:10′	9:30′	7:50′	5:30′	7:50′	9:28′	12:10′	14:50′	17:24′	18:30′	17:24′	14:50′

shown in *Table IX*, taken from *Waldo's Elementary Meteorology*. The vertical thickness of the atmosphere is taken as 1:00, and the amount of sunshine received from the zenith on the outside of the atmosphere is also represented by 1:00.

2. *How does the distribution and quantity of sunshine received by the different crops vary within the United States?*

Consider:

  (a) The cotton crop.
  (b) The rice crop.
  (c) The corn crop.
  (d) The wheat crop.
  (e) The oats, rye, flax and barley crops.

3. *How does the distribution and quantity of sunshine vary with the seasons in different latitudes?*

Consider:

  (a) The conditions shown in Tables VIII, IX, and X.
  (b) How these conditions must enter into the climate of Quito, Vera Cruz, New Orleans, Chicago, Winnipeg, and St. Petersburg.

NUMBER WORK.

1. From the standpoint of distribution, express, by ratios, the sunshine intensity at Chicago, compared with that at other points in the latitudes mentioned in *Table X*.

2. Express the same from the standpoint of day's length.

3. Express the same, taking the thickness of the atmosphere into account.

4. Express, by ratio, the relation of the quantity and intensity of sunshine received in June, by a cotton field in Mississippi, to that received by a wheat field in Minnesota.

5. Express, by ratios, the relative distribution of sunshine, in the latitudes mentioned in Table IX; how are these ratios modified, when the length of day is considered? When the relative thickness of the atmosphere is considered?

6. By means of the skiameter, find out the relative distribution of the sunshine, for the different hours of the day; by means of Table IX, show how the results must vary, owing to the thickness of the atmosphere.

REPRESENTATIVE EXPRESSION.

1. *Drawing.*

    (a) In accordance with suggestions, (see page 37, chapter IV), draw a series of rectangles, which will show the sunshine distribution in your latitude, each month of the year.

    (b) By calculations, construct other series of rectangles, which will show sunshine distribution, each month of the year, in the latitude given in Table X.

2. *Painting.*

    (a) Landscapes; particularly, those show-
ing cloud and sky effects, in the different seasons.

INDEX.